Strategic
Design Thinking

28 July 2016
Nelson,
Remain inspired,
to inspire!
Enjoy,
Natalie

Strategic
Design Thinking

Innovation in Products, Services, Experiences, and Beyond

Edited by

Natalie W. Nixon
Philadelphia University

Fairchild Books
An imprint of Bloomsbury Publishing Inc

BLOOMSBURY
NEW YORK · LONDON · OXFORD · NEW DELHI · SYDNEY

Fairchild Books

An imprint of Bloomsbury Publishing Inc

1385 Broadway	50 Bedford Square
New York	London
NY 10018	WC1B 3DP
USA	UK

www.bloomsbury.com

**FAIRCHILD BOOKS, BLOOMSBURY and the Diana logo are trademarks
of Bloomsbury Publishing Plc**

First published 2016

© Bloomsbury Publishing Inc, 2016

Library of Congress Cataloging-in-Publication Data

Strategic design thinking : innovation in products, services, experiences
and beyond / edited by Natalie W. Nixon.
pages cm
ISBN 978-1-62892-470-1 (paperback) — ISBN 978-1-62892-495-4 (ePDF)
1. Creative ability in business. 2. Creative thinking. 3. Design. 4. Organizational change. I. Nixon, Natalie W.
HD53.S757 2015
658.4'094—dc23
2015019185

ISBN: PB: 978-1-6289-2470-1
ePDF: 978-1-6289-2495-4

Typeset by Lachina
Printed and bound in the United States of America

Table of Contents

PART III: THE WHAT 143

Acknowledgments

Over ten years ago, I met Olga Kontzias, who was an editor at Fairchild. I was a budding academic and reviewer of many texts for Fairchild's fashion studies titles, and Olga saw in me the promise of a book. She was a big supporter of my foray into the field of design management during my doctoral studies and the first to get the ball rolling in formally establishing me as the editor of what has become *Strategic Design Thinking*. For this, I am very grateful to Olga.

No endeavor like this is a solo job. I thank all of the contributing authors to this book for their hybrid thinking, keen sensibility, and awesome points of view.

I am eternally grateful to my family for their support of my desire to stretch myself professionally. A big thanks goes to my husband, John, one of my greatest encouragers. I cherish his partnership and friendship.

Dedication

I dedicate this book to my students, especially the Strategic Design MBA students of Philadelphia University. Their wit, intellectual curiosity, and creativity inspire me always. They are my best teachers.

—Natalie W. Nixon, April 2015

Foreword

We begin with two commentaries in this book's foreword. Given the integrative nature of strategic design, it is essential to reflect the voices of an academic perspective and a practitioner's—a business perspective and a design perspective. Jeanne Liedtka and Bob Schwartz do just that. Enjoy!

PART I
WHY STRATEGIC DESIGN NOW?
Jeanne Liedtka, DBA

 **Jeanne Liedtka** (United Technologies Professor of Business Administration, Darden Graduate School of Business, University of Virginia) is a thought leader on the integration of design thinking into business problem-solving processes. Jeanne has authored a number of books, including *Designing for Growth: A Design Thinking Tool Kit for Managers* and *Solving Business Problems with Design Thinking: Ten Stories of What Works*. Her forthcoming book, *Designing for the Greater Good*, moves her work into the social sector.

Almost fifty years ago, Nobel Prize–winning economist and business school professor Herb Simon pointed out that the act of *designing* was core to management, because anyone interested in turning an *existing* situation into a *preferred* one had to pay attention to design. And for the next forty years at least, those of us who study, teach, and practice management proceeded to ignore completely what he said. Not because we disagreed—we just couldn't quite figure out how to translate that lofty idea of designing better futures into a different reality at the front line of organizations. Until now. Until design thinking, with its pragmatic practices and toolkit, flashed the management landscape like a new star making its first appearance.

But it's not new, of course. Not even to management. Designers have been toiling away in organizations, creating better products and services for a long time. So why now? And what does it all mean for designers?

You will get a much better and deeper answer as to "Why now?" as you read this book, but for now, let's just say it's because innovation has never mattered more to business than it does today. And business thinking and traditional tools don't help us to do innovation very well. In fact, they approach the world in ways almost opposite to design—and therein lies business's great problem and your great opportunity.

Business thinking, for instance, assumes rationality and objectivity. Its decision driver is cold, clean, economic logic. Reality is precise and quantifiable. There is "truth"—and answers are "right" or "wrong." Design, on the other hand, takes human experience, always messy, as its decision driver and sees true objectivity as an illusion. Reality, for designers, is always constructed by the people living it. In this world, there is only our individual truth—and answers are "better" or "worse."

These stark differences, you can argue, provide the reason why business and design have so much to offer each other: To create innovation within an ever-changing and unpredictable environment, business *needs* design, with its emphasis on exploration, learning by doing, and using data from actual customers instead of from market reports. And design needs a dose of traditional business thinking, as well, to ensure that new ideas can actually create value not just for customers, but also for the organizations that commit the investments that turn ideas into action. So they'll be around to turn more ideas into action tomorrow.

Seems obvious, doesn't it? Yet most business people are still struggling to understand what design thinking even *is*. You can blame Apple for this, I believe. Apple put design on the radar of organizations when they demonstrated how very valuable it could be to establishing a clear competitive advantage. Unfortunately, the hype that accompanied how they did this led most business people to believe that it was only rare creative geniuses like Steve Jobs who could make this happen.

I call this the "Moses Myth": this idea that great design only happens in the hands of holy men, anointed with the ability to perform miracles. Moses—or Steve Jobs—just had to raise their hands for the Red Sea to part. Mere mortals like the rest of us are more likely to drown.

The authors of this book—along with an increasing number of people in business organizations—know this isn't true. What makes design thinking so powerful is that it can teach us mere mortals how to build a bridge to cross the Red Sea, instead of standing on the sidelines waiting for a miracle.

And you'll understand why—and how to get some of that magic for yourself—when you read this book!

PART II
DESIGN'S ENSEMBLE APPROACH: A GAME CHANGER
FOR BUSINESS INNOVATION
Robert T. Schwartz, FIDSA, DMI

Bob Schwartz is the general manager of Global Design & User Experience at GE Healthcare, leading six studios in five countries. He's held similar positions at Procter & Gamble, Motorola, and the Industrial Designers Society of America, among others. Bob is a member of the Board of Trustees of the Milwaukee Institute of Art & Design and the Executive Board of the Design Management Institute. He has a master's in industrial design from the Rhode Island School of Design, where he was a Roddy Scholar, and a BFA in industrial & graphic design from the Kansas City Art Institute.

What if I asked you to just close your eyes and breathe? Please think about a time when you or someone you care about felt most supported or least supported during a healthcare experience. C'mon, you can do it. When I do so, I think about my eighty-six-year-old mother, who for a decade was the caregiver of my stepdad, who had Alzheimer's disease. We all have stories like this, and you are thinking about them now.

This reflection you are having is likely welling up a sense of *empathy* for what you and/or the people around you experienced during such a hardship. Seeing through the eyes of another and walking in their shoes can elicit a powerful human response.

In a large company like GE, we use the concept of empathy as a very personal "front door" to remove barriers and create an understanding of how we apply the broader context of design thinking.

For a big, global, industrial company like GE, helping all the business and technical disciplines connect the functional features of amazing technology to the emotional benefits we want to deliver to the human beings who will encounter our products and services is essential. We call it "The Magic of Science and Empathy."

Regardless of the category, it's no surprise that it can be a struggle to get teams to understand that their work is not for some faceless throng or about numbers on a spreadsheet. It's about our families, friends, and the communities where we live.

Never mind getting a team to a place where they can discover and leverage their group genius and work together cross-functionally. The concept of empathy can be used to help them accept and add to each other's ideas and become a single-minded ensemble of players.

This ensemble approach heavily leverages theatrical improvisation techniques. How did you feel the last time you were told can't; won't; don't know how; been there, done that? In improvisation, it's all about "Yes, and …" There are no silly ideas, only ones to pile on and add to quickly, to make them stronger.

Another tool that we use to break down barriers to innovation, creativity, and imagination is to give grown-ups back the tools they had when they were kids. When you were seven, you could draw, make things, imagine, and tell stories. What's four chairs and a bed sheet? Yes, it's a fort! No one had to tell you how to build it or how to play in it. You created a world of imagination with your siblings and friends and kept building on your ideas until mom said, "Clean up that mess!"

When we use these simple techniques, the smiles return, and by the end of the week, even some of the toughest hombres don't want to go home.

Of course, design-thinking tools are not only about feelings and play. The serious business of delivering world-class and differentiated innovation against a timeline and cost always remains at the heart of our focus.

With a foundation, such as that described above, teams are then guided to developing contextual, ethnographic, and behavioral research protocols, to begin understanding opportunity spaces and the unmet needs of users. It's interesting how the conflict between what people will tell you versus what you observe them doing may reveal the innovation opportunity.

Often, we first take teams into worlds outside of their own and ask them to explore. This helps inspire and embed the tools without the blinders that may come from working inside a familiar category. Sometimes, powerful insights can be derived by looking somewhere else. What can you learn about healthcare delivery by studying spiritual places, for example?

Translating what is learned into useful problem statements and opportunity spaces is the most difficult part of innovation. We are so often compelled to want to leap to the idea before truly understanding the challenge that needs to be solved. Quickly creating many, very low resolution prototypes brings early concepts to life, and by the way, anything can be prototyped! Business and product ideas are both easily made when the stuff you created with as kids is in your hands.

From there it's about iterating and refining and testing and validating with users to get to the doorstep of serious product development or service innovation.

This process—of story, ethnography, lateral thinking, translation and prototyping, testing and refining—is the foundation of strategic design. We have realized at GE Healthcare that it is an essential component to innovation, and I am thrilled that this book, *Strategic Design Thinking: Innovation in Products, Services, Experiences, and Beyond*, will be a means to spread this gospel to both the business and design communities. Its value is in its integrative approach. In the end, design must go far beyond aesthetics, to shaping products and services that are inviting ("I *want* to work with it"), intuitive ("I *get* it"), exciting ("I can do things I couldn't do before!"), innovative ("This is *different*"), inspirational ("I am *delighted and empowered*"), and localized (*integrated*) into the user's life. The pages that follow are the road map for that very shift.

Introduction

AN INTRODUCTION TO STRATEGIC DESIGN THINKING:
INTEGRATION, OWNERSHIP, AND LANGUAGE

Natalie W. Nixon

THE NEW PARADIGM OF SHARING

The design field is emerging out of an identity crisis. The overwhelming crisis in the field has been one of ownership: namely, "Who 'owns' the innovative processes and frameworks that are promoted by design thinking? Design, or business?"

The better question to address is how do we shift away from the old paradigm, one of ownership, to a newer paradigm of sharing? *Strategic design*—the process of developing strategy as informed by the design-thinking processes—is at the nexus of design thinking and strategy, and in many ways resolves this dilemma because it is a shared platform, integrating design and business principles. The first three words of this book's title—"strategic design thinking"—capture that nexus and the integrative nature of this approach. Embedded in strategic design is the design-thinking process; by combining those three words "strategic design thinking," we give a nod to both strategic design and design thinking, where notably, design is the literal, actionable, and figurative bridge. As you immerse yourself in both, you will come out the other end fluid in strategic design thinking.

Design management researchers and practitioners alike have beleaguered conversations about having "a seat at the table." Some designers take a purist stance and are fearful that design thinking will dilute the value of design. There are emerging camps based around those practitioners who value a more open-sourced approach and are fearless about "giving it away." Meanwhile, the business press and trends in higher education reflect a more open stance. Strategic design ultimately is a potent new space, a heuristic and a lens, informing innovation for very ambiguous environments.

There are three major insights that we must embrace when acknowledging the relevance of strategic design: First is the importance of the *integration* of design, design thinking, and business strategy. Second is that *ownership* of this discourse is being negotiated. And third is that *language* is the key to navigating a worldview, and strategic design offers a new language. This book, at various points in each chapter, will convince you of strategic design's relevance to your studies and practice in design and business.

In March 2013, *Fast Company's Co.Design* published a provocatively titled article by Brian Gillespie: "Should Designers Fear Design-Thinking MBAs?"

Outsiders may think "Gee whiz, that's a really strong word: 'fear.'" Even more fascinating than the article were all of the comments posted afterward. Brian's short answer was no, we shouldn't fear design-thinking MBAs. This is great from my perspective, because the graduates of programs, such as Philadelphia University's Strategic Design MBA program, have a lot to offer! But it is really significant that what is surfacing in our popular culture are these realities of angst that a lot of designers have felt as we attempt to become more integrated.

I have tested my observations on integration, ownership, and language with a range of practitioners, including Harold Hambrose, the CEO and founder of Electronic Ink; Valerie Jacobs, vice president of trends at LPK; Keith Scandone, a partner at the digital media firm O3; Surya Vanka, former director of user experience at Microsoft; and Bob Schwartz, general manager of design at GE Healthcare. Harold Hambrose says that "the designer's job is to make the process transparent, inviting and inclusive." What is really interesting about his comment is this focus on transparency. Valerie Jacobs pointed out that designers struggle with design's "return on investment." This comment really helped me to think about "What is the perceived value of design and what is the real value? And how do you find metrics for the value of design? Is it actually possible?" The Design Management Institute has embarked on this query and has discovered some important insights through their research.

Keith Scandone, a partner at O3, a digital media design firm in Philadelphia, has a background in marketing, and he works with a lot of UX designers, graphic designers, and design managers. He noted that the more diverse the team, from the beginning of the process, the better the results. I also interviewed Bob Schwartz, the general manager of the Global Design and User Experience at GE Healthcare. He has remarked that "Ultimately, I clear weeds, I lay pipe, I am a diplomat." And Surya Vanka, who was a director of user experience at Microsoft, emphasizes that designers "have to own it!" They have to own their value and own what it is that they are contributing and "have the confidence to challenge. One of the limitations in design education as compared to business school education is that designers do not tend to be educated specifically for leadership—if they trip upon it … great! But you don't really see that in the forefront as a goal—it's pretty rare."

Social media has also revealed some very interesting public discourses about strategic design. Pinterest, LinkedIn, and Twitter reveal a sense of humor among designers and design managers, which is refreshing. These social media platforms also highlight a significant amount of scholarship and contributions to the field of knowledge in strategic design. Sites such as LinkedIn have become forums for discussion, debate, and professional networking. Twitter reveals linkages between strategic design and social innovation, social entrepreneurship, service design, and public policy. So these platforms have practical *and* philosophical applications.

Design has also had a huge role in influencing public policy around the world. Now the World Economic Forum has a Global Agenda Council on design and innovation. They have highlighted that design can innovate policy, urbanization, and education. Additionally, cities can now be selected as world design capitals: Helsinki, Finland; Seoul, South Korea; and Capetown, South Africa have all been World Design Capitals. This shows the greater opportunity and breadth of strategic design's application.

INTEGRATION AND STRATEGIC DESIGN

Strategic designers are in a holonic space: They simultaneously build bridges and are also bridges themselves. This can create complexity, frustration, and difficulty. Don't assume that all designers are good at design thinking. Designers who are also good at design thinking in, for example, the business realm, have to be *meta*-designers: For example, they must operate and execute some of the design-thinking principles, such as empathy, when they are meeting with business leaders. Being self-aware enough to apply on a meta-level the principles that make designers distinctive in their own practice is essential.

It is important to note that assimilation is not equivalent to integration. Too frequently, we conflate the two. What do I mean by that? Assimilation is a one-way street; integration is a two-way street. Integration requires curiosity on both sides, from both partners, about the other. It requires commitment, communication, and dialogue. If the assimilator is always in the position of learning about the other and from the other, translating for the other and figuring out how to navigate that—it is not yet integration.

If we plot integration over time, we can see three iconic stages of design's evolution, which may not necessarily be integrated into an organization.[1] In the first stage, design and strategic design management are treated as eye candy. It's an icing-on-the-cake type of strategy: "What can you designers come in and do for us?" Design is an afterthought. That is the very early stage, and it certainly is not integration; it is assimilation.

---

1. This schema is a recombination of one from Bob Schwartz, general manager of design at GE Healthcare, and one from Sabine Junginger, of Macromedia University.

The second stage is designers as "influencers." Designers may be invited to a meeting or two, but they aren't necessarily brought in at the beginning of a process. Perhaps they are brought in at the end, and even then, they aren't given public credit. This is still not integration.

Then we get to the third stage, where designers and design managers are "collaborators" and partners with business strategists. This is a little better, and frankly, this is where a lot of mainstream companies, which we think offer great design, exist.

The real goal, which is the truly integrated moment in the history and lifespan of a company, is when strategic design is part of the DNA of an organization. So Apple and the usual suspects are at this stage—and that has everything to do with leadership.

Harold Hambrose of Electronic Ink made this comment, which I think is really significant: "If I move as many disciplines as possible through the process, I get much richer problem definition." Harold was trained as a graphic designer, and he has observed that one of the big shifts for a design manager is that they have to learn how to manage "the other." When you are required to work with "the other"—those who have a different background, discipline, lens, or worldview than you—you have to be very clear about what you are bringing to the table in order to understand what the added value is. When Harold first started his practice he hired designers, anthropologists, psychologists, MBAs, and everybody got the role of "designer." And they loved it—to a point! There really is a cool factor with design that can't be underestimated. Jennifer Merchant, a designer at Procter & Gamble, has noted that "integration elevates design—it doesn't mean that we don't have a seat at the table but that we are now part of the conversation." This is a wonderful, poetic way to understand this integration.

Education has an important role in how design gets integrated into business at large. This is a big take-away from the design school versus business school debate. The challenge that some design school education has is that students become fascinated with the artifact and not the *path* to the artifact. They are completely enraptured with this object; an industrial designer, for example, may become fixated on "How do I make a million units?" However, the understanding of the process, that path to the object, is transferable to scientists, engineers, policy workers, and to business.

At the other end of the spectrum, most business schools aren't currently equipped to apply and scale the design process. By scaling the design process, we mean, "So, now you think you have learned the basics steps and methodology involved with design thinking— how do you apply that process in five days versus how do you apply it in five months? And how do you apply it in different contexts?"

I really took these kinds of ideas and criticisms to heart when developing the Strategic Design MBA at Philadelphia University. I wanted to be certain that in our attempt to bridge the traditional silos in academia, we learned from this healthy critique.

OWNERSHIP AND STRATEGIC DESIGN

A lot of the struggle about who owns design and the conversation about design, design thinking, and design management is really about transparency. The veil has been removed from the face of design, because of design thinking. Suddenly design's problem-solving process has become more accessible to a wider range of people.

At the same time, the veil has also been pulled away from business. All of the convoluted algorithms and overly complex financial operations and statements that few could penetrate are actually quite accessible now due to gamification and great user-experience design and social media platforms.

What are we actually talking about when we discuss ownership? Robert LeFevre, a libertarian and a pacifist, wrote some interesting things about the philosophy of ownership—specifically, the ownership of the intangible. For example, once we share ideas, and we open up who owns an idea or a process or a space, it is a bit like emptying water from a bucket. So when you empty water out of a bucket, there are still droplets of water left, yet the boundaries of the idea have expanded. Another concept that LeFevre explored is that ideas are constituted by multiple things—in other words, no idea is truly new. He also wrote about sharing being predicated on ownership. So in order to share something, we first must own it. What an even better outcome if a multitude of people own it!

Nathan Hendricks, a creative director at LPK, gave a talk on "Design as the Fourth Estate." The fourth estate is typically thought of as an institution of society that is not credited as being very influential. Usually the fourth estate is considered the media, but what Nathan put forth is that the fourth estate is actually design—and that design is not credited for the influence that it has on society. Nathan hones in on the feeling of angst that is very alive in this conversation about who owns design.

Bruce Mau quotes Leonard Cohen in his "Design Manifesto" when he remarks upon the dichotomy between "The Suits" and "The Creatives" as a "charming artifact of the past." There is no such division anymore. We have to move beyond that.

We can learn a lot from fashion. There is a big debate going on in fashion about ownership of ideas and intellectual property. One camp, headed by Diane von Furstenberg, supports trademark and copyrights and increasing the legal barriers to entry, which has all sorts of cost ramifications if you are a young, emerging designer. Tom Ford on the other hand is part of that camp that says "Give it away!"; the threat of fashion knock-offs actually helps us to be more innovative and on the verge on what's new and what's next. This philosophical stance of opening up the playing field, which is what we see in fashion, may be helpful for the rest of the design world to borrow.

LANGUAGE AND STRATEGIC DESIGN

There are several levels of language. There is the language among designers, and there is also the language and translation that happens between non-designers and design. I have considered that perhaps there needs to be a lingua franca, one that integrates business and design. After speaking with a number of people, I realized that we don't need to complicate things that much, but we do need to distill concepts to a common denominator. Perhaps the issue is less about confusion over terms and more about confusion over value and time commitment. That is where the breakdown really happens.

There are examples of how other industries distill concepts down to a simpler common denominator. Twyla Tharp's *The Creative Habit* successfully translates the tenets of creativity to the "non-creatives." Tharp does a really good job at this, partly under the assumption that we all are creative at our core. Another good example of translation on very simple terms is Daniel Pink's *To Sell Is Human*. Pink translates the value of sales and selling to wider audiences, some of whom may cringe at the idea of being a salesman. He really is broadening the conversation. Translation is occurring even in the legal field. Law is certainly a profession that is bogged down by jargon that most of the time seems impenetrable, but "legal rebels," as these practicing attorneys are called by the American Bar Association, are doing things differently and integrating—wait for it—design thinking into law.

BLURRED LINES

Interestingly, if you compare visual representations of design thinking and of lean start-up, you won't actually see much of a distinction. There seems to be a bit of a merger. For example, a visual by Thoring and Müller, where they break down the distinction between design thinking and a lean start-up, they purposefully have mapped them out very similarly. They then took things a step further by asking what might "lean design thinking" look like. So they truly integrated the two and tried to create a visual language that shows the overlap and integration.

Bob Schwartz has said, "We are in this business to deliver shareholder value and improve the lives of people." This is a twofold mission that designers have. Perhaps we should not be asking about the ROI (return on investment) of design, but rather the ROE (return on equity) of design. If we start to shift the conversation to ROE instead of ROI, then we begin to understand, in very real terms, that it is design that makes business visible, viable, and feasible.

ROI is a very external conversation with external influences. Return on equity is a much more internal conversation; it is net income divided by shareholder equity. The equity piece is the craft, skills, and ideas that designers contribute. So equity is really the melding of value, meaning, craft, skills, and ideas. To take it a step further, designers' ROE is really about sensemaking. It is really about being able to attach meaning to what is experiential.

Strategic design is the perfect opportunity to embrace a blurred line that formerly separated design and business. This book offers some foundational ideas and provocative insights to help you reframe the value of design thinking and ultimately become a better designer, a better strategist, and a better strategic design thinker.

—Natalie W. Nixon
Philadelphia, PA
November 2014

PART I

The Why: Introduction to Part I—Chapters 1, 2, and 3

Simon Sinek (2010) said it best in his explanation of the Golden Circle and his "Start with Why" premise: "Words may inspire, but only action creates change," and we take his lead by framing this book in terms of the Why, the How, and the What of strategic design thinking. With each sequential chapter, we hope that you will be inspired by the words that explain the foundations of strategic design and then go on to change the ways that you think, act, and relate to others in your work and personal lives.

In part I we give you a theoretical grounding upon which to start your exploration of strategic design. We explore "The Why" of strategic design by examining the impetus for this approach to problem solving. We begin in chapter 1 with a thorough, detailed, and robust explanation of design thinking, the core of strategic design, by Alison Rieple of the University of Westminster School of Business in London. I always highlight that design thinking is a problem-solving process, borrowed from the field of design, and applied to the design of services, experiences, and processes. It uses empathy, lateral thinking, prototyping, and story to compellingly unravel insights that are embedded in complex systems. Alison does a deep dive into the theoretical parameters of design thinking, while accessibly unpacking what it is about the designer's problem-solving process and abductive rationale that is distinctive and adds value to business strategy. It is essential that you understand design thinking because it is fundamental to and at the core of this creative approach to strategy for marketing, operations, and organizational design.

In a saturated market and VUCA (volatile, uncertain, complex, and ambiguous) business environment, your organization will need more than a SWOT (strengths, weaknesses, opportunities, and threats) analysis and focus group to connect meaningfully to your consumer. In chapter 2, Joe Hancock of Drexel University explains meaning and meaningful connections to customers by examining semiotics. Semiotics is the study of sign and symbol, and it is the theoretical underpinning to all branding strategy. Joe takes us on a journey of semiotics by focusing on the fashion industry. This is an exciting and important lens because the fashion industry excels at the aspirational—after all, no one in the Western world really needs another T-shirt or pair of jeans—and yet we clamor for more! Semiotics in the context of fashion also highlights the value and power of story.

Story is indeed the Why of your brand and causes people to lean in; it is a vehicle for authenticity, distinctive from a narrative or a dry mission statement. Story is one of the reasons companies such as Dove and Chipotle lead in their respective market categories with short films that focus on their Why—without once mentioning product. In a saturated market, people are vying for authentic messaging. Joe leaves you with introductions to cultural anthropologist Grant McCracken and theorist Jean Baudrillard, to ensure that you are grounded in the theory behind the practice.

We end part 1 with a colorful and broad exploration of the brand, because in the strategic design view, branding is not some frilly add-on at the end of a process; branding is core to strategy, and in fact, it is a strategic endeavor. Valerie Jacobs, vice president of trends at LPK, and Michael Wintrob, vice president of strategy at LPK, have coauthored a vibrant and thorough essay on the history of brands, again pointing out the key component of story, integrating a good dose of theory on rhetoric, and explaining the strategic advantage of incorporating trends research when developing brands. Valerie and Michael point out forward-thinking uses and cases of brands that are actually platforms, co-created with the customer.

In part I, you will be fully excited with each new concept, suggested reflection, and exercise that will set you up for the rationale of why strategic design matters and is significant for any strategic endeavor today.

Reference

Sinek, S. (2010), "How Great Leaders Inspire Action," TED Talk. Available online: http://www.ted.com/talks/simon_sinek_how_great_leaders_inspire_action?language=en

Alison Rieple

Dr. Alison Rieple is a Professor of Strategic Management at the University of Westminster in London. She is the coauthor (with Adrian Haberberg) of *The Strategic Management of Organizations* (2001) and *Strategic Management: Theory and Application* (2008). She is also currently coediting two books on design management for Edward Elgar (forthcoming, 2015 and 2016/17). Alison's research interests include the management of design process; the management of innovation, especially in the cultural and creative industries; and the processes of resisting, adopting, and institutionalizing innovation.

Focusing Question: What is distinctive about the design-thinking lens and how might design thinking contribute to organizations' decision-making processes?

In this chapter we look at the concept of design thinking and its contribution to creativity and organizational problem solving. The concept of design thinking attempts to capture what it is about what designers do that is distinctive and different.

This chapter explores the key questions:

· What is design thinking?

· What do designers do that is different from other people?

· How can design thinking improve decision making in organizations?

INTRODUCTION

Design thinking is a fairly recent concept, and there is no real consensus as to what it is. Early definitions focused on designers' activities, and writers in the design community still tend to concentrate on identifying what it is that designers do. Many of the leading design consultancies, such as IDEO, and universities, such as Stanford's Design School, have websites offering extensive descriptions of their views of the process and "toolkits" for those interested in using design thinking (see box). More recently, the term has entered mainstream business writing, and authors have started to focus on how design-thinking approaches might usefully be applied to more general business problems.

IDEO's Design-Thinking Methodology

"Design thinking is a human-centered approach to innovation that draws from the designer's toolkit to integrate the needs of people, the possibilities of technology, and the requirements for business success."
—Tim Brown, president and CEO

Thinking like a designer can transform the way organizations develop products, services, processes, and strategy. This approach, which IDEO calls design thinking, brings together what is desirable from a human point of view with what is technologically feasible and economically viable. It also allows people who aren't trained as designers to use creative tools to address a vast range of challenges.

Design thinking is a deeply human process that taps into abilities we all have but get overlooked by more conventional problem-solving practices. It relies on our ability to be intuitive, to recognize patterns, to construct ideas that are emotionally meaningful as well as functional, and to express ourselves through means beyond words or symbols. Nobody wants to run an organization on feeling, intuition, and inspiration, but an over-reliance on the rational and the analytical can be just as risky. Design thinking provides an integrated third way.

The design thinking process is best thought of as a system of overlapping spaces rather than a sequence of orderly steps. There are three spaces to keep in mind: *inspiration*, *ideation*, and *implementation*. Inspiration is the problem or opportunity that motivates the search for solutions. Ideation is the process of generating, developing, and testing ideas. Implementation is the path that leads from the project stage into people's lives.

Under this system, IDEO uses both analytical tools and generative techniques to help clients see how their new or existing operations could look in the future—and build road maps for getting there. Our methods include business model prototyping, data visualization, innovation strategy, organizational design, qualitative and quantitative research, and IP liberation.

All of IDEO's work is done in consideration of the capabilities of our clients and the needs of their customers. As we iterate toward a final solution, we assess and reassess our designs. Our goal is to deliver appropriate, actionable, and tangible strategies. The result: new, innovative avenues for growth that are grounded in business viability and market desirability.

Source: "Our Approach: Design Thinking," IDEO.com. Available online: http://www.ideo.com/about/ (accessed July 9, 2015).

Horst Rittel (1972) was an early advocate of designers' difference when he identified the "wicked nature" of many design problems. These are characterized by ambiguous or unclear boundaries to the problem and high uncertainty as to what might be the most successful solution. For example, a municipal government might ask "How do we end homelessness?" or a hotel might ask "How might we anticipate our customers' needs?" Both of these questions point to wicked problems. Linear, analytical approaches were unlikely to be able to resolve such problems; they needed an experimental approach in which multiple possible solutions could be explored. Many have now taken up this baton and pointed out that many organizational problems are similarly "wicked." For that reason, understanding what designers do and applying it as a methodology to complex organizational problems that require creativity and inspiration might be quite a good thing to do.

So in this chapter, we will attempt to define the term and show how it has developed over time—and from this show how thinking like a designer can be helpful to organizations as they seek to develop creative solutions to organizational problems, such as decision making and strategy development.

History of the Concept

Design thinking as a term appears to have been first mentioned in 1987 by Peter Rowe, a professor of architecture at the Harvard School of Design. His intention was to "account for the underlying structure and focus of inquiry directly associated with

those rather private moments of 'seeking out,' on the part of designers" (Rowe 1987: 1). In 1991 the first formal academic research symposium on design thinking was organized by Nigel Cross, Norbert Roozenburg, and Kees Dorst (http://design.open.ac.uk /cross/DesignThinkingResearchSymposia .htm). These workshops have continued since, and in recent years have examined things such as:

- turn-taking in design focused discourse
- sketching and gesture as a means of communicating design ideas
- emergence as a property of designing

This stream of thinking emerged from designers and design educators trying to understand what it is that designers do, so they could pass on these skills through education and training to newcomers.

Probably the first effort to move design thinking to a more mainstream audience happened when IDEO executives David Kelley (Kelley & Littman 2005) and Tim Brown (2009) attempted to show how design thinking—what designers do, their principles, methods, and tools—could be applied to innovation development and organizational problem solving. Since then it has become an increasingly popular topic in mainstream business publications, such as *Business Week*, *The Economist*, *Harvard Business Review*, *Fast Company*, the *New York Times*, and the *Wall Street Journal*. Such publications have taken an interest in the subject because their readers are interested in what makes some companies more successful than others—so that they can achieve the same success. The basis for competing effectively is about implementing strategies that confer some sort of distinctiveness on the organization—something that no one else can do as well. And it's very hard to achieve. Competitive advantage can come from producing goods at a lower cost than your rivals (and therefore charging lower prices or making higher profits), or from producing better quality or novel products, or from making highly desirable products. Or, in a perfect world, a mixture of all three. These choices are what are known as the organization's competitive stance, and designers can play a strategic role in each of them.

For organizations wishing to produce at lower costs than their competitors, designers can:

- Design products that can be manufactured cheaply and reliably and transported cheaply and reliably. This means choosing materials carefully and taking care to cost in such issues as wastage and damage. H&M were able to reduce their transport costs significantly by designing their logistics systems so that they transferred most of their clothes in sealed containers. This resulted in fewer items being damaged, and losses were much lower from pilfering and losing items along the way.
- Design the layout of the organization so that communications are efficient and quick and materials can be transported to the right place at the right time. This may mean visualizing the value chain of the organization so that gaps in communication and delays in the movement of goods can be seen easily.
- Design the value and supply chain and logistics systems so that goods can be bought and obtained by customers quickly and effectively. This may mean designing a website, so that goods can be "seen" almost as well as in real life, or designing a store, so that the most important and profitable goods are at eye level or accessible via a "footfall" path that captures the places where the most people pass.

Designers can help to produce better quality products by:

- Knowing about the best quality materials—how to source them, how to integrate them in the manufacturing process, and how to combine them with other organizational assets to produce the best quality, or perhaps most reliable, finished goods.
- Helping to develop innovations that bring new features to existing offerings, or by developing entirely new products that competitors cannot yet offer.

And designers can help to create desirable products by:

- Designing brands that symbolize the organization's values and product characteristics, and in so doing, save customers search costs.
- Creating products that customers "must have," either because all their friends have them, or because they

want to show off, or because they are products that customers just *love* to have: They have an emotional bond with them. Girls and shoes are just one example. Men and cars are another! (Not that we are stereotyping anyone here, you understand!)

In order to contribute to such strategic directions, designers have to grapple with the unknown—whether consumers will buy the product, whether it will fulfill the needs that it promises, and whether the product will work or not. This is where design thinking comes in, and it is also where the designer's ability to imagine, to visualize, and to empathize and understand consumers' behavior comes in.

Two prominent academics who have advocated design thinking for mainstream business use are Roger Martin and Jeanne Liedtka. Martin (2009), dean of the Rotman School of Management at the University of Toronto at the time, advocated breaking down the dichotomy of instinctive/original/creative and quantitative/analytical thinking on the basis that organizations need both types but typically, because of their risk aversion, focus more on analytical processes. He advocated organizations using a design-thinking type of process to solve wicked problems by moving systematically through a "funnel" from the "mystery" of the problem through a "heuristic" process to an "algorithm" that developed solutions (see Figure 1.1). Doing so would allow organizations to embrace both the creative and analytical aspects of problem solving, a process of *abductive* reasoning (we

return to these concepts below). Quoting Tim Brown (Brown 2008: 86), Martin said that design thinking was "'a discipline that uses the designer's sensibility and methods to match people's needs with what is technologically feasible and what a viable business strategy can convert into customer value and market opportunity.' A person or organization instilled with that discipline is constantly seeking a fruitful balance between art and science, intuition and analytics, exploration and exploitation" (Martin 2009).

Jeanne Liedtka, along with her coauthor Tim Ogilvie (Liedtka & Ogilvie 2011), developed a design-thinking toolkit for organizations that operationalizes the principles of design thinking into a form that mainstream organizations can use. They begin by imagining what would be different if managers thought more like designers. Their answer: empathy, invention, and iteration. They identify four stages to problem solving: (1) **what *is*** explores current reality; (2) **what *if*** envisions a new future; (3) **what *wows*** makes some choices; and (4) **what *works*** takes us into the marketplace (see Figure 1.2). Mapped against this are ten tools that are used to a greater or lesser extent in each of the four stages:

- visualization, a "meta" tool "so fundamental to the way designers work" that it is used in most of the stages
- ethnographic tools, such as customer journey mapping
- value chain analysis
- mind mapping
- brainstorming

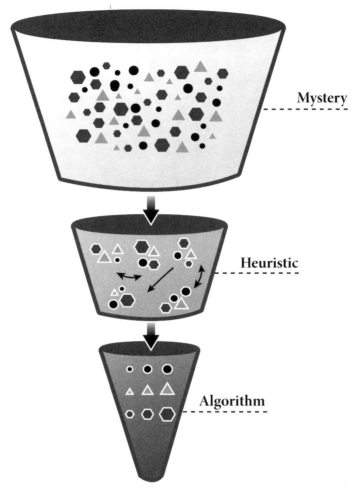

Figure 1.1 Moving systematically through a funnel going from an ambiguous mysterious stage to the clearer algorithmic stage is one way to think through wicked problems.
(Source: Martin 2010: 38)

- concept development
- assumption testing
- rapid prototyping
- consumer co-creation
- learning launch

We return to examine some of these elements of design thinking in more detail below. But first, let us look at why design thinking might be a useful thing for organizations to embrace.

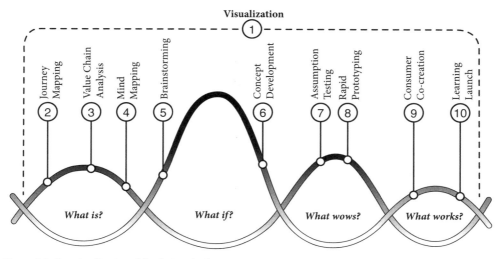

Visualization

(1)

(2) Journey Mapping

(3) Value Chain Analysis

(4) Mind Mapping

(5) Brainstorming

(6) Concept Development

(7) Assumption Testing

(8) Rapid Prototyping

(9) Consumer Co-creation

(10) Learning Launch

What is?   *What if?*   *What wows?*   *What works?*

Figure 1.2 One visualization of the design-thinking process
(Source: Liedtka & Olgilvie 2011)

Why Design Thinking May Help Problem Solving in Organizations

The world has changed. Arguably the business environment has changed more in the last ten years than has ever happened before. Two major forces have had an impact on all organizations: (1) the internet and electronic communications technology and (2) the increasing internationalization of business activities. Given these two massive, and linked, forces, organizations need to behave in very different ways from the ways that they would have behaved twenty or more years ago. This requires a different way of solving organizational problems—problems that forecasting, planning, and measuring are less likely to solve. Traditional metrics, methods and ideologies—as epitomized by traditional MBA courses and a focus on rational analysis—just won't work as well any more.

Liedtka and Ogilvie compare two approaches—one by a student team of MBAs and another of design students—to a typical challenge faced by a leading consumer products firm: how to respond to changes in the retail marketplace over the next ten years. They suggest the MBAs would research trends in the marketplace, read analysts' reports, and benchmark performance against competitors. They'd produce forecasts and recommend a set of strategies, complete with ROI (return on investment) and NPV (net present value) calculations. The design students would approach the problem very differently. They might begin with a similar understanding of trends but use this to develop scenarios of possible futures instead of spreadsheets. They would hang out in stores and talk to shoppers and employees to understand their experiences. Perhaps they'd model potential changes in their lives and shopping habits over the next ten years and present not solutions but a small number of concepts to be prototyped. These would be explored with users to see how they felt and reacted. Any changes in expected reactions could be accommodated by altering the prototypes until one could be found that worked. Now no one is saying that organizations are going to give up the MBA's approach any time soon, or that they should, but the design students will bring a different, fresh, and complementary look at the same problem.

There is some evidence that the design students' approach will produce more, and more novel, solutions. Where a creative approach is required, they are more likely to be successful. Some powerful voices have argued that creativity (the ability to create new meaningful forms) and innovation (the creation of a new product, technology, or business model) has now become the decisive source of competitive advantage in virtually every industry (Florida 2002; Pink 2005). This suggests that design thinking is becoming more important as it can be a catalyst for innovation productivity, increasing the rate at which good ideas are generated. If creativity is now the key element of global competition, more than the traditional selling of goods and services made in economically advantageous locations, then traditional hierarchical organizations are likely to be replaced by creative workplaces of intrinsically motivated, self-managed, and independent workers who have blurred traditional notions of time, work, and leisure and in so doing have changed the workplace and the community. Project-based working, temporary contracts, and flexible hours are increasingly common. This is both the cause and effect of a work environment that values solutions rather than turning up and staying at the office for eight hours. In this type of environment, design thinking matters because it allows for user- and experience-based solutions, rather than those based around budgets and unit-based targets.

In this rather unstable environment, many of the problems that are encountered are "wicked." Wicked problems (Rittel & Webber 1973; Conklin 1996, 2001; Conklin & Weil 1997; Pries-Heje & Baskerville 2008; Marshak 2009; Napier et al. 2009; Peters 2012; Fyke & Buzzanell 2013) are those that are essentially unique and novel. Their boundaries cannot be seen, and they have no discernible end. They can be explained in different ways, and the choice of explanation determines the nature of the problem's resolution. There are no right and wrong answers. In fact, the problem may not be understood until after the formulation of a solution. Planning and rational analysis are only of limited use in these circumstances. Planning works best when the future is likely to resemble the past.

GO DEEPER
Read the following:
- "Wicked Problems in Design Thinking" by R. Buchanan in *Design Issues*.
- "Risk Preventative Innovation Strategies for Emerging Technologies: The

Cases of Nano-textiles and Smart Textiles" by A. R. Köhler and C. Som in *Technovation*.

- "Perspective: Linking Design Thinking with Innovation Outcomes through Cognitive Bias Reduction" by J. Liedtka in *Journal of Product Innovation Management*.
- "Reflections on Wicked Problems in Organizations" by R. J. Marshak in *Journal of Management Inquiry*.

REFLECTIONS
- Think of an example of a wicked problem in your own life. Describe in as much detail as you can what characterizes it as wicked. What steps are you taking to try to solve it?
- Try to describe the typical problem-solving process in your organization (your school, college, or workplace)— in as much detail as you possibly can.
- Have you seen anyone solve a wicked problem in your workplace successfully? What did they do to solve the problem?

Solutions to wicked problems are not true or false, but good or bad—and sometimes this cannot be judged until after the event. There is no immediate test of a solution; each solution is a "one-shot operation"; because there is no opportunity to learn by trial and error, every attempt counts. Arguably all strategy problems have always been wicked. After all, companies have never been able to predict what competitors would do, in reaction to a change of direction perhaps, or what new products and services competitors themselves were going to bring out. However, wicked problems seem to be more commonplace and are found at many levels in the organization.

Another reason why design thinking may be helpful is that decision makers often find it difficult to come up with new, groundbreaking ideas (Loewenstein & Angner 2003). In the traditional "rational" organization, the ideas that are generated tend to emerge from within the existing paradigm and suffer from a number of individual and organizational sociopsychological constraints and biases. There are many of these. In the first place, we tend to think that the future will resemble the past (Gilbert, Gill, & Wilson 2002) and be more positive than it actually will be (Larwood & Whittaker 1977; Kahneman & Tversky 1979). These perception biases severely restrict the decision maker's ability to consider left-field threats or the possibilities of radical change.

Part of the problem is that people find it difficult to accurately describe their preferences or describe their current behavior, much less make reliable predictions about how they will react to something in the future, for example, a new product or a new way of working. The user cannot always articulate the need. This problem has been well documented in relation to market research and buying behavior; consumers cannot predict how they will react to an innovation (Rogers 2010; Slater, Mohr, & Sengupta 2014). Decision makers therefore find it difficult to predict users' future behavior, whether these are customers or colleagues. This is a potential problem when something new is proposed, and it tends to push decision makers to choose something less risky or unpredictable.

Other biases that affect decision choices are the tendency to project thoughts, preferences, and behaviors onto other people (Van Boven et al. 2000; Van Boven & Loewenstein 2003). There is a well-recognized "hypothesis confirmation bias," where decision makers seek explanations that are congruent with their own preferences. This means that they become attached to the solution they already have created (Kahneman, Knetsch, & Thaler 1991). Other research (e.g., Loewenstein & Angner 2003) describes how mood and affective state influence the assessment of the value of an idea. In stressful situations, such as the need to respond to a changing environment or deal with a threatening competitor, necessary risks may not be taken because of fear of failure or because of the emotional load that would be required to do something different (Morgan & Laland 2012).

GO DEEPER
Read the following:
- "The Future Is Now" by D. Gilbert, M. Gill, and T. Wilson in *Organizational Behavior and Human Decision Processes*.
- *Thinking, Fast and Slow* by D. Kahneman.
- "Intuitive Prediction: Biases and Corrective Procedures" by D. Kahneman and A. Tversky in *Management Science*.
- *Diffusion of Innovations* by E. M. Rogers.
- "Radical Product Innovation Capability: Literature Review, Synthesis, and Illustrative Research Propositions," by S. F. Slater, J. J. Mohr, and S. Sengupta in the *Journal of Product Innovation Management*.

REFLECTIONS
- Think of a decision that you have made that you decided subsequently had been a mistake. What influenced your choice? How could you have made a better decision?
- Bad decisions can also be made by firms. Think of a bad decision made by a company—one that affected its profits or its reputation perhaps. Find out what was written about this decision on websites and in social media, newspapers, business magazines, and books. Look for evidence of bias, emotions (hubris, competitiveness, anger, pride, etc.), or other types of cognitive processes in the decision-making process.
- Describe how you would try to ensure that a brand new idea that you want friends (or work or college) to agree to gets accepted successfully.

In an unknown, unknowable future full of wicked problems, decision makers need to consider alternative futures, paying attention to opportunities not just constraints. But because the sorts of biases described above can be overconfident in their chosen future, the search process tends to terminate prematurely and firms overinvest in early solutions. Design thinking has been suggested as a way of breaking down such cognitive biases and reaching more and better quality decisions.

Design-Thinking Methodologies

We return to discussing design-thinking methods and how they are used in real situations in chapter 6. Here we look at some of the underlying principles of design-thinking methodologies and how these may help organizational decision processes, given the organizational contingencies just described.

As we said earlier, there are many different aspects to design thinking, and there is no real agreement yet as to what it is; however, in this section we focus on what seem to be the most important elements—those that are mentioned by most people and that seem to have the most potential benefits to organizations at large. Tom Lockwood summarizes it well in describing design thinking as "a human-centered innovation process that emphasizes observation, collaboration, fast learning, visualization of ideas, rapid concept prototyping, and concurrent business analysis" (Lockwood 2009: xi). We will now look at design-thinking elements in more detail.

Visualization

Visualization involves the use of imagery, either visual or narrative. It is arguably the most significant difference between designers and other people; designers simply have to represent their thoughts. In addition to traditional drawings, charts/graphs, mock-ups, and photography, visualization includes such tools as the use of metaphor and stories. These latter elements are not unique to designers, but they are a verbal expression of the same visualization imperatives as the more graphical techniques.

Visualization not only helps people to communicate their ideas, it also helps them to generate them, as well as helping potential users understand what a new idea will involve. Like prototyping, which we return to below, it is a way of seeing what might be possible rather than simply trying to imagine it. Visualization is also linked with designers' interest in storytelling (which we also return to below) as a way of creating a vision of the future.

In terms of strategy formulation, people need to be able to see why you've chosen a certain strategy and what you're attempting to do with it. It is no accident that strategists are told to think about setting a *vision* for the future. But most senior managers tend to do this in words—how much more compelling could this be if this vision could be transformed into a form that can be seen and stimulate the generation of vivid mental images (Liedtka & Ogilvie 2011).

Visualization also helps people to focus on a single interpretation of an idea. Designers, by making a film, scenario, or prototype to illuminate a vision, can help people emotionally experience the thing that the strategy seeks to describe. If, say, Motorola unveils a plan to create products that have never existed before, everyone in the organization will have a different idea of what that means, and what they will do. But if Motorola creates a video so people can see those products, or makes prototypes so people can touch them, everyone has the same view. As Tim Brown says, "Because it's pictorial, design describes the world in a way that's not open to many interpretations. Designers, by making a film, scenario, or prototype, can help people emotionally experience the thing that the strategy seeks to describe" (Wroblewski 2006a).

Most companies use design during the implementation phase (Figure 1.3b) to improve the usability and aesthetic aspects of a product, but as Luke Wroblewski (2006b) says, design's potential value is often ignored: Companies that recognize the strategic value of design know its power lies in communication. These companies include designers and design artifacts

(prototypes, mock-ups, concept models) when communicating or developing a vision to help an individual, team, or an entire organization understand something visionary (Figures 1.3a and 1.3b).

Abduction

Abductive thinking is a type of logical reasoning that goes from observation of data to the development of hypotheses that can explain this evidence. According to Wikipedia, the American philosopher Charles Sanders Peirce (1839–1914) first conceived of the term as "guessing" the most

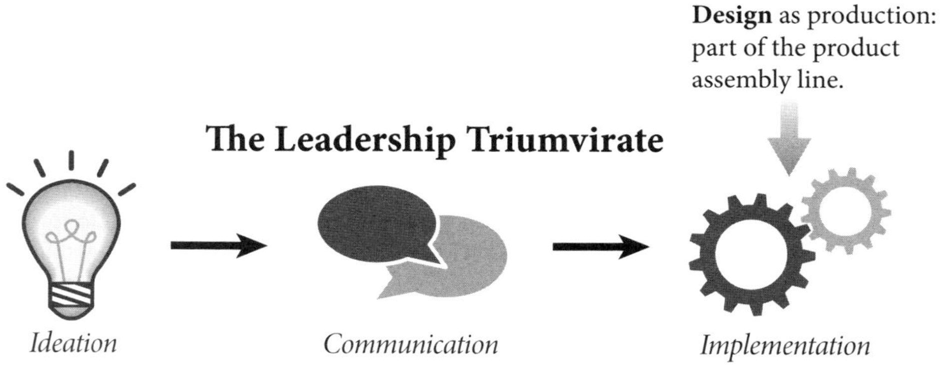

Figure 1.3a Design as production
(Source: Wroblewski 2006b)

Figure 1.3b Design as strategy
(Source: Wroblewski 2006b)

plausible explanation for what is seen. In more recent times, design-thinking theorists (notably Roger Martin) have used abduction to mean a process of inferring, developing plausible solutions to solving the problems that the data present, and visualizing what those solutions might be. Where deduction takes existing data and creates an explanation for what is seen and induction attempts to prove that this explanation works, abduction *synthesizes* knowledge to create something plausible and coherent.

The style of thinking in traditional firms is largely inductive and deductive; the business approach is definitive, seeking for proof. In contrast, abductive reasoning is arguably one of the most important aspects of designers' thinking. Strongly linked with the use of prototyping and experimentation that we return to below, designers use an intense focus on problem exploration and use iterative cycles of exploration to develop insights and then build criteria to test these insights (Cross 2001, 2004).

Design thinking relies on a "build to think" process dependent on trial and error and an ability to move between intuitive and analytic modes (Martin 2007, 2009; Liedtka & Ogilvie 2011). This is characterized by a dialectical problem-centered focus and the recognition that alternative solutions must be invented, compared with the "decision attitude" characteristic of business thinking, in which alternatives are treated as already known and choices are rational (Boland & Collopy 2004). We return to discussing such integrative, holistic systems and thinking approaches in more detail in chapter 7.

Experimentation and Prototyping

As suggested in the previous section, a corollary of abductive reasoning is **experimentation**. Designers love to play around with ideas—mock-ups, prototypes, models. As Roger Martin says, the philosophy in design shops is "try it, prototype it, and improve it" (2004: 10). Design thinking is inherently a prototyping process: Designers build in order to think. Another way of putting this is to say that designers learn by doing (Cross 2004; Bogers & Horst 2013). It involves actively avoiding making choices for as long as possible (Cross 2001; Olins 2005). Sometimes this is not such a good thing: Designers are not always great at knowing when enough is enough!

An organization in which design thinking is embedded has an environment in which personnel at all levels experiment with new ways of doing things, realizing that some new ideas will fail, but that in failing these efforts will bring benefits. Experiments allow the designer/design thinker to test the underlying assumptions of a hypothesis out in the real world—or as close to the real world as one can get without actually being there. These assumptions may be made by the designer, who overestimates the attractiveness of a new idea; by the consumer or potential user, who misunderstands how he or she will behave in a given situation or with a given artifact; or by the manager, who assumes that a product will be more popular (or less!) than hoped. This allows the organization to manage risk. Prototypes are a relatively low-cost way to learn from failure.

In a design-thinking approach to strategy development, the organization's strategy is refined early and often, in effect prototyped, and the strategy evolves, bringing in multiple contributors to the process. This has a number of effects. In the first place, those that are involved are "brought in" to the decisions that are taken, helping to minimize the "not invented here" mentality that is often responsible for resistance to any new directions. Involving collaborators also typically leads to better solutions: They bring new insights into the process—ones that a single person, however imaginative, could not have contemplated. In corporations, most decisions are not tested (Martin 2005) but are made by a small number of people (too often the CEO alone) and are based on suboptimal decision-making processes that rely on bias and instinct, as described so powerfully by Daniel Kahneman (2011). Prototyping unlocks people's unconscious biases. People can *feel* how they will react to a change and therefore understand it. This allows the initiator to react to powerful emotions and rework the idea if necessary. But also, when external circumstances change, the strategy can change more easily along with it. The organization has the ability and flexibility to uncover problems and fix them in real time, as the situation unfolds.

As we discussed earlier, visualization techniques are useful for helping people to understand a new idea. Prototyping takes that a stage further. Physical techniques, such as storyboarding, scenario planning, and experience journey mapping, are all useful for making abstract ideas tangible (Liedtka 2013).

This process brings us to the next big design-thinking element—the involvement of multiple participants in a decision process. As described in this section, this mostly applies to internal organizational members, but design thinking explicitly brings in everyone who is likely to be affected by a decision. This requires certain skills—those of ethnography and anthropology: observation, empathy, interpretive sensemaking expertise, and the ability to create a conductive context for understanding people's behavior.

Ethnography and Interpretive Sensemaking

Empathy is a relatively recent addition to the design thinker's toolkit (Patnaik & Mortensen 2009), but it is an important one. As Tim Brown describes it, "At IDEO, a design thinker must not only be intensely collaborative, but empathic" (2006); this is design thinking as human-centered and user-driven. Collaborative work, especially with others having different and complementary experiences and skills, is necessary to generate better ideas and to achieve agreement on decisions. Nora Madjar, Greg Oldham, and Michael Pratt (2002) found that interactions with others from diverse backgrounds improved the creativity of individual responses.

GO DEEPER
Read the following:
- "Using Ethnography in Strategic Consumer Research" by R. Elliott and

N. Jankel-Elliott in *Qualitative Market Research*.

- *101 Design Methods: A Structured Approach for Driving Innovation in Your Organization* by V. Kumar.
- "A Difference of Design" by L. Wroblewski. Available online: http://www .lukew.com/ff/entry.asp?205

REFLECTIONS

- Using a storyboard tool, such as the one available at https://www .storyboardthat.com/storyboard-creator, create your own storyboard about a new product or service that you would like to develop. Think about who you would encounter along the way. What would they think? How would they behave?
- Imagine that you want to research whether consumers are likely to buy a new product. List the sorts of things that you would find out by using (a) market research techniques and (b) ethnographic techniques.
- Think of how you might counter a CEO who says that prototyping is a waste of time and money.

Choosing how to frame the problem and judge possible solutions requires a sensitivity to otherness and the ability to use a range of qualitative research methods. These focus on developing a deep understanding of users by observing and interacting with them in their native habitats and interpreting their behavior. Such ethnographic methods allow the observer to discover the (often hidden) meanings and feelings behind behavior: Ethnography uncovers needs that users cannot articulate. This process produces much better, and more real, information than focus groups and quantitative market research methodologies, which are so problematic when innovative insights are required (Bogers & Horst 2013). By immersing themselves in the user's experience, decision makers become less reliant on their biases as a source of new ideas (Liedtka & Ogilvie 2011) and can perceive opportunities that were not previously evident.

Reality, for designers, is always socially constructed, rather than an objective reality "out there" that can be discovered through statistical techniques. A design-thinking viewpoint looks at a situation subjectively, participating in it from the inside. "We're making the world up by the choices, stories, products, and experiences we make. If they are compelling enough, other people will want to join in" (Wroblewski 2006a). Ethnographic sensemaking and interpretive techniques are used to structure and analyze the copious qualitative data obtained by the design-thinking team to look for patterns and insights. These include techniques such as observation and the mapping of the product or service utilization, as well as the use of cognitive techniques, such as metaphors, storyboarding, mind mapping, and brainstorming.

Metaphors play a major role in helping make sense of experiences; metaphors are some of design thinking's most important sensemaking and visualization tools. By helping to stimulate participants' imaginations, metaphors help reduce decision makers' reliance on the past, broaden their field of vision, and produce more novel ideas (Liedtka 2013). Metaphorical language is inherently emotion laden. Talking in metaphors, analogies, and stories is more compelling than purely analytical logic and reasoning (Pugmire 1998). Decisions driven by emotion rather than logic can be a far more powerful motivator than so-called objective goals (Liedtka & Ogilvie 2011).

Such techniques generate multiple, more compelling options. As decision makers have to consider—and explain—a range of possible options, this also helps to improve the accuracy of predictions. It forces thinkers to consider what Kahneman (2011) calls system 2, or less instinctive, thinking, rather than jumping to obvious or biased

conclusions. In experiments conducted by Dale Griffin, David Dunning, and Lee Ross (1990), when subjects were asked to come up with multiple potential future situations, they were far less likely to show the overconfidence that is characteristic of most subjects in these types of studies.

To summarize, design thinking is fundamental to the way that designers think and behave. It underpins strategic design processes and is an important potential tool to help "normal" managers improve their decision making in a world full of wicked, unknowable problems. In the remainder of this book, we look in more detail at specific examples of design thinking in practice in strategic design decision making and in wider organizational and social contexts.

Acknowledgments

To the many people who have inspired me to get involved in design management theorizing and education. But especially to Jeanne Liedtka and Natalie Nixon, for their enthusiasm and commitment to the development of design thinking. And of course to my husband, Gordon, who has been a constant source of support and encouragement throughout.

References

Bogers, M. and W. Horst (2013), "Collaborative Prototyping: Cross-Fertilization of Knowledge in Prototype-Driven Problem Solving," *Journal of Product Innovation Management*, 31 (4): 744–64. Available online: http://onlinelibrary.wiley.com/doi/10.1111/jpim.12121/full

Boland, R. and F. Collopy (2004), *Management as Designing: Exploring a New Vocabulary of Practice*, Palo Alto, CA: Stanford University Press.

Brown, T. (2006), "Innovation through Design Thinking" (address to the Dean's Innovative Leadership Series at the MIT Sloan School of Management),

Cambridge, MA: March 16, 2006. Available online: http://video.mit.edu/watch/innovation-through-design-thinking-9138/

Brown, T. (June 2008), "Design Thinking," *Harvard Business Review*, 84–92.

Brown, T. (2009), *Change by Design: How Design Thinking Transforms Organizations and Inspires Innovation*, New York: Harper-Collins.

Buchanan, R. (1992), "Wicked Problems in Design Thinking," *Design Issues*, 8 (2): 5–21.

Conklin, J. (1996), "Wicked Problems," CogNexus Institute. Available online: http://www.cognexus.org/cco-wpdm.pdf

Conklin, J. and W. Weil (2001), "Wicked Problems and Social Complexity," CogNexus Institute. Available online: http://www.accelinnova.com/docs/wickedproblems.pdf

Conklin, J. and W. Weil (1997), "Wicked Problems: Naming the Pain in Organizations," CogNexus Institute. Available online: http://www.ideapartnership.org/documents/wickedproblems.pdf

Cross, N. (2001), "Designerly Ways of Knowing: Design Discipline Versus Design Science," *Design Issues*, 17 (3): 49–55.

Cross, N., ed. (2004), "Expertise in Design," special issue of Design Studies, 25 (5).

Elliott, R. and N. Jankel-Elliott (2003), "Using Ethnography in Strategic Consumer Research," *Qualitative Market Research*, 6 (4): 215–23.

Florida, R. L. (2002), *The Rise of the Creative Class: And How It's Transforming Work, Leisure, Community and Everyday Life*, New York: Basic Books.

Fyke, J. and P. Buzzanell (2013), "The Ethics of Conscious Capitalism: Wicked Problems in Leading Change and Changing Leaders," *Human Relations*, 66 (12): 1619–43.

Gilbert, D., M. Gill, and T. Wilson (2002), "The Future Is Now," *Organizational Behavior and Human Decision Processes*, 88 (1): 430–44.

Griffin, D., D. Dunning, and L. Ross (1990), "The Role of Construal Process in Overconfident Predictions about The Self and Others," *Journal of Personality and Social Psychology,* 59 (6): 1128–39.

Kahneman, D. (2011), *Thinking, Fast and Slow*. New York: Farrar, Straus and Giroux.

Kahneman. D. and A. Tversky (1979), "Intuitive Prediction: Biases and Corrective Procedures," *Management Science*, 12: 313–27.

Kahneman, D., J. L. Knetsch and R. H. Thaler (1991), "Anomalies: The Endowment Effect, Loss Aversion, and Status Quo Bias," The Journal of Economic Perspectives, 5(1): 193–206.

Kelley, T., and J. Littman (2005), *The Ten Faces of Innovation: IDEO's Strategies for Beating the Devil's Advocate and Driving Creativity throughout Your Organization*, New York: Doubleday.

Köhler, A. R. and C. Som (2013), "Risk Preventative Innovation Strategies for Emerging Technologies: The Cases of Nano-textiles and Smart Textiles," *Technovation*, 34 (8): 420–30.

Kumar, V. (2012), *101 Design Methods: A Structured Approach for Driving Innovation in Your Organization*, Wilmington, DE: John Wiley & Sons.

Larwood, L. and W. Whittaker (1977), "Managerial Myopia: Self-serving Biases in Organizational Planning," *Journal of Applied Psychology*, 62 (2): 194–98.

Liedtka, J. (2013), "Design Thinking: What It Is and Why It Works," Design at Darden Working Paper Series. Available online http://www.designatdarden.org/academic-papers/

Liedtka, J. and T. Ogilvie (2011), *Designing for Growth: A Design Thinking Tool Kit for Managers*, New York: Columbia Business Press.

Lockwood, T., ed. (2009), *Design Thinking: Integrating Innovation, Customer Experience, and Brand Value*, 3rd edn, New York: Allworth Press.

Loewenstein, G. and E. Angner (2003), "Predicting and Indulging Changing Preferences," in G. Lowenstein, D. Read, and R. Baumeister (eds.), *Time and Decision: Economic and Psychological Perspectives on Intertemporal Choice*, 351–91, New York: Russell Sage Foundation.

Madjar, N., G. R. Oldham, and M. G. Pratt (2002), "There's No Place Like Home? The Contributions of Work and Nonwork Creativity Support to Employees' Creative Performance," *The Academy of Management Journal,* 45 (4): 757–67.

Marshak, R. J. (2009), "Reflections on Wicked Problems in Organizations," *Journal of Management Inquiry*, 18 (1): 58–59.

Martin, R. L. (2004), *The Design of Business*, Cambridge, MA: Harvard Business Review Press.

Martin, R. L. (2005), "Why Decisions Need Design," *Bloomberg Business.com*, August 31. Available online: http://www.bloomberg.com/bw/stories/2005-08-31/why-decisions-need-design (accessed June 4, 2015).

Martin, R. L. (2007), *The Opposable Mind: Winning through Integrative Thinking*, Boston: Harvard Business School Press.

Martin, R. L. (2009), *The Design of Business: Why Design Thinking Is the Next Competitive Advantage*, Boston: Harvard Business Press.

Martin, R. L. (2010), "Design Thinking: Achieving Insights via the 'Knowledge Funnel,'" *Strategy & Leadership*, 38 (2): 37–41.

Morgan, T. J. H. and K. N. Laland (2012), "The Biological Bases of Conformity," *Frontiers in Neuroscience*, 6 (87): 1–7.

Napier, N. K., P. R. Bahnson, R. Glen, C. J. Maille, K. Smith, and H. White (2009), "When 'Aha Moments' Make All the Difference," *Journal of Management Inquiry*, 18 (1): 64–76.

Olins, W. (2005), *Wally Olins on Brand*, New York: Thames & Hudson.

Patnaik, D. and P. Mortensen (2009), *Wired to Care—How Companies Prosper When They Create Widespread Empathy*, San Mateo: Jump Associates.

Peters, L. (2012), "The Rhythm of Leading Change: Living with Paradox," *Journal of Management Inquiry*, 21 (4): 405–11.

Pink, D. (2005), *A Whole New Mind—Why Right Brainers Will Rule the Future,* New York: Penguin.

Pries-Heje, J. and R. Baskerville (2008), "The Design Theory Nexus," *MIS Quarterly*, 32 (4): 731–55.

Pugmire, D. (1998), *Rediscovering Emotion: Emotion and the Claims of Feeling*, Edinburgh: Edinburgh University Press.

Rittel, H. (1972), "On the Planning Crisis: Systems Analysis of the 'First and Second Generations,'" *BedriftSokonomen*, 8: 309–96.

Rittel, H. W. J. and M. M. Webber (1973), "Dilemmas in a General Theory of Planning," *Policy Sciences* 4: 155–69.

Rogers, E. M. (2010), *Diffusion of Innovations*, New York: Simon & Schuster.

Rowe, P. (1987), *Design Thinking*, Boston: MIT Press.

Slater, S. F., J. J. Mohr, and S. Sengupta (2014), "Radical Product Innovation Capability: Literature Review, Synthesis, and Illustrative Research Propositions," *Journal of Product Innovation Management*, 31: 552–66.

Van Boven, L., D. Dunning and G. Loewenstein (2000), "Egocentric Empathy Gaps between Owners and Buyers: Misperceptions of the Endowment Effect," *Journal of Personality and Social Psychology*, 79 (1): 66.

Van Boven, L., and G. Loewenstein (2003), "Social projection of transient drive states," *Personality and Social Psychology Bulletin*, 29 (9), 1159–1168.

Wroblewski, L. (2005), "A Difference of Design." Available online: http://www.lukew.com/ff/entry.asp?205

Wroblewski, L. (2006a), "Defining Design Thinking." Available online: http://www.lukew.com/ff/entry.asp?357

Wroblewski, L. (2006b), "It's Simple. Design Communicates." Available online: http://www.lukew.com/ff/entry.asp?287

2 Relating Semiotics, Hyperreality, and Meaning to Design

Joseph H. Hancock II

**Joseph H.
Hancock II**

Joseph "Joe" H. Hancock II, of Drexel University, focuses his research in the area of popular culture as it relates to transnational mass-fashion garments, world dress, and aspirational fashion branding, as well as men's fashion and lifestyles. He has published peer-reviewed works in the journal *Fashion Practice, Clothing Cultures, and Critical Studies in Men's Fashion*. His book *Brand/Story: Ralph, Vera, Johnny, Billy and Other Adventures in Fashion Branding* (2009) is now to be released in a second edition through Bloomsbury Academic. He has completed two coedited books, *Fashion in Popular Culture* (2013) and *Global Fashion Brands* (2014), with Intellect UK and is the principal editor of the indexed peer-reviewed journal *Fashion, Style and Popular Culture* (Intellect Publishers). He is working on an authored book *Jeans* with Bloomsbury Academic.

Focusing Question: How can semiotics be optimized in strategic design so that consumers deem products and services meaningful?

This chapter will define semiotics and how it is used to deconstruct meaning. Through various design examples, the reader will gain an understanding of how meaning is crucial for designers who wish for their goods to be consumed by individuals.

This chapter explores the key questions:

· What is semiotics and how did it become an important field of study?

· How have marketers benefited from the field of semiology?

· What is hyperreality and how is it used to promote design?

· How did the postmodern era impact the way we understand design?

· How do consumers relate to symbols and signs that are utilized in contemporary design?

INTRODUCTION

For many of us, our choice of clothing is but one way we choose to visually express our identity. But what makes some products, styles, and fashions more appealing to us than others? Our relationships with a particular garment are special; and through strategic methods, the designer, retailer, manufacturer, or stylish brand label must create an emotional attachment in consumers to elicit a response so that they will purchase a particular item and incorporate it into their lives. Using familiar signs and symbols that relate to consumers, in order to trigger such a response, contributes to this process because we are able to understand or read what the marketer is trying to tell us. The term *reading* implies the ability to understand what is going on in a particular advertisement or perhaps a visual display in a store.

For instance, the Ralph Lauren brand's Fall 2014 collection included a black Western-style leather jacket, retailing for $1,600 USD. What would compel a consumer to pay $1,600 for this black distressed Western leather jacket? The Double RL Company enforces a strong presence of historicism based in Americana and is enriched with the clothing that was historically worn by men who represent an outdoorsy and rugged demeanor. Most of this clothing line uses styles from the military, blue-collar workers, and the American cowboy—icons of American popular culture that are prominent in men's sportswear. One symbol, the cowboy, is such a prominent recurring theme of this fashion brand that it has been blatantly featured in the windows of the Double RL Company stores (Figure 2.1). This simple symbol communicates a lot about the brand and even conjures up a story in my mind, as it is supposed to do.

As consumers, we can read what is being communicated to us and how a particular division of Ralph Lauren inspires a need to buy. But what compels the desire to purchase is more than individual components of the ideology behind the brand that include the marketing of the brand, the clothing, sales assistants, and the actual store space; it is these parts combined and more.

The collaboration of each part of a brand's context generates and communicates to a customer to purchase the goods and services of a particular retailer or designer if that individual understands it. The relationship to Ralph Lauren's Double RL Company can be a symbolic and emotional tie to the brand. For example, if you grew up in the Midwestern region of the United States in Kansas, where cowboy culture is historically prominent and part of a personal internalization process, then this historicism is enjoyed and romanticized. But before we go too far, let's start from the beginning by defining some basics about semiotics, signs, meaning, and consumption.

Understanding Semiotics through Design

Semiotics is the study of signs and the ways they produce meaning. A major concern in semiotics is the way that signs function in our global and cultural environments and how they are systematized into codes that

Figure 2.1 Ralph Lauren Double RL Company store in New York's Nolita area. Note the various icons associated with the American West and the blatant use of the cowboy as a marker of acceptable men's fashion.
Photo courtesy of Joseph H. Hancock II, 2012. All Rights Reserved.

communicate a form of language, as well as their dissemination into mainstream society (Childers & Hentzi 1995: 272–73). Philosophically, while the concept of signs has received attention from academics for hundreds of years, it is only really during the twentieth century that there has been a concerted effort to truly develop a system for the study of semiology because marketers and advertisers have become aware of the potential to earn consumer dollars by constructing meaning in their products.

The word "semiotics" comes from the American philosopher Charles Sanders Peirce, who examined the signs as a system of relationships. He developed a system based on the relation between the thing and what it signifies. A signifier (one thing) *signifies* (represents) a sign or symbol (something else); for example, the word "star" could signify either a celestial body up in the sky that shines at night or a famous person, like James Dean, Madonna, or Ryan Kwanten (see Figure 2.2).

Peirce developed three major types of signs: **symbols**, **indexes**, and **icons** (Childers and Hentzi 1995: 272–73). The symbol's relationship to the signified is a

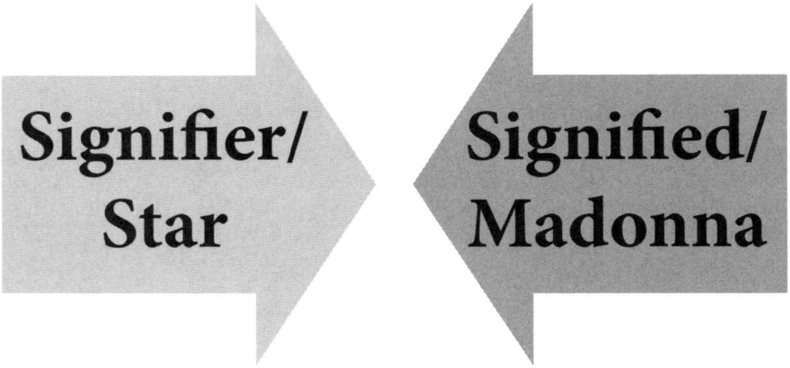

Figure 2.2 A visual representation of Peirce's Signifer/Signifed model

contemporary one and is truly arbitrary; for example, if you see a red, octagonal-shaped sign while driving in the United States you think "stop sign." The index bears a casual relationship to the signified, such as a thermometer and your body temperature. The icon's relationship is founded on similarities and shared features, such as that between a designed object and its placement in an advertisement. In Figure 2.1, the cowboy is an icon for the clothing line Ralph Lauren RRL.

Peirce's work was further developed by a Swiss linguist, Ferdinand de Saussure, who is perceived as more esteemed in the field of semiotics. Saussure's ideas are based upon the concept of a connection between the signifier and signified (remember the star example or the cowboy in Figure 2.1); he believed that because there were relationships between these two that a language is formed between actual objects and words. Voilà! The science of semiology was created.

In the 1960s, another philosopher by the name of Roland Barthes (1985: 3–18) tested the notions of semiology using his three favorite subjects: striptease, professional wrestling, and fashion. For the purpose of this chapter, we will look at fashion. According to Barthes, in the design process, clothing garments are created and stylized to suit current styles. This can include color, silhouette, finishing, pattern, or whatever is currently the trend. Barthes (1985: 3–18) believes that a garment is actually present in the fashion system at three distinct levels: the *real garment* or actual garment itself (it is what you see on the hanger); the *terminological garment* that signifies the written word used to describe the object, such as T-shirt or denim jeans, and finally the *written rhetorical garment*, which includes how the garment is described and portrayed in photographs (the advertising). While Barthes's work demonstrates that the consumer desired the real garment, his research helped scholars and advertisers understand that it is the rhetorical written garment in photos or on the fashion runway (where the actual garment is either presented as real or manipulated to create a fantasy garment) that is important for stimulation of consumption (Barthes 1985: 3–18). This principle demonstrated that advertising and various forms of mass media are crucial connections for selling and the distribution of designed objects.

GO DEEPER

Read the following:
- *The Language of Fashion* by R. Barthes.
- *Semiotics: The Basics* by D. Chandler.
- *Introducing Semiotics* by P. Cobley and L. Jansz.
- *Glossary of Semiotics* by V. M. Colapietro.

REFLECTIONS
- How do signs and symbols communicate to you in your daily life? Did you use a public restroom today? How did you know which bathroom to use? How was it marked? Words or a symbol? Did you drive to class? Did you stop at a red traffic light? Why?
- In class or as a group give some common examples of signifier/signified relationships.
- Think of a time when you saw an advertisement for a product you thought you just had to have. Once you actually saw the product, did it even look like the one in the ad? Did you still want it? Discuss how this scenario

reflects the thoughts of Roland Barthes on fashion.

Meaning and Hyperreality

During the 1960s, the era of postmodernism emerged, and mass media began to influence consumer culture through various types of distribution channels. Postmodern ideology and concepts are borrowed by these media outlets and presented to consumers in products such as motion pictures, television, and fashion advertising. Examples include movies, such as *Blade Runner* (1982); television series, such as *Twin Peaks* (1990–91); performers, such as Madonna; and the shopping channel QVC. For instance, QVC's branding techniques contextualize fashion products through storytelling and meanings, creating fantasies to entice consumers to buy more fashions.

Jean Baudrillard (1988), an influential postmodernism theorist, defines postmodernism as a time of simulation where the boundaries between what is real, and perceived as real, have been conflated. This conflation blurs the lines between what an individual knows as reality, and what is reality, thus causing confusion (Best & Kellner 1991: 119). An individual's inability to distinguish between what is real and attainable versus fantasy is what Baudrillard calls **hyperreality**. Those having **social standing** (Baudrillard's words for people of cultural and social power, money, or influence) at the macro-levels of consumer culture create the distortions between reality and hyperreality (1988: 19). Baudrillard contends that the sign (the real), or the image, is distorted by moving through the following stages:

1. It is a reflection of basic reality.
2. It masks and perverts a basic reality.
3. It masks the absence of a basic reality.
4. It bears no relation to any reality whatever: It is its own pure simulacrum (simulation) (Baudrillard 1988: 170).

In the first stage, the object is shown in what Baudrillard calls the natural state; for example, a tablet computer displayed alone without context or verbal or visual presentation. In stage two, the tablet computer is aesthetically presented in a contextual state with verbal and visual cues that have been created by those of social standing (such as advertisers) who distort the object (tablet computer) and give it new meaning. For example, the tablet computer may be presented in an ad that features people from all over the world using the tablet computer or demonstrating various usages, thus indicating it is a versatile tablet computer. Stage three represents the absence of all previous reality of the object (tablet computer). The origins, the use, histories, functions, and ideologies of a tablet computer are erased by those of social standing; moreover, the tablet computer is placed in a fantasy context (e.g., an Apple ad showing people at events, going on safari, and in various elite situations, such as sitting next to the Eiffel Tower in Paris, sipping cappuccino, while using an Apple iPad). This type of ad gives consumers an impression that having this device alone will allow

them to travel the world without a care. In stage four, the object (tablet computer, now an Apple iPad) is part of a whole new reality and has almost no relation to its origin. This is hyperreality.

Baudrillard believes hyperreality presents itself to consumers through media. Television, print advertising, computers, and other forms of communication create surreal life situations but present them to consumers as real (Best & Kellner 1991: 119). Don't think you would fall for such a ploy? Do you have an iPad? Can you really afford to own a device that costs $499 USD, plus perhaps cellular data plans that cost an additional $25 a month? Does it have a fancy cover? Or did you buy the Apple iPad or your tablet computer using a credit card? In addition to your computer, cellular phone, and any other gadget you have purchased, did you use credit or did someone else buy it for you because you could not afford it? Do you buy anything you cannot afford? If so, then you have been a victim of hyperreality.

Airbrushed models in magazines, bogus internet dating services, as well as distorted lenses on television cameras alter the real appearances of their subjects, all while alluding to the viewer that the subject is natural. Another example of hyperreality is internet dating websites, such as Match.com, that allow individuals to create conflated autobiographies: By posting an airbrushed photo and writing a colorful autobiographical story, an individual tries to attain a mate. The person who views the ad may fantasize about the Match.com computerized image and autobiography, but then when the two individuals meet, the real person reveals himself. Person A (who posted the ad) may disappoint person B (who desired the hyperreal or internet person) when the true image and personality are actually seen; instead, the hyperreal is fantasy, while the person standing in front of you is reality. Reality is sometimes less attractive.

Baudrillard (1988) believes that consumer goods are the principal concepts of advertising culture and that they constitute a new discourse in the order of consumption. According to Baudrillard, those of social standing have repackaged consumer products in hyperreal scenarios in order to generate continuous consumption. Since those of social standing use media to create advertising and marketing to sell products, they are influenced by postmodern popular culture and consumer lifestyles. Also, with the development of postmodern brand culture, ideas continue to surface; postmodern ideological concepts, such as *fragmentation*, *de-differentiation*, *chronology*, and *pastiche* have become applicable to current advertising campaigns. Postmodern theory and branding discourse assimilate into a contemporary vocabulary that is now considered everyday business semantics. Arthur Asa Berger (1991: 87) states that retailers, marketers, and branding executives incorporate postmodern concepts to create their own definitions and meanings of these terms. Reflecting current postmodern aesthetics and ideology, marketers brand designs borrowing from postmodern semantics. Examples of how these words are used in current fashion marketing follows.

Fragmentation describes the separation of similar, mass-oriented groupings into smaller, specialized product ranges. Moreover, mass-produced items are tailored to specific consumer segments. In retailing, phrases such as "target market" or "market niche" describe the end result of fragmentation. These notions of fragmentation reflect a diverse marketplace where the level of each consumer's taste is unique and individualized.

De-differentiation suggests the blurring of high and low cultures. What have been previously notions of high or low art and culture have been altered in the minds of consumer culture. With regards to design, the fuzzy lines between design-as-art and art-as-design are perfect examples. Target and Walmart have commissioned renowned designers, such as Rachael Ray and Alexis Taylor, to design home goods and fashions for their stores. Where formerly these retailers may not have been viewed as high end, some critics may expand their understanding to design being available for the masses after seeing some of the products in those stores. Another example is when stores such as Marshalls, T.J. Maxx, and HomeGoods present themselves as high-end retailers to give the impression that they are luxury: Are you a Fashionista or a Maxxinista?

Chronology explains a consumer's preoccupation with nostalgia and an interest in the past. A consumer may become enchanted with a hangtag that states that a design is "authentic." Despite the language retailers use to reference "vintage," the products in fact are often knock-offs or brand new. While sometimes the word "authentic" is used, the consumer must be aware that the standards of authenticity are not necessarily related to traditional standards of design. By using words such as "original," "authentic," or "real," some consumers may become confused on the actual origins of products. It becomes the consumer's own responsibility to know if he or she is buying a quality good. An example of this is Levi's, traditionally known for high-quality denim with "Made in the USA" labels. However, due to high labor costs, during the early 1990s most of their jeans began to be manufactured in other countries. The company still continued to brand their jeans as "Original Levi's" and as "authentic," when in reality these new jeans were not the same. They were sewn and produced in countries like Mexico and China instead of the United States. Consumers were no longer supporting the local US market as Levi's had historically done, but an import one instead. Now, the company has begun reproducing their jeans in the United States, but it charges over $200 USD a pair because of labor costs in the domestic market.

Pastiche can almost be a synonym for the word "collage." In postmodern consumer culture, pastiche relates to the use of mixing traditional and nontraditional items in order to create context. Actress Sharon Stone demonstrated postmodern fashion techniques when she wore her Gap turtleneck with an Armani couture jacket to the seventieth Annual Academy Awards. By mixing a mass-fashion garment with couture, Stone created a postmodern look. Additionally, Target's own home design line by Threshold carried a "Modern Vintage" theme in 2014, combining two words that are complete antonyms for one another and conflating the notions of what is modern and what is vintage in design: This is true postmodernism.

In the late 1990s, scholar Jean A. Hamilton (1997: 165) addressed the transfer of individual designs and their meanings from the macro (global) interface to the micro (individual) level. Her study delves into how cultural arbiters globally influence consumers' interpretations of ideas associated with designed goods and branding. Hamilton touches on issues of *how* and *why* merchandise is made and distributed. Hamilton's innovative argument focuses on the use of storytelling to create brand concept of continual consumption (Hamilton 1997: 165–71). Hamilton's theoretical ideology suggests that through storytelling, a context is created to entice consumers to repurchase mass-produced items.

Hamilton's work illustrates a model (Figure 2.3) based on the notion that macro influencers affect the micro-level meanings that consumers associate with their personal products. Her theoretical framework identifies the micro-to-macro movement from negotiations with the self to negotiations with others to fashion system arbiters to cultural system arbiters (macro) (Hamilton 1997: 165). The following list includes the cultural system arbiters (macro) that underlie this process:

MICRO --MACRO

Negotiations with Self----Negotiations with Others ---Fashion System Arbiters---Cultural

System Arbiters

Figure 2.3 A rendering of Jean Hamilton's macro-micro interface model
(Source: Hamilton 1997)

- Designers, product developers, and state planners in controlled economies. An example would be the recent growth of hybrid cars to give consumers the perception that we are being fuel efficient.
- Style forms and ideas created by designers and product developers. An example would be a silhouette fashion change over specific periods of time, for instance how women's and men's fashions have gotten slimmer over the last few years.
- The spontaneous, free-flowing interaction of components on the delivery side (supply side) of the production system, for example, designers, media, producers (including manufacturers), and distribution (including retailers).
- The interaction of components that work in collaboration in the fashion system; these range from major events/phenomena in the cultural system that influence fashion system participants and institutions, as well as individual consumers. Examples of these are war, national elections, political revolution, and economic recession/depression.

- Trends in the cultural system (or in subcultural systems) may influence all or some participants in the fashion system or some individual fashion consumers, for example, Eastern religions, avant-garde music, art, films, or literature.
- Any or all of the above in combination with one another (Hamilton 1997: 167).

Hamilton recognizes the ambivalence of designed products in the consumerist society, but her article emphasizes the importance of decisions made by the cultural system influencers/intermediaries. These decisions serve as persuasive devices for consumers. All products carry only a certain amount of meaning and are signifiers of only the styles they represent. It is the arbiters who give them meaning through the selling context, merchandising, and visual display. Moreover, the arbiters must be aware of what will appeal to a particular consumer or niche market for their styles to become fashion; failure to do so could result in lost sales.

As Hamilton notes, a great vehicle for demonstrating her theory are television networks designed to sell goods and products to their viewers. International networks, such as QVC (quality, value, convenience) and HSN (Home Shopping Network), connect meaning to their fashion goods by displaying them and creating "selling stories" about the products' function and aesthetics. The consumer listens to the story and begins to relate to the item. The item begins to have meaning associated with it, and the consumer feels the need to add it to his or her collection. This collection of goods serves to establish the individual's identity (Hamilton 1997: 168).

One example of successful system arbiters creating a contextual meaning for products is found in the Joan Rivers line of jewelry that is still promoted on QVC. Joan Rivers (an international megastar and icon) and QVC were fashion arbiters of her jewelry collection. QVC has a database of information about previous customers who have purchased Rivers's jewelry. The company also knows what previous scripted segments of its show sold the most jewelry. Therefore, when Rivers was on QVC discussing her jewelry line, she referred to topics and the characteristics of her market niche. Also, when she was on the air, Rivers listened to and spoke with callers who had previously brought her jewelry. These callers told Rivers about their experiences with the jewelry and how to wear it. The viewer who was watching at home may have related to Rivers, her jewelry, or the stories, as well as the discussions she had with the callers and other QVC employees on the air. The jewelry gained significance through the selling context that was created around it. Without the context, Rivers's name, or the television channel popularity, the jewelry is less enticing for consumption. Another

approach to understanding storytelling is to focus on the meaning and relationships connected to brands.

Grant McCracken a cultural anthropologist' continually investigates consumption as an essential component of the cultural evolution of society. According to McCracken, meaning moves from the "culturally constituted world" to the "gatekeepers" of products and services to the "individual consumer." All three add meaning to a brand as it passes through their domains. McCracken's theoretical models suggest that through social interaction, individuals (and eventually society) assign status to branded products (McCracken 1988: 71–89).

In his scholarship, McCracken's research connects meaning to brand management. He emphasizes the need for brands to be studied from a meaning-based model instead of the traditional information basis (conventional branding methods), because meaning-based models are more intricate, allowing for nuanced understandings of what consumers want and desire. For the consumer market to evolve, meaning will become more effective in determining consumer patterns of consumption. Branding is one key to the creation and generation of future consumer consumption (McCracken 2005: 162–70).

McCracken suggests that context creates meaning for design. He identifies nine different types of meaning (typically targeted by clothing companies): gender, lifestyle, decade, age, class and status, occupation, time and place, value, and fad, fashion, and trend. For McCracken, the company, its competitors and collaborators, customers, marketing segmentation, product and service positioning, marketing mix, and price of each consumer item determine meanings. He suggests that future brands study the various types of meaning used to create context around fashion goods as if they were a culture unto themselves. By examining each aspect of a business, an individual can see how the brand story reflects the products and services specific to that retailer.

GO DEEPER

Read the following:

- *The Portable Postmodernist* by A. A. Berger.
- *Postmodern Theory* by S. Best and D. Kellner.
- "The Macro-Micro Interface in the Construction of Individual Fashion Form and Meaning" by J. Hamilton in the *Clothing & Textiles Research Journal*.
- *Culture & Consumption* by G. McCracken.
- *Culture & Consumption II* by G. McCracken.
- *Jean Baudrillard: Selected Writings* edited by M. Poster.

REFLECTIONS

- Think about a time when you purchased a particular item. What was it? Why did you buy it? What made you purchase that particular one in that particular store? Did it have meaning for you? Discuss.
- What is your favorite brand? Why do you buy that brand? How does that brand advertise or promote its product? How does that brand's method of advertising and promotion appeal to you?
- Give examples of how meaning is associated to brands through consumer use.
- In what ways do social media platforms such as Twitter and Instagram serve as cultural arbiters? Find three examples of the ways in which these platforms influence meaning and culture.

Consuming Design through Storytelling

The major function of advertising is to provide a structure capable of transforming the language of objects into meaningful products for people to buy. Judith Williamson (2002) suggests that while an advertiser's main goal is to sell products, good advertising requires marketers to not only take into account the inherent qualities of the products but to also generate a meaning to the consumer. Williamson believes that advertisements are selling more than just the consumer goods in the ads. By providing a structure, method, and function for using a product, the connections between the consumer and product are made. These connections generate associations of both identity and forms of status in consumer culture.

As stated, semiotics and deconstruction provide a structure that uses images and language to impart meaning in design. Once the design is completed, an advertiser's main goal is to sell it. Good advertising requires the marketers' ability to take into account the inherent qualities of products and to generate a specific meaning for the consumer. Advertisements should consist of more than consumer goods in ads; there should be connections between the consumer and the products; these connections generate associations of identity and status in consumer culture (Williamson 2002: 12). For example, Starbucks' ability to elevate a cup of coffee (more than $2 for a small coffee) to an ideology of superior quality is not only done by having fabulously displayed retail stores but also by connecting the object (coffee) to a high-end image that shows global stories, where attractive individuals of different nationalities, races, and lifestyles are chatting with others in their stores, while friendly and happy employees serve a variety of coffee drinks. They are selling an experience. Additionally, Starbucks continually presents new lines of coffee drinks and various coffee blends with each season. In the fall there is pumpkin spice latté, then they transition to the Thanksgiving and Holiday Blend coffees; in the spring there are Frappuccino-blended fruit drinks, not to mention the Starbucks gift cards that change with each holiday to give their counters an essence of style and decor. The company continually allows its coffee to change season to season—similar to the ways that a fashion designer changes his or her clothing line. This gives Starbucks a quality of high design and style that is internationally understood by consumers.

Conventional design development is actually more physical and "hands on" in the actual creation of the product, in order to differentiate it between similar styles and build a relationship to a particular branded designer, retailer, or manufacturer's assortment. As most of us know, this is usually done by managing each step of actual design and production processes to create the style, specs, and finishes, and most importantly, a pleasing aesthetic to the customer. Additionally, each design must be "brand correct," consistent with the culture of the retail establishment. Successful styles are then incorporated into the specific retailer's assortment and selling season.

As in the Starbucks example, in today's market, most designed products are like mass-fashion apparel and are created for established selling seasons. We see the continuous creation of product lines for multiple seasons, beyond the Autumn, Holiday, Spring, and Summer quarterly calendars, to compel us to buy the new one/what's next. With the largest seasons for most retailers being Autumn and Holiday, because of back-to-school for youth and the celebrations that occur during November and December, such as Christmas and Hanukkah, companies have learned to release new models in conjunction with the annual calendar. Spring and Summer are usually defined by such themes as Resort and Family Vacation, with designs and items to reflect these seasons. These types of annual patterns can be seen in almost all types of designed products, from patio furniture to print designs on paper towels.

With a design system working on an annual cycle, the role of manufacturers and sometimes merchandisers are to micro-manage each step in the production process and facilitate the physical branding, such as creating the proper finishes, features, tags, packaging, and in-store marketing for the items that make it unique from the previous year. Additionally, ensuring that price points are in perfect alignment to the retailer's brand image and target market is very important so that consumers will want to buy the item. More importantly, this newly produced item must meet upper management's specifications for a proper brand presentation on the selling floor. For example, when you shop a retailer such as The Gap, there is an aesthetic that you expect to find at that particular store. If you suddenly walked into The Gap and the assortment did not fit the image of the retailer, you might stop shopping there. It is the branded garments, along with the store image, marketing, and sales associates that generates the nontraditional emotional component of shopping—the storytelling.

For branding, the storytelling process relies on a company's ability to make an emotional connection through its brand to build target markets. A retailer, manufacturer, or designer reaches full potential when an emotional attachment to consumers is attained and when the consumer and employees of the brand are able to understand the company's values and messages (remember the example from Figure 2.1?). Storytelling is the vehicle that communicates these values in a process that is easy for consumers to understand (Fog, Dudtz, & Yaka: 2005: 13–25). Globally, most individuals understand the processes of storytelling—advertisers, marketers, and merchandising strategists use the basic concepts of storytelling for fashion branding. Even the simplest fashion advertising reflects the basic framework of a story that includes a message, conflict, characters, and plot. Fashion advertisers and merchandisers use this same formula and are able to pique consumer interest while building associations to their products and creating emotional meaning.

Referring back to The Gap, an example of this type of brand building and storytelling can be seen in the product promotion of women's skinny black pants in September 2006 advertising campaigns. In the ads, The Gap featured the legendary actress Audrey Hepburn, bringing her back to life through digital methods. The ad for the slim leg pants creates a narrative story that most women would relate to in their own lives, with Hepburn dancing around the screen in pants that appear to be stylish and chic, yet practical to wear. Images of the iconic Audrey Hepburn make these pants a must-have fashion item. Older consumers or those who might recognize Hepburn from her famous films, such as *Funny Face* (1957) or *Breakfast at Tiffany's* (1961), immediately relate to the actress and the importance of these pants in fashion. However, those younger consumers unfamiliar with Audrey Hepburn might be interested enough to investigate further, and young hipsters might connect to the bygone era. The music played in the ad is the heavy metal band AC/DC's hit song "Back in Black," which gives the ad a contemporary vibe and allows the ad to stand out. The story becomes one of Audrey Hepburn dancing to a heavy metal song, thus creating a new selling story for skinny black pants. The message and plot for consumers is to go buy these pants, done through the conflict and character of Hepburn and her dancing in the ad (see this ad at: http://www.youtube.com/watch?v=T_K-GxEk3K0).

Meaning in Design through Brand/Story

Brand/story implies that all those related in the creation, buying, and selling of goods to consumers need to engage in the cultural and social zeitgeist of the times in which their products are consumed to maintain a competitive edge. By telling good stories to the consumer and through various signs and symbols, the company can gain a competitive edge in the market by associating meaning to its products.

To demonstrate how design utilizes brand/story, let's look at two examples of the same type of design: one from low end and one from high end. In the late 1990s, cargo pants became all the rage in the mass consumer market. While the garment had been around since the late 1930s, it really was associated with the military, army surplus shopping, and subcultural style up until the late 1990s. This is when retailers like Abercrombie & Fitch and Ralph Lauren prominently displayed the garment in their assortments. At one time Ralph Lauren was featuring over twenty styles of the pant in one season through his Polo Ralph Lauren line, Black Label, Denim & Supply, as well as his Double RL line. Competition among retail stores is fierce in this pant and short category. With that in mind, design becomes the key to distinguish each garment from one

another. Some garments go so far as to include brand/story in the actual design. Here are two examples.

Target: "All the World's Dreaming" by Keanan Duffty

Keanan Duffty is a former British singer and songwriter who became one of Britain's high-end designers in the early 2000s, specializing in clothing that resembles garments from other fashion designers, such as Vivienne Westwood. Duffty graduated from St. Martins in London and has shown his clothing on the runways in Italy, England, and the United States. Besides fashion design, Duffty produces and directs music videos. His personal mission is to build a brand that is heavily influenced by both music and fashion.

In July of 2006, Target began to feature a special line of clothing that was designed by Keanan Duffty. This line included a pair of ripstop khaki cargo pants that have a large patch of the Union Jack flag sewn onto the seat of the garment (Figure 2.4) and adjustable waistband and leg openings. Target's description of the pants suggests they are 1980s rocker-chic inspired—all for the Target price of $29.99 USD.

Other brand detailing of the pants includes a red patch above the right pocket that states: "England's Dreaming Keanan Duffty." This patch has a coat of arms with a large *KD* in the center. Target has attached a paper waistband tag above the left pocket that mimics the previously mentioned patch. There is a hangtag attached to the

Figure 2.4 Keanan Duffty for Target. Cotton ripstop cargo pant, $29.99, Fall 2006

Courtesy of Joseph H. Hancock II. All Rights Reserved.

pants: The front features a skull and cross-bones, guitar, and a background of the Union Jack flag with the words, "England's Dreaming Keanan Duffty." The backside of the hangtag features a biography of Duffty with his photo and the price of the cargo pants.

What makes these otherwise insignificant cargo pants unique is the Union Jack sewn onto the seat of the pants. The Union Jack is a blatant signifier to England, since it is the official flag of the country. The red patches, sewn above the British flag patch that has the words, "England's Dreaming

Keanan Duffty," reinforce the connections to England and the Union Jack. What influenced Target to feature a male British designer that fall? What connections to culture and fashion was Target trying to make?

That year, the Spring/Summer issue of *VMan* magazine predicted that Anglomania would be one of the hottest trends that fall:

> *Perhaps in anticipation of the upcoming "Anglomania" show at New York's Metropolitan Museum of Art, British inspired menswear is flying its flag high. At Burberry, Christopher Bailey continued to reference dandyism with sharply tailored suits and coats, now accessorized with silver chains. Dsquared went for an over-the-top investigation of landed gentry and their old-world accoutrements. With sharp tailoring and immaculate pinstripes, Ralph Lauren proved once more that he gives the Brits a lesson or two in traditional English dressing. Paul & Joe chipped in with an homage to John Steed, the iconic bowler-hat-wearing character of '60s cult TV show* The Avengers. *Emporio Armani also celebrated London's swinging '60s by focusing on richly colored velvets and tartan trousers.* (VMan 2006: 197)

In their referral to Anglomania as a hot trend for fall fashions, *VMan* suggests that the Metropolitan Museum of Art's exhibit *Anglomania: Tradition and Transgression in British Fashion*, which had its run from May 3 until September 4, 2006, was one of the inspirations for British fashion influence. While many of the women's fashions were historical references to the past, the room titled *The Gentleman's Club* not only featured men's clothing dated from 1938, but most of the men's garments were brand new! The museum displayed over fifteen new styles of men's garments, with only three outfits consisting of historic costumes. Menswear designers were obviously influenced by the new designs.

Burberry and Condé Nast publications, both of which are major influences in current fashion and style, sponsored the exhibit. Target's blatant referral to England through Keanan Duffty's Union Jack flag allows the retailer to support a market niche in current high fashion. This is cultural branding that demonstrates how design incorporates and reflects the current zeitgeist.

Energie: "Godzilla! We Want Only, Only Toy Tanks"

At first glance, the Linwood long cargo shorts by Energie that retailed for $125 USD seem to reflect fun popular culture; however, the branding details of the shorts reveal a serious political statement (Figures 2.5a and 2.5b). This garment is a capri style, running longer than most other cargo shorts. Very similar to original military-style fabric, these shorts are made of 100 percent ripstop cotton. The major branding details visible on the outside of these shorts are the Energie label and Godzilla!

The Godzilla theme is reinforced on the inside pocket linings of the shorts. Each pocket is lined with a woven cotton

Figures 2.5a and 2.5b Energie ripstop long, cotton cargo short, $125, Summer 2006
Courtesy of Joseph H. Hancock II All Rights Reserved.

fabric that has toy tanks, maps of countries, and the phrase "We Want Only, Only Toy Tanks" embedded in the cloth. The historical significance and cultural references of this garment are quite compelling. This garment makes references to antinuclear testing and the removal of weapons of war, while reflecting current fashion style (Figures 2.6a and 2.6b).

Godzilla first appeared in 1956 in the motion picture *Godzilla, King of the Monsters!* Godzilla was resurrected from the relic Jurassic age due to a nuclear explosion off the coast of Japan.

The moral of the Godzilla story is based upon the negative effects of nuclear testing. The movie reflects the horrific attacks in Nagasaki, Japan, in 1945, where up to 80,000 people were killed by an atomic bomb. Godzilla becomes the messenger of postnuclear blast destruction, warning everyone that nuclear testing and war must stop.

While the Godzilla story can be taken seriously, it was also given a camp-like quality among other fans. The technical qualities of *Godzilla* relied on 1956's special effects. Miniature replicas of cityscapes and road vehicles were used in almost all movies. The tanks that Godzilla destroyed in his hands resembled toy tanks. This political statement references Energie's pocket lining that, "We Want Only, Only Toy Tanks," but it keeps the shorts fun without becoming too serious at referencing the theme of war. However, the shorts do make a statement about military weapons and their

Figures 2.6a and 2.6b Design details of the Energie cargo shorts: interior lining (left) and Energie label and Godzilla (right)
Courtesy of Joseph H. Hancock II. All Rights Reserved.

manufacturing by suggesting that we no longer want real tanks only toy tanks. Additionally, with the recent revival of *Godzilla* (2014) in theaters, it becomes clear that Godzilla is easily recognizable across all cultures and that using this icon in the design of a short is ingenious and could help to sell the garment.

Like the cargo pants by Keanan Duffty, the actual cargo shorts are fairly insignificant without the branding details. Without the references to Godzilla, these Energie shorts could not have possibly commanded the $125 USD price tag. While Energie has been identified as a luxury brand, what really appeals to individuals are these shorts' pop cultural and political themes. Those whose personal milieu reflects a connection to Godzilla or a political stance on nuclear disarmament may think that these shorts represent their individualism.

GO DEEPER

Read the following:

- *Brand/Story: Ralph, Vera, Johnny, Billy and Other Adventures in Fashion Branding* by J. Hancock.
- *How Brands Become Icons* by D. Holt.
- *Decoding Advertisements: Ideology and Meaning in Advertising* by J. Williamson.

REFLECTIONS

- How do garments, like graphic T-shirts, tell brand/stories like the cargo example? What are other designed products that tell brand/ stories?
- Do any of the items you own in your personal collection reflect the zeitgeist? Discuss.
- How have you created your own visual milieu and how does it convey your brand/story?

Conclusion

Semiotics is the study of signs and symbols within our global and cultural contexts. Whether we are Eastern or Western, from the northern hemisphere or southern, we all have symbols, icons, and indexes that are understood. Each has been deconstructed to denote meaning and how it is understood in our culture. This pastiche of signs, symbols, and meaning creates narratives and stories that most of us understand because we all understand the art of storytelling. Advertisers and marketers rely on this type of understanding, so we will buy and purchase goods and services—and it works!

Let's take a step out of fashion and examine Coca-Cola's use of semiotics to build a compelling business case. This company reaches a global market and has created an iconic image with their red-and-white label that people know as Coke. However, did you know that Coca-Cola is responsible for creating the familiar American Santa Claus in the red-and-white suit? In 1931, Coca-Cola introduced the character, and by including him over the years in various poses, with elves, and in different scenarios, Coca-Cola has not only generated stories about the American Santa Claus, but it actually also co-branded him with its product and spread him all over the world, making him an international icon. That's spectacular branding.

The next time you go shopping, remember that branding is not a trend. It will continue to communicate through methods of storytelling—print media, in-store environments, the internet, mobile devices, and even through sales associates and their own customers. Brands will continue to create exclusive notions about their mass-produced products through strategies, such as limited production, unique design, and other methods of product development. Branding will continue to create experiences that have to be physically experienced by consumers for their essence to be understood. And finally, branding will always give customers the feeling that they are not part of a group, but are special individuals. That's the most important part about good storytelling in brand practices.

Acknowledgments

I would like to thank my family for supporting me through all my hours of writing scholarship: My partner, Eddie Augustyn, who reads and edits almost everything I write; my mother, Peggy Miller, who has supported me throughout my entire career—first as a retailing professional and now as an academic; and our dog Ruby, who went without walks while I was writing this chapter. For this particular work, I would also like to acknowledge those who continuously help me build my personal milieu that tells my brand/story, including my personal trainer, Reuben Wouch, my hair stylist, Sandi Wenger, and my personal shopper, Anthony Maitoza.

References

Barthes, R. (2013), *The Language of Fashion*, trans. A. Stafford, edited by A. Stafford and M. Carter, New York: Bloomsbury.

Barthes, R. (1985), *The Fashion System*, Cape (orig. 1967), New York: Columbia University Press.

Baudrillard, J. (2003), "The System of Objects," in M. Poster (ed.), *Jean Baudrillard: Selected Writings*, Stanford, CA: Stanford University Press.

Berger, A. A. (1991), *The Portable Postmodernist*, Walnut Creek, CA: AltaMira Press.

Best, S. and D. Kellner (1991), *Postmodern Theory: Critical Interrogations*, New York: The Guilford Press.

Chandler, D. (2007), *Semiotics: The Basics*, 2nd edn, New York: Routledge.

Cobley, P. and L. Jansz (2010), *Introducing Semiotics: A Graphic Guide*, London: Icon Books.

Colapietro, V. M. (1998), *Glossary of Semiotics*, St. Paul, MN: Paragon House.

Childers, J. and G. Hentzi (1995), *The Columbia Dictionary of Modern Literary and Cultural Criticism*. New York: Columbia University Press.

Fog, K., C. Dudtz, and B. Yaka (2005), *Storytelling Branding in Practice*, Denmark: Springer.

Hamilton, J. (1997), "The Macro-Micro Interface in the Construction of Individual Fashion Forms and Meaning," *Clothing and Textiles Research Journal*, 15 (3): 165–71.

Hancock, J. (2009), *Brand Story: Ralph, Vera, Johnny, Billy and Other Adventures in Fashion Branding*, New York: Fairchild Publications.

Holt, D. (2004), *How Brands Become Icons: The Principles of Cultural Branding*, Boston: Harvard Business School Press.

McCracken, G. (1988), *Culture and Consumption*, Bloomington: Indiana University Press.

McCracken, G. (2005), *Culture and Consumption II*, Bloomington: Indiana University Press.

Metropolitan Museum of Art (2006), *Anglomania: Tradition and Transgression in British Fashion*, New York: Burberry.

Poster, M., ed. (1988), *Jean Baudrillard: Selected Writings*, Stanford, CA: Stanford University Press.

VMan (2006), "Fall Forecast," *VMan*, Spring/Summer (6), 197.

Williamson, J. (2002), *Decoding Advertisements: Ideology and Meaning in Advertising*, New York: Marion Boyars Publishing.

Valerie Jacobs

Valerie Jacobs is vice president and managing creative director of Trends at LPK. Her trend analysis for LPK clients is grounded in a strategic approach of research, analysis, and translation of trend data into actionable strategies. Valerie has taught at the University of Cincinnati College of Design, Architecture, Art, and Planning for more than a decade.

Michael Wintrob

Michael Wintrob leads the strategy discipline at LPK, where he uses approaches and methodologies informed and inspired by design. He has developed best-in-class practices for a wide variety of leading global brands during his fifteen-year career. He also serves as an adjunct instructor at the University of Cincinnati's Lindner College of Business.

Focusing Question: How might we highlight the shift in the role of branding from an agent of financial value to one that is derived from design thinking, focused on consumer connectedness and the power of human values?

This chapter explores the key questions:

- What is the relationship between brands and rhetoric?
- How has the role of design and design thinking changed over time in the creation and management of brands?
- What is the new paradigm of branding, and why does that matter?

INTRODUCTION

Brands are more important than ever to the creation, distribution, and viability of products, services, and experiences. As the central framework for the marketing of businesses, brands allow firms to differentiate products that are often functionally similar. For consumers, the role of brands has gone far beyond simple identification or reducing perceived risk. Today the purchase and consumption of brands often has a role in an individual's construction of identity, and even as a creator of happiness. In fact, in 2013 *The Guardian*'s Mood of the

Nation survey showed 67 percent of the British population can name a brand that makes them happy. Incredibly, more than 600 brands were named in total.

Defined as the promise of an experience, brand is not superficial, but rather it is integral to the meaningful production of value and identity formation and function in people's lives. As in a woven cloth, brand is the warp and design is the weft, leading ultimately to the interwoven experience.

We cannot understand business without understanding brands. This chapter will explain how brand has been elevated to the rhetoric of our day—its style and identity driving compelling messages to persuade consumers. Additionally, the approaches and processes long practiced by designers have become central to the creation of the modern brand and thus deserve to be explored.

Since the turn of the millennium, design has been in its ascendancy as a function within the business community, gaining traction as a differentiator and value creator. One need look no further than the singular success story of the first fifteen years of twenty-first-century commerce: Apple Inc. Led by the keen eyes of founder Steve Jobs and design guru Jonathan Ive, Apple turbo-charged its product line with an unmatched attention to design, resulting in landmark offerings like the iMac, iPod, and iPhone. While Apple has often leaned on iconic product and interface design to build its brand, other businesses have leveraged graphic or digital design as a means to ensure memorability and to forge a human connection. The most evolved firms now look to employ design thinking as a means to create value. Design thinking enables and empowers integrative approaches, while focusing first and foremost on the needs of the user. This is essential in a business environment that is increasingly complex, networked, global, and ever changing. Powered by an attention to trends and a foundation rooted in design thinking, a strategic design approach more effectively projects the wants and needs of the consumer in the future compared with many of the traditional analytical methods long taught by business schools around the world.

Rhetoric: From Fifth Century BCE to the Twenty-first Century

Taking a step back in time, we can follow the ascendancy of rhetoric from persuasive speaking to its current role in brands' meaning-making, wayfinding, and style. The art of persuasion is at the root of all definitions and theories on rhetoric, and uses three modalities: authority (ethos), emotion (pathos), and logic (logos). When a new form of government—democracy—emerged in fifth century BCE Athens, there came a demand for broader participation of the population in government and legal affairs. Suddenly, the skill of rhetoric was the most important measure for success. Sophists, educators who specialized in using the techniques of philosophy and rhetoric, introduced one of the most important aspects of rhetoric—that the notions of truth must be adjusted to fit a particular audience at a certain time.

Little has changed. As Edward McQuarrie and David Mick (1996) stated: "when persuasion is the overriding goal, the rhetorical perspective suggests that the manner in which a statement is expressed may be more important than its propositional content" (424). Jump to the twenty-first century—past the influences of Plato and Aristotle, past the tweaks from rhetoricians along the way—and you see that although in a different setting, rhetoric is not a lost art but is alive and well. Barry Brummett (2014) defines rhetoric as the "ways in which signs (meaningful images and items) influence people" (4). According to Brummett, this influence is closely linked to power management, just as it was in the early years of Grecian democracy. Those with the ability to build a strong argument hold the power.

The mid-twentieth century saw brands so strongly focused on their influence to drive sales that they began to drive people away from the truth. Cigarette companies boasted "doctor recommended" packs, and beauty and food products offered claims they could not deliver, like "get all the nutrients you need" (Figure 3.1). Plato experienced a similar dilemma criticizing the sophists for projecting deceit instead of honest facts. Consumers today desire the transparent truth, looking to credible authority (*ethos*), logical claims (*logos*), and more so now than ever, a strong emotional connection to the source (*pathos*). However, unlike its foundation in oration, twenty-first-century rhetoric is grounded more in persuasive visual and written cues.

Using rhetorical principles, brands create attention-directing word and image patterns or indirectly communicate meanings that customers must infer and connect with in a positive manner. "Companies do not design meaning; rather, they design the conditions and context to evoke meaningful experience" (Nixon & Corlett 2013: 109). A favorable attitude toward the message has an effect on the attitude toward the brand and thus influences the purchasing intention. For example, the Advertising Research Foundation found "liking" to be the strongest determinant of persuasion and the primary driver of advertising effectiveness (Huhmann & Albinsson 2012).

In our global world of infinite brands and companies, thoughtful rhetoric serves to distinguish a successful business venture. Providing consumers a framework for seeing and experiencing their offerings, successful brands help consumers sift through all of the false promises, products, and results. We see that rhetoric has three functions in today's brand-filled market:

1. Meaning-making
2. Societal navigation and wayfinding
3. Style—a brand's aesthetic taste, point of view, and expression

Today, a brand's style and identity are the rhetoric that drives the compelling message to consumers. Natalie Nixon and Tod Corlett (2013) assert that "style is a key signifier of group identification; as such it can be used to identify brands … pointing to the intangible qualities that lead consumers to form meaningful connections to products and services" (100). Brands

Figure 3.1 Rhetorical devices challenging consumer credulity were a staple of mass advertising in the mid-twentieth century.

1946, Dr. Robert K. Jackler, Stanford University School of Medicine

like Nike, Coca-Cola, and Disney all point away from the product and focus on the experience that the consumer will have with the product. Coke's "Share a Coke" campaign insists on the people-to-people connection that will result from buying into the brand, not the product itself. The idea of designing for experience is to "persuade, stimulate, inform … events, influencing meaning and modifying behavior" (Jones 2011), the same purpose of traditional rhetoric. Branding has been elevated to the rhetoric of our day.

GO DEEPER

Read the following:

- *Rhetoric in Popular Culture* by B. Brummett.
- *Rereading the Sophists: Classical Rhetoric Refigured* by S. Jarratt.
- *The Substance of Style: How the Rise of Aesthetic Value Is Remaking Commerce, Culture and Consciousness* by V. Postrel.
- *Defining Reality: Definitions and the Politics of Meaning* by E. Schiappa.

REFLECTIONS

- Explore more deeply the proposition that brands serve as the rhetorical devices of today. How do brands embody the ethos, pathos, and logos of the day?
- Compare two brands in the same category. Which is the more effective brand? How does each brand connect to consumers using the principles of ethos, pathos, and logos?

Backcast: A Brief History of the Evolution of Branding

Before we can truly understand the ways in which brands and culture are evolving today and why that matters, we must first be grounded in the origin of **branding**— defined as the process of attaching an idea to an object, service, or organization—as a tool, discipline, and meaning-maker.

The word "brand" originally comes from the Norse "brandr," though the concept of branding originated more than 4,000 years ago with the Egyptians who had special markings on their tombs to indicate identity. Throughout history, tribal affiliations, coats of arms, flags, and a myriad of other tangible indicators did the work of today's brands— communicating to audiences who they were, what they did, and even what they believed. By the 1500s, cattle owners were burning simple, unique marks on their livestock as a means to show ownership. In the late eighteenth century, the Industrial Revolution, with its mass production and complex transportation infrastructure, caused a broadening of the concept to fill the need for product differentiation, distinguishing commodities as production moved from local communities to centralized factories. Eventually the marks stamped on shipping crates began to evolve from signals of ownership to ones of quality and provenance, as sellers looked to charge a premium for one brand versus another.

This long history supports the notion that there is a human need to express identity, ownership, and status through symbols, names, colors, and stories. Broadly

Figure 3.2 Procter & Gamble has long been acknowledged as the inventor of modern brand management.
P&G Heritage & Archives Center, 1879, https://www.pg.com/Heritage/branding.php

speaking, these are the same tools used by designers today in brand construction.

The practice of modern branding can be credibly traced all the way back to 1837, when William Procter, an immigrant from England, and James Gamble, originally from Ireland, married sisters in Cincinnati, Ohio, and—with a little encouragement from their new father-in-law—went into business together. The new company, Procter & Gamble (P&G), began making candles and soap and would eventually become ground zero for the creation and deployment of many of today's most fundamental approaches to brand building (see Figure 3.2). Most notably, in 1931 the seeds of the brand-management system were planted when a young executive named Neil McElroy wrote an internal memo arguing that there should be a dedicated team of people focused on marketing each brand owned by a manufacturer and tasked with ensuring the long-term success of that individual brand, even if competitive with another brand in that company's portfolio. This suggestion was adopted by P&G and quickly became the default structure used by the large majority of consumer-goods companies. Throughout the twentieth century, P&G turned branding into an art, becoming home to successful household product names, such as Tide, Pampers, Folgers, Swiffer, Olay, and Mr. Clean. Many companies regard this technique of brand management as one of the seminal innovations in American marketing during the twentieth century.

The conclusion of World War II saw the rise of a new middle class optimistic about the future and flush with disposable income. Advertisers used more sophisticated methods to appeal to this desirable audience in new ways, while also using the invention of television to get right into the family rooms of millions of homes. More than ever, marketers attempted to separate their brands from competition by suggesting emotional benefits rather than simply functional ones. Commercials promised a particular brand would make you cooler, more attractive, or even happier, as Coca-Cola and Mean Joe Greene promised with "Have a Coke and a Smile!"

As manufacturers increasingly learned to build a brand's identity and personality beyond product function, the brand name along with associated ideas and imagery came to be a true creator of financial value. Evidence of this was clear in October of 1988, when Philip Morris, the country's largest tobacco manufacturer, decided to diversify its cigarette-heavy portfolio with the purchase of Kraft Foods. While Kraft was home to a stable of well-known grocery brands, such as Kraft Singles, Velveeta, and Miracle Whip, these brands were only modestly profitable. So why did Philip Morris pay $13 billion USD for Kraft—more than six times what the company was worth on the balance sheet? In essence, it bought the value of the brands. At the time, one analyst said: "You don't spend $13 billion for brain power, you spend $13 billion for brand power" (Widder & Key 1988).

During this time, the role of the "designer as brander" took on some additional meaning. Most packaged goods were now sold in a self-select environment, increasing the importance of making a brand easily identifiable and understandable. Iconic expressions—such as the Morton Salt girl with her umbrella, the red-and-white Marlboro carton, or the silver-wrapped Hershey bar package—became valuable unto themselves, assets to be managed as surely as a plant or fleet of trucks. Though the designer increasingly played a more valuable role, his or her integration into the conceptualization, creation, and marketing of a product was typically limited to authoring visual language and aesthetic styling. Rarely integrated or central to the brand's development process, design choices were often subjective and rarely focused on the user.

From the Egyptian kings to Burger Kings, the evolution of branding is eloquently summed up by Philip Kotler, professor of international marketing at the Kellogg School of Management at Northwestern University, who said, "The art of marketing *is* the art of brand building. If you are not a brand, you are a commodity. Then price is everything, and the low-cost producer is the only winner" (Kotler 2012: 63).

GO DEEPER

Read the following:
- *A New Brand World: Eight Principles for Achieving Brand Leadership in the Twenty-First Century* by S. Bedbury and S. Fenichell.

- *Ogilvy on Advertising* by D. Ogilvy.
- *Buying In: The Secret Dialogue between What We Buy and Who We Are* by R. Walker.
- *Designing Brand Identity: A Complete Guide to Creating, Building, and Maintaining Strong Brands* by A. Wheeler.
- Mean Joe Greene's iconic advertisement. Available online: http://www.youtube.com/watch?v=xffOCZYX6F8&feature=kp

REFLECTIONS
- Compare the earliest forms of branding with modern business's sophisticated approach to identity construction. What is the same? What has changed most dramatically?
- Discuss examples of memorable brand design. How are these elements managed by brands to deliver long-term value?
- Consider some memorable forms of brand advertising or marketing. Discuss which brands communicate using functional benefits and which use emotional benefits? Do any use both?
- Select three product categories and brainstorm examples of commodities versus brands in each.

The Changing Nature of Brands

Given a solid background in the historical function of brands and how their role has evolved, we now arrive at the recent past and recognize the power of context and cultural forces. While the practice of "branding" emerged and took root during the twentieth century, this is not just the concern of academics and businesses, nor does it exist in a vacuum.

At a macro level, the recent tectonic shifts in our culture—driven by globalization, economic and geo-political power dynamics, technological ubiquity, and increased connection (digital and social media)—have had myriad effects on the business and practice of branding. These forces have arguably served to empower people now more than at any other point in history. This level of interconnectedness on a global scale, as well as unprecedented power in the populace, has altered the dynamic between brands and people. Observing that we are emerging from an era where many people in developed nations question the role of consumerism, and perhaps are less concerned with "consuming," we begin to consider that brands have a greater responsibility. It is in this context that many branding professionals have begun to make the case that brands are a path to meaning-making and that brands must bond emotionally with people and serve as builders of our very culture.

As brands move beyond a single vector of financial-value creation, we see another shift occurring that reflects the needs of brands to offer not only value but also to serve up and reflect our own values. "People no longer accept fake offerings from slickly marketed phonies; they want real offerings from genuinely transparent sources." James Gilmore and Joseph Pine (2007) continue in *Authenticity: What Consumers Really Want*, "Buyers view offerings that conform in both depiction and perception to their self-image—their perceived state of being, including aspects real, representational and aspirational—as authentic" (5).

Driving Values: Authenticity, Social Responsibility, Localization, Human Relevance

As we observed a deep sociocultural shift toward meaning-making and authenticity, so too did we see the rise in an era of corporate social responsibility. The movement toward ethics and transparency took off in the 1990s, and it was followed more recently by the sustainability movement. Together these movements strove to wake up businesses, brands, and people to the intangible costs of the previous eras of unbridled consumerism.

Written about in *Authenticity: Brands, Fakes, Spin and the Lust for Real Life* by David Boyle in 2003, as well as in Gilmore and Pine (2007), the demand for authenticity from consumers was obvious, but making a brand "authentic" became an increasingly vexing problem. Brands at the time were not authentic, soulful, or compassionate; they were the imprimaturs for business and tools for value creation—simply the means to create authentic, soulful, or compassionate connections for users.

This new want for authenticity and transparency might have been met with mere lip service from companies if not for the simultaneous advancements in technology and the internet that enabled a world where there are no more secrets.

Further, while consumers craved brands with more meaning, businesses struggled to create them in a quickly globalizing culture where "one size fits all" became "one design/meaning fits all cultures" as the growth philosophy. The leaders of culture, global brands expanded in a tried-and-true model of consistent replication for profit generation, yet branding consistency eventually became monotony for designers and consumers alike. In his book *Beyond Trend* (2008), design forecaster Matt Mattus examines the current state of pop culture and design, its effect on consumer behavior, and what the future of our over-branded and globalized culture may look like. He posits that a "global sameness" is afoot and that "the gigantic influence of big business on our culture today is, in fact, arresting the very culture it is trying to market to" (25). As a result, brands arrived at a seemingly precarious position as both the agents of business and the creators of culture. Mattus states that corporate inventions like "global efficiencies" could be culture killers and that "business isn't interested in moving the human experience forward but, instead, moving the bottom line forward, and bottom lines love efficiency" (25). Business and brands have left us in "low culture."

Other cultural indications for this change in business approach were signaled by the likes of thought leaders such as John Seabrook. He delves into the history of our cultural hierarchy and its evolution. Historically, high-society culture fed into the middle-brow and then trickled down to influence the masses. Across the United States, the 1990s saw a shift to a new hierarchy, the end of an old aristocratic culture, leading to the advent of a new democratic culture where a commercial elite was being born. This new hierarchy holds identity at the top, and niche subcultures influence the mainstream. Instead of relying on the distinction of high-brow versus low-brow culture, Seabrook believes we are in an era of "Nobrow"—the exact place where culture and marketing converge. To fulfill our needs as creative, constantly evolving humans (not just "consumers"), we must move to a higher culture.

Ultimately, the rise in authenticity and sustainability trends, along with the emerging reality of radical transparency, was the underpinning of the business movement that led to purpose-driven brands. This all served to shape a new paradigm wherein people, planet, and purpose were considered alongside profit in the analysis of a company's performance. Connecting to the ethos of emotions and desire for truth and logic of the early twenty-first century, brands successfully swayed consumers by forming associations with good causes or by using sustainable practices,

like Patagonia. The emergence of companies such as TOMS shoes, with its one-for-one business model, took branding to new heights by bringing "values" to the forefront of the business proposition (see Figure 3.3).

GO DEEPER

Read the following:

- *In Search of Authenticity* by R. Bendix.
- *Authenticity: Brands, Fakes, Spin and the Lust for Real Life* by D. Boyle.
- *Authenticity: What Consumers Really Want* by J. Gilmore and J. Pine.

REFLECTIONS

- What brands that are currently on the market deliver the feeling of authenticity? What brands build authenticity for you personally?
- When have you observed a brand that does *not* feel authentic or transparent? How do you and others relate to this

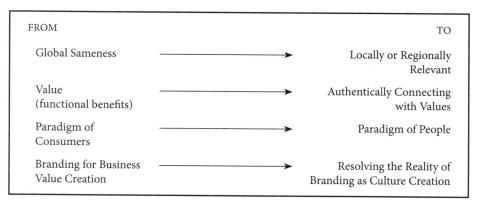

Figure 3.3 The changing nature of branding in the 21st century.

brand compared to the brands identified in the previous question?

The "Why"

As we exited the first decade of the twenty-first century, the desire for authenticity began to take shape in another dimension of branding. As people quested for their personal authenticity, they also grappled with their reason for being. People began to move beyond using brands for status and identity and looked to brands as a path to meaning. At the same time, the business world was experiencing a similar evolution.

Simon Sinek's TED Talk and subsequent book, *Start with Why* (2011), encapsulated this message, suggesting that most brands had inverted the equation when communicating with consumers. They begin by talking about what they do and how they do it, but they rarely share why they do it. For example, a computer company could state that it builds great computers (what) that are beautifully designed, simple to use, and user friendly (how) (Figure 3.4). But from the consumer's point of view: So what? Sinek brought to the fore the equation that brands should start from the inside out, from the why to the how to the what.

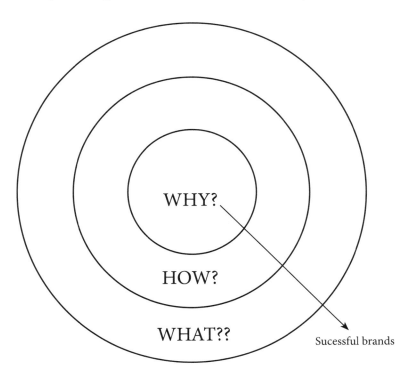

Figure 3.4 Sinek's Golden Circle, as found in his book *Start with Why: How Great Leaders Inspire Everyone to Take Action*
(Source: Sinek 2011)

Sinek (2010) shows how back in the 1980s, Apple started with the why in saying: "everything we do, we believe in challenging the status quo, we believe in thinking differently (why), the way we do this is by making our products beautifully designed, simple to use and user-friendly (how), we just happen to make great computers (what)." By starting with why, Sinek posited that brands attract people through the congruence of values and purpose: "people don't buy what you do, they buy why you do it … the goal is to do business with people who believe what you believe." Jim Stengel, previously the global marketing officer of P&G, conducted a survey with Millward Brown and used the results to inform his own brand-building framework, a process that puts purpose at the center of the brand-design process. By connecting consumers with the "why," he claims in his book *Grow* (2011) that there is a direct correlation between brand purpose and financial performance, stating that "those who center business on improving people's lives have a growth rate triple that of competitors" (1). Brands need to connect and engage with consumers based not only on shared values, but also on a shared and resonating purpose.

Jerry Kathman, president and CEO of LPK, the largest independent brand design agency in the world, has said, "We are engaged in helping our clients replace the transaction-focused communications of old with meaningful social interactions, leading to a more personal, human brand expression and experience" (2013: 76).

The Rise of "Citizen" Branders

From the advent of the internet search and all sorts of digital publishing, we have seen a transformation in our world from one of information storage and retrieval to one of sharing and socializing. This shift in how people use technology has served to irrevocably alter the dynamic between the people and practically every long-standing power structure (governments, corporations, institutions). This new era embraces an ever-evolving mix of platforms that harness the power of network effects (the positive impact and value creation that results as people join and expand a network). People immediately found ways to utilize these innovative platforms, but most corporations (brands) were far behind the populace in terms of understanding how to use these developments in the context of business. In that regard, business was no longer leading the people; people in many ways left brands and businesses behind—or at best wrested the power for themselves. This in no way squared with the "push marketing" advertising modality of the past where brands operated in a broadcast paradigm, projecting a prescriptive point of view in one direction to consumers.

Now, instead of constructing brands for consumers, we must coevolve brands with people and further embed the ability for meaning-making into our brand-building process. However, we must acknowledge that the act of meaning-making occurs within the individual and is not something we can actually control. At best we can use design to create the opportunity, context, and tools for meaning-making and put them into the hands of people. In this sense we treat our work as the "scaffolds for experiencing" (Sanders 2002: 1). Whereas in the past, brand building relied largely on consistency and repetition, the new paradigm lends itself to a less controlled, less dictatorial, and less monotonous approach. Brands create the construct that empowers people to be, experience, and become whatever they desire (versus the old paradigm where brands told people who they should become).

This cultural shift toward co-creation brings the practice of brand building into literal contact with people. This has made understanding consumers and trends more important than ever. Professionals not only have to practice the emerging fundamentals of brand building that have resulted from this shift in context (macro trends), but they must also understand the relevant social and cultural dynamics (micro trends). For example, Coca-Cola as a brand knows that it needs to be in dialogue with consumers through a variety of social media on a multitude of platforms, and it needs to understand social and cultural trends in order to connect with consumers through its campaigns. By sensing the unfolding future, this intelligence can ensure that when brands enter into dialogue with people they are relevant at the moment and don't feel dated or out of step with the lifestyle of the consumer. When we do not continually mine for insights from consumers or follow trends in the marketplace, brands/companies run the risk of being the next Blockbuster or Blackberry. There are a number of techniques to obtain

insights and to understand the trajectory into the future of the hopes, dreams, and desires of people. It is here that we begin to see how the power of design, and more specifically, design thinking, can fuel this new paradigm.

Alongside the marketing era of the mid-to-late twentieth century, design mostly was seen as the last station in brand design, "the cake decorating." In the 1990s, however, the idea of design thinking began to gain steam powered by the design firm IDEO. As we entered the 2000s, the concept of design thinking moved beyond the design world and began to be embraced by the business world with the intent of adding value to brands throughout the entire brand-building process. By the mid-2000s many had embraced the philosophy including the celebration of whole-brain engagement, bringing the consumer into the process, prototyping, and fast learning. This new design-centric or even design-led approach flipped traditional branding in a fundamental way. According to Nathan Hendricks, CCO of LPK, "for the most part, traditional marketing and branding existed in service to the [stock] market, but when design entered the picture, branding had to be in service to people" (Jacobs 2013).

As we practice in this new design-led paradigm, we look beyond the traditional frameworks that favor control and strict consistency (Figure 3.5). In an age that favors diasporas over demographics, we toss out the idea of efficiency and monotonous, one-size-fits-all theories and approaches in favor of design thinking (as explained in chapter 1)

Principles to consider

Tools for control e.g, models, standards, protocols	vs	Tools for co-creation e.g, open source, generative platforms
Efficiencies e.g, global deployments, one-stratrgy- fits-all	vs	Opportunities e.g, culturally relevant, co-opt friendly
Proprietary e.g, tightly held, protective of IP, secretive development	vs	Plentiful e.g, peer fed, sharable/spreadable

Figure 3.5 As we evolve the paradigm for branding, new principles emerge.
Content created by Valerie Jacobs and Michael Wintrob, Figure created by LPK

and more context relevance, including the dimensions of both spatial/location and temporal/timing. BMW Mini demonstrated this bespoke branding with its "Not Normal" campaign that generated one-off messages via billboards aimed directly at a single Mini driver that led him or her to an experience at a nearby gas station. We also eagerly invite people into the brand as passionates, hackers, and co-creators, such as with Mountain Dew's "Green Label" initiative.

We need to create opportunities for people to co-opt the messaging, to encourage more customized and personal storytelling with the brand in order to engage in the brand experience, socially and personally. In a way, we are suggesting the rise of "citizen" brand managers, allowing corporate brand managers to become more like brand curators and conductors. People develop deeper, more personal brand equity, achieving that ephemeral emotional connection with the brand, elevating the brand to a more consumer-driven and more consumer-centric entity. Ultimately this evolving role of brands and designers legitimately enables higher culture, deeper emotion, realized ideals, and self-actualization.

GO DEEPER

Read the following:
- "The Timely Death of the Imperious Global Design Agency" by J. Kathman in *Design Intelligence*.
- *Beyond Trend* by M. Mattus.
- *Start with Why* by S. Sinek.
- *Grow* by J. Stengel.
- Review the following websites and talks:
  - http://green-label.com/legacy/gla/
  - http://www.jimstengel.com
  - http://www.maketools.com/articles-papers/ScaffoldsforExperiencing_Sanders_03.pdf
  - http://www.outputmagazine.com/digital-signage/applications/dooh/

bmw-mini-targets-drivers-directly-
with-new-digital-billboard-campaign/

- http://www.ted.com/talks/simon_
  sinek_how_great_leaders_inspire_
  action/
- Coca-Cola Small World Machines—
  Bringing India and Pakistan
  Together: http://www.youtube.com/
  watch?v=ts_4vOUDImE

REFLECTIONS

- How might businesses better incorporate consumers to have more real-time
  influence in the brand?
- Is there an opportunity to utilize
  design thinking in your own field?
  What is the opportunity?

Vignettes

The following comments are from interviews conducted by the authors in 2014.

*Drew Boyd, Assistant Professor
of Marketing and Innovation at
University of Cincinnati; Coauthor
of* Inside the Box: A Proven System
of Creativity for Breakthrough Results

I see a significant shift happening in the
role of design in brand strategy based on
an experience I had while at Johnson &
Johnson. Our industrial design team was
aligned functionally to our R&D [research
and development] team. Their primary
focus was taking the medical devices created by R&D and building in the aesthetics
and human factors into the products. The
design team had little interaction with marketing. When we launched a new corporate
branding initiative, we included the head of

design on the cross-functional team. What
became evident early on is that the "voice of
design" was very influential in how the team
thought about brand. The design group
had already created a design language for
our products, and we were able to transfer
and embed that language into our brand-
building efforts. Because of this initiative,
the company moved to align the design
team closer to marketing and give it a stronger voice in shaping and managing brand.

*Dave Knox, Chief Marketing Officer,
Rockfish Interactive*

Back in 2010 when we started the Brandery, our hypothesis was: "Could design be
used to give a competitive advantage to
start-ups?" When you look at the words
"marketing" and "design," essentially they
are simple words for user acquisition and
user experience, both of which are vitally
important to successful start-ups. With
that in mind, the Brandery became about
bringing the power of design into the
world of start-ups using the principles of
design and marketing to give competitive advantage. Fast-forward five years,
we are fortunate enough to report that
our hypothesis works as the Brandery is
in the top ten programs in the country for
business acceleration. The difference of
applying the design-thinking mind-set to
build clients versus just putting a logo on
a brand is apparent. An example of bringing design into the branding experience is
Frameri, a start-up alum of the Brandery.
Frameri is an eyeglass company that offers
interchangeable lenses. Because they come
from the fashion realm, design was very

important from the beginning. One of the challenges of the eyeglass industry is that it is very difficult to tell the brand of eyeglasses unless you ask. A design concept that came up was offering a series of different distinct colors that will go around the lenses, so from a distance, you can always tell that it is a Frameri pair of glasses. Emphasizing design from the beginning is not something most startups that come to the Brandery think of including. But I have noticed a growing acceptance of paying attention to design from the first day. It matters how early design thinking is introduced to a developing brand because it is often one of the largest drivers for success.

Jeff McFarland, Director of Strategy in Greater China, Landor Associates

My career path has taken me from design school and design management to marketing school and brand management. So to me, one of the most interesting evolutions I've observed through these years has been the acknowledgement of design being in the service of building brands. A traditional goal of design taught to me in school was to achieve certain aesthetic principles. Another tradition I learned was "form follows function"—design as engineering, as industry. Later I witnessed marketing trying to become more of a science and research testing becoming a normal part of any development process. From this perspective, a primary goal of design was to please consumers. While all of these traditions or criteria remain present, increasingly we make design decisions based on whether or not it will support a desired brand perception or goal. So, in my early client-side work with automotive brands, we might have introduced a new interface in an automobile even though it appeared out of place, and may not have been requested by drivers yet. But we design it this way because it will position our brand as a leader, link our brand to technology and performance, and make our products more identifiable. The concept of the brand acting as an organizing principle, as the "North Star" guiding a company, insists that design and other disciplines be in service of the brand. This is a perspective I have come to appreciate over the years, and have sought to add in my work with companies in Asia and beyond.

Jack Rubin, Associate Brand Director, Procter & Gamble

This example was from the time I was working on Folgers, and it's one I often use with new hires. I walked in my first day of joining the brand, and my manager at the time said, "Welcome to Folgers, it is your job to turn around the flavored-coffee business." Great. So I gathered our reports and saw that Folgers flavored coffee was declining by double digits year after year, while the flavored-coffee category was growing by leaps and bounds, including our main competitor Maxwell House. After printing out the share report for every item in the category, I went to the grocery store to walk down the aisle and just see what was happening. The first thing I noticed was that we couldn't find

Folgers flavored coffee. Every other flavored coffee you could see a mile away. All other brands had some indication of premium cue with bold printing, images that evoked the flavor you were going to experience, and an easy-to-read name of the flavor. The other thing we noticed in the report was that the fastest growing flavors in the category were chocolate, caramel, and cinnamon. Not only did Folgers have no premium cues, no images of the flavor and printed names just a little bigger than the font on this page, but guess which three flavors we did not have? Needless to say, we took heed of our observations and, in the following fiscal year, Folgers flavored coffees grew 43 percent. The amazing part of this relaunch is that it was not major product innovation of any sort, everything we did was pure design and branding. This is the power of branding, marketing, and design thinking—observing what is going on and discovering how, with holistic design, you can improve the total experience.

Leigh Bachman, Owner, Crimson Blue Brand Consulting; Former Executive Director, Strategy & Research, Interbrand
One of the most fun and interesting projects that I led around the changing role of design was for a gum brand that needed to rediscover its connection with teens and twenty-somethings who no longer viewed the brand as cool. We had just learned that the brand had a new capability that would allow it to print color graphics on the outer plastic wrap (rather than just using a transparent plastic, as was typical in

the category). This meant that the branding and design on the outside no longer had to match the branding and design on the inner pack—the one that consumers would carry with them in their pockets or purses. This innovation meant we had an opportunity to change the game: design the outer pack based on the rules of what would work in a shelf context, but then design the inner pack on a new set of rules—what consumers really wanted to carry with them—a set of rules most CPG [consumer packaged goods] brands never get to explore. Because we were no longer designing a gum brand, but rather an accessory, the process for approaching this was equally game changing. Research now involved sitting around a comfortable room with teens and twenty-somethings, asking them to use patterns and prints we had created to design their own iPod cases, or finding out which patterns were cool enough to be associated with their favorite celebrities. From this approach we were able to launch three to four rotating designs for each flavor of gum—raising the social currency of the brand almost overnight, while also increasing share.

Conclusion
We are at a time in history where traditional "broadcast" branding is losing its foothold. While brands are still modern-day rhetorical devices, used as a means to persuade, we are in the midst of a shift from our siloed business activities to integrative approaches enabled and empowered by design thinking. Design represents people, thus providing agency

for individuals, who are gaining more and more control as the power dynamic shifts away from the previous power structures. It is therefore design's role to represent and include people in the development of products, services, and experiences. Creativity, the process of translating new and imaginative ideas into the tangible, will drive these developments, as strategy and business are increasingly seen as creative endeavors. Design and design thinking remain in their ascendancy. As compared to traditional analytical approaches focused on known-knowns, design is able to hypothesize against known-unknowns and connect dots to uncover unknown-knowns, thus making it more powerful and more appropriate for the twenty-first-century's high-speed, highly networked, highly unpredictable environment. It's an exciting time because this new way offers unprecedented creative potential and opportunity.

Acknowledgments

Foremost, we would like to thank Cristina Sanders for her many and always excellent contributions in ensuring the completion of this chapter. Additionally, we send a special thank you to the friends and colleagues who contributed personal vignettes detailing their own experiences on this topic.

References

Bedbury, S. and S. Fenichell (2002), *A New Brand World: Eight Principles for Achieving Brand Leadership in the Twenty-First Century*, New York: Viking Penguin.

Bendix, R. (1997), *In Search of Authenticity: The Formation of Folklore Studies*, Madison, WI: The University of Wisconsin Press.

Boyd, D. and J. Goldenberg (2014), *Inside the Box: A Proven System of Creativity for Breakthrough Results*, New York: Simon & Schuster.

Boyle, D. (2003), *Authenticity: Brands, Fakes, Spin and the Lust for Real Life*, New York: Harper Perennial.

Brummett, B. (2014), *Rhetoric in Popular Culture,* Thousand Oaks, CA: Sage.

Gilmore, J. and J. Pine (2007), *Authenticity: What Consumers Really Want*, Cambridge, MA: Harvard Business Review Press.

Huhmann, B. and P. Albinsson (2012), "Does Rhetoric Impact Advertising Effectiveness with Liking Controlled?" *European Journal of Marketing*, 46 (11/12): 1476–1500.

Jacobs, V. (2013), In-person interview with Nathan Hendricks on December 10, 2013.

Jarratt, S. (1998), *Rereading the Sophists: Classical Rhetoric Refigured*, Carbondale, IL: Southern Illinois University Press.

Jones, R. (2011), Lecture at the University of Kentucky College of Design, October 10, 2011. Available online: http://www.uky.edu/design/index.php/events/lecture/ronald_jones/

Kathman, J. (2013), "The Timely Death of the Imperious Global Design Agency," *Design Intelligence*, 19.5 (2013): 74–78.

Kotler, P. (2012), *Kotler on Marketing*, New York: Simon & Schuster.

Mattus, M. (2008), *Beyond Trend: How to Innovate in an Over-Designed World*, New York: Oxford University Press.

McQuarrie, E. F. and D. G. Mick (1996), "Figures of Rhetoric in Advertising Language," *Journal of Consumer Research*, 22: 424–38. Available online: http://jcr.oxfordjournals.org/content/jcr/22/4/424.full.pdf

Muminova, O. (2013), "Mood of the Nation Survey Says People Still Care about Brands' Ethics," *The Guardian*. Available online: http://www.theguardian.com/sustainable-business/consumers-care-about-brands-ethics

Nixon, N. and T. Corlett (2013), "Articulating Style and Design in Strategic Ventures," *Conference Proceedings of the 2nd Cambridge Academic Design Management Conference*. Available online: http://www.cadmc.org/CADMC2013Proceedings.pdf

Ogilvy, D. (1985), *Ogilvy on Advertising*, New York: Vintage Books.

Postrel, V. (2004), *The Substance of Style: How the Rise of Aesthetic Value Is Remaking Commerce, Culture and Consciousness*, New York: Harper Perennial.

Sanders, E. B.-N. (2002), "Scaffolds for Experiencing in the New Design Space," *Information Design*, Institute for Information Design Japan (editors), Graphic-Sha Publishing Co., Ltd. (in Japanese).

Schiappa, E. (2003), *Defining Reality: Definitions and the Politics of Meaning*, Carbondale, IL: Southern Illinois University Press.

Seabrook, J. (2001), Nobrow: *The Culture of Marketing, the Marketing of Culture*, NY: Vintage.

Sinek, S. (2010), "How Great Leaders Inspire Action," TED Talk. Available online: http://www.ted.com/talks/simon_sinek_how_great_leaders_inspire_action?language=en

Sinek, S. (2011), *Start with Why: How Great Leaders Inspire Everyone to Take Action*, New York: Portfolio.

Stengel, J. (2011), *Grow—How Ideals Power Growth and Profit at the World's Greatest Companies*, New York: Crown Business.

Walker, R. (2010), *Buying In: The Secret Dialogue between What We Buy and Who We Are*, New York: Random House.

Wheeler, A. (2006), *Designing Brand Identity: A Complete Guide to Creating, Building, and Maintaining Strong Brands,* New York: Wiley.

Widder, P. and J. Key (1988), "Phillip Morris, Kraft Seen as a Good Fit," *Chicago Tribune*, November 1. Available online: http://articles.chicagotribune.com/1988-11-01/business/8802120126_1_general-foods-kraft-philip-morris-cos-merger

PART II

The How: Introduction to Part II—Chapters 4, 5, and 6

In a continuation of Simon Sinek's Golden Circle paradigm (see Figure 3.4), "the How" is just as essential as the Why, because it contains more of the tactical aspects of how we can operationalize and actualize strategic design and shape our thinking. We structure this section of the book in a meta-design-thinking way by first doing some divergent thinking: exploring design research in chapter 4, then converging on some worm's-eye view and tactical tools in chapter 5, and culminating with another divergent and bird's-eye view of perspectives on the organization through chapter 6.

The research methods employed in strategic design are directly linked to design research, and understanding design research is central in chapter 4. Steve Wilcox, the president and founder of the design research firm Design Science, explains, with wonderful practical and real-world examples, what design research is and why its process is critical to framing the problem. One of the crucial and distinctive approaches that strategic design adopts is to be human-centered in investigating a marketing, operational, or systems challenge. It prioritizes doing the background research in defining the user, the stakeholders, and the actual problem you are investigating. Design research applauds getting out of the office, embracing tenets of ethnographic research methods, and asking "Why?" over and over again.

People are at the core of any strategic design process. In chapter 5, Cindy Tripp gets down to brass tacks and delivers to us a plethora of practical tools, frameworks, games, and methods that assist in teaming, ideation, and problem definition. Cindy has led design-thinking initiatives at Procter & Gamble; she is now a full-time consultant. She well understands how crucial it is to get the right people in the room, at the right time, and connect them so that they wantonly and creatively suspend judgment and explore a range of possibilities without being restricted by constraints, at least initially. Such a creative process is the only path to getting to innovative insights.

We culminate part II of this book with chapter 6, authored by Michelle Miller, a consultant with 2nd Road, a strategic design firm created to help its clients design, build, and learn using design-thinking principles. Michelle will help you to go from the tactical and applied tools that Cindy outlined to some bigger picture frameworks that are essential for organizations to evolve and grow. The frameworks that Michelle reviews gives you the bird's-eye view to explore three critical assets for strategic design: organizational, social, and human.

Enjoy and study the practical examples, creative exercises, and compelling frameworks that will help you to implement strategic design principles.

Stephen B. Wilcox, PhD, FIDSA, the founder of Design Science, has thirty years of experience working in product development. He was the chair of the Human Factors Section of the Industrial Designers Society of America for several years and has written extensively on design research. His book, *Designing Usability into Medical Products*, with Michael Wiklund, was published in 2005.

Stephen B. Wilcox

Focusing Question: What is design research and how is it used as part of the product-design process?

This chapter explores the key questions:

- What are the foundations of design research?
- What are some of the basic requirements for design research?
- What are the various types of design research?
- How does design research integrate with product design?

INTRODUCTION

Design research, as I will broadly define the term here, is research about people that is used to support the development of products. The purpose of design research is to guide the design process toward solutions that fit with the wants and needs of the people who will use the products.

While it is true that versions of design research are also applied to other design problems besides product design (e.g., architecture, signage, and the workplace, as well as service design), this chapter will restrict the focus to product design in order to keep the discussion manageable.

It follows, logically, from the definition above that there are two categories of people who have to be considered, although in different ways:

1. The people who are being designed for (*users*)—the ultimate beneficiaries of the design process, and
2. The people who are doing the designing (*designers*)—the designers, engineers, marketing specialists, and so on, who are the executors of design efforts.

In order to be useful in helping to meet the needs of users, design research has to be, first of all, *accurate*, and second of all, *thorough*. It has to be accurate for the obvious reason that it cannot help to meet the wants and needs of users unless those wants and needs are accurately identified. Indeed, a key function of design research is to replace false assumptions, based on the designer's intuitions and biases, with accurate information, based on evidence.

But accuracy is not enough. Design research also has to be thorough enough to provide the level of detail necessary to really inform the variety of design decisions that will have to be made. To give a simple example, imagine setting out to design a skateboard, a product that is used by a particular young subculture, a subculture that the members of the design team are unlikely to be members of (see Figure 4.1). Design research might be used to explore the way the product will be used in order to create the proper geometry: Will it be picked up by hand or will users expect to spring it up

Figure 4.1 Skateboarders
Courtesy Depositphotos, Inc.

by stepping on it? How will it be carried? Do users prefer to lean forward or back? What type of shoes will they be wearing?

However, accurate research that limits itself to these types of "functional" questions is unlikely to provide the designer with what he or she needs to fully fit the wants and needs of users. In such a product category, it is necessary for the product to be "cool" in order to be successful, so the designer also has to know what colors, surface treatments, overall geometries, and so on that the target users will find "cool." The point is that "getting it mostly right" is not enough. In this example, getting it mostly right is a sure prescription for failure.

In sum, good design research has to be accurate, and it also has to be thorough so that it answers the full array of questions that the designer uncovers in order to successfully tailor a product to its intended users.

As mentioned, though, there is, in effect, another user that has to be considered—the designer. In order to avoid unnecessary confusion, I will use the term "users" to refer to the people who will use the product that is being designed and the term "designers" to refer to the people who are doing the designing (actually, in the typical case, an interdisciplinary team with various backgrounds, including, but not limited to, design). However, it is important not to lose sight of the fact that designers are actually the users of design research.

The other requirement for design research, then, is that it must be capable of being used effectively by designers. In the same way that products need to be tailored to the wants and needs of their users, design research has to be tailored to the wants and needs of its users. This means, in practice, that it must be both accessible and useful to the people from the different backgrounds who will participate in a given design process. In other words, design research must be understandable to the design team and, once understood, must prove useful in helping the team to successfully meet the wants and needs of product users.

The primary mission, then, for this chapter, is to describe the various forms of design research and to provide advice about how to make it, on the one hand, accurate and thorough, vis-à-vis users, and, on the other hand, accessible and useful vis-à-vis designers.

But first, let's briefly examine where design research came from.

The Origins of Design Research

Design research, as a discipline, emerged from a need—the need for product designers to understand users. What follows is a broad-stroke historical overview of design research (summarized in the timeline shown in Figure 4.2). That said, the first real design researcher was Alvin Tilley, who worked for Henry Dreyfuss Associates for over forty years. As Henry Dreyfuss and his colleagues tackled the design of products for people—creating classic Bell telephones, Hoover vacuum cleaners, Polaroid cameras, Westclox alarm clocks, Honeywell thermostats, John Deere tractors, and so on—they recognized the need for better information about the people for whom they were designing. Alvin Tilley, who was trained as a mechanical engineer, came

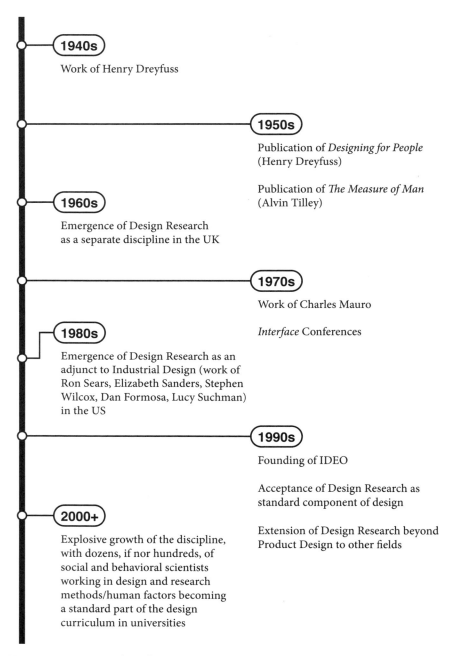

Figure 4.2 Design research timeline
Courtesy Design Science

forward to fit that need. He began collecting information from various sources to support the design efforts, which resulted in, among other things, the publication of *The Measure of Man* in 1959. *The Measure of Man* was a compendium of useful information, particularly **anthropometry** (the study of the shape and size of the body), which, in a revised form, remains a useful tool for designers today.

Tilley was clearly ahead of his time. The field of design research did not really begin to gel as a discipline until years after he began his work. During the 1960s, the field of design research began to emerge in the UK, including the founding of the Design Research Society in 1966. However, the primary focus at that time was on research about design as opposed to research as a component of design. There are few significant contributors to the latter field until Charles Mauro founded what was then Mauro and Associates (now MauroNewMedia) in 1975. Mauro is an industrial designer, co-trained in ergonomics, who had worked for Henry Dreyfuss and Raymond Loewy prior to establishing his own firm. Mauro began applying research methods to design and writing about these methods. Then, as the 1980s began, the field really started to emerge. Ron Sears, a PhD psychologist, joined the design consultancy, Richardson Smith, in 1980, followed by Liz Sanders, another PhD psychologist, the next year.

Sears and Sanders were the first PhD-level social/behavioral scientists to be employed by product-design consultancies. Around the same time (1981), Dan Formosa, like Charles Mauro, trained in both ergonomics (the application of knowledge about human beings to design—also called **human factors**—and, in his case, the subdiscipline of ergonomics called **biomechanics**, which is the study of the physics of animal or human movement and posture) and design, was one of the founders of Smart Design, a firm that integrated (and continues to integrate) research with design. In the meantime, Lucy Suchman, an anthropologist from the UK, was working at Xerox Parc. She began there as an intern in 1979 and became a staff member of PARC in 1984.

Then throughout the 1980s, the population of social/behavioral scientists in design continued to increase. I joined Herbst LaZar Bell (HLB) in 1984; Jane Fulton Suri joined Bill Moggridge's firm, ID Two, soon after. ID Two went on to be merged into IDEO in 1991. Bill Moggridge, although not a social scientist, per se, was a designer who deserves special mention vis-à-vis design research. From the founding of his first design consultancy in London in 1969, Moggridge Associates, he saw the value of design research and incorporated early versions of it into his work. Throughout his career, he wrote and spoke about the value of research in design.

One important development in the late 1970s and through the 1980s was a series of conferences called "Interface" that were jointly sponsored by (what was then) the Human Factors Society and the Industrial Designers Society of America. These conferences provided a forum for designers and design researchers to meet each other and compare notes. Many of the methods that we use today—ethnographic research, participatory design, usability testing—were presented at those conferences, perhaps for the first time.

Today design research is recognized as a key component of product design. It has evolved into two forms: (1) research done by designers to support their own efforts and (2) research done by social/behavioral scientists to support designers' efforts. There isn't space to delineate the differences between these two approaches in what follows, and, in fact, the methods are not necessarily particularly different. It is just that trained social scientists tend to be able to apply more rigor to research efforts: For example, they tend to incorporate more quantitative methods.

Regardless of who performs it, design research involves a number of methods, as described in the next section.

GO DEEPER

Read the following:

- *Developments in Design Methodology* by N. Cross.
- *Creating Breakthrough Ideas: The Collaboration of Anthropologists and Designers in the Product Development Industry* edited by S. Squires and B. Byrne; particularly see William Reese's chapter: "Behavioral Scientists Enter Design: Seven Critical Histories."
- "Design Research Has Come a Long Way" by S. Wilcox in *Innovation*. See also the other articles in this special issue of *Innovation* devoted to design research.

REFLECTIONS

- To turn the clock back, imagine how you would approach redesigning an everyday object without doing any research into how it's used. How would you expect your process to change if you could do any research you wanted?
- Try reading some of the articles in Jones and Thornley (1963) to see how design was approached prior to the incorporation of a research phase.

Design Research Methods

Design research methods fall into four basic categories:

- Observational research. This is generally conducted as the first step of product development to provide a foundation of "real-world" information to support the design process.
- Secondary research. This uses published technical information about human beings to inform design decisions.
- Usability testing. This entails using empirical testing of prototypes to "work out the bugs."
- Participatory design methods. This brings product users into the design process.

Let's explore each of these in turn.

Observational Research

Observational research evolved from the ethnographic research used by cultural anthropologists. The purpose of observational research is twofold: (1) to determine the "facts on the ground" that constrain a new product and (2) to learn to see things from the point of view of product users. In the broadest sense, observational research entails watching what people do in the real world and extracting design-related information from it.

In terms of establishing the facts, the observational researcher has to answer three families of questions:

- Who are the users?
- What is the use environment?
- What are the procedures that the product category is used for?

While answering these objective questions, the researcher attempts to answer the more subjective question of what makes the user tick—how he or she sees things. The latter can be difficult, since the designer's viewpoint is inevitably dramatically different from that of the user. The designer knows the systems by which the product is made, the strategies by which pricing is determined, what the marketing infrastructure is, and so on, but except in rare cases, the designer does not use the product on a regular basis, as the user will. The irony is that, as the designer learns more and becomes more sophisticated, he or she becomes even more different from the people for whom he or she is designing. Thus, it becomes necessary to use research to "step into the user's shoes," as mentioned, one of the central purposes of observational research.

Conducting good observational research requires a number of steps, which I will briefly describe:

1. Determining what to observe and obtaining access to it. The key is to observe people using products that are akin to the one being designed. It is important that observations be made of realistic conduct in realistic environments. So the first step is to determine who the target users are and where a product will be used. The next step is to figure out how to get access. One possibility is to create a screener that can be used by a professional recruiter to obtain sites for observation.

2. Preparing for the research. There are two things that are nearly always necessary in order to conduct good observational research: (1) studying the phenomena beforehand so that the research team is adequately knowledgeable and (2) creating a research protocol. In the absence of prior research, the team is unlikely to be able to understand what it is seeing in enough depth to be useful. The purpose of a research protocol is to provide structure to the research, to elevate it above simply "going out and looking." The protocol specifies what will be observed and the questions that will be asked. For observational research, there is usually not a fixed order of events, but it should act as a check list to assure that the right information is being gathered. A good criterion for inclusion of observations or questions in the protocol is whether or not the results are likely to affect design decisions.

3. Conducting and documenting the research. Observational research usually has two parts: (1) "fly on the wall" observations that attempt to avoid interfering with the phenomena that are being observed and (2) questioning that follows this initial observation.

It is often possible, at some point in the research, for users to narrate their activities. However, this can alter their behavior, so it should not precede the "neat" observations.

Another important requirement is to collect video. Video documentation is nearly always necessary to obtain adequate observational research because it is usually impossible to fully see what is happening in real time. It simply happens too fast, and there are too many things going on. Video documentation allows the researcher to study the captured procedures in depth.

4. Analyzing the data, thus obtained. Observational research typically yields two forms of raw data: the video record and the researcher's notes.

5. Presenting the results. Observational research gives complex, "messy" results, creating a challenge for presenting findings in a way that is clear and actionable but without "dumbing it down" and without doing violence to the actual complexity of the observed phenomena. One trick is to use "information graphics" (cf, Tufte 2001) to show patterns. A simple heuristic is to imagine a road map without graphic content, having only text and numbers. Without the graphic content, it just isn't usable. The same is true of observational research. There are various types of graphic tools for making sense of complicated information, including:

- A *matrix format* (as shown in Figure 4.3) shows the steps of a procedure on one dimension (with time translated into horizontal distance) and the tools that are used on the other dimension. All sorts of additional information can be layered onto this type of graphic summary.
- A *flow chart* (see Figure 4.4) is particularly useful in capturing where decision points are and what the overall logic is of a given domain.
- A *storyboard* (see Figure 4.5) provides for an intuitive understanding of the components of a procedure. (See chapter 5 for more information on storyboards.)

Another valuable approach is to use a multimedia presentation tool in which video illustrations of observed phenomena can be embedded. In general, it helps to think of the presentation as a pyramid, the top of which consists of the key design implications of the research, with the bottom being the raw data that a design team may want to wallow in—video, coded data in spreadsheets, and so on.

Here is a real example of contextual inquiry applied to product development; it is somewhat altered because part of the story remains the intellectual property of the client for whom the research was conducted.

The project involved a new technology that allowed a device, used for "transecting" (i.e., cutting) human tissue, to be made smaller. The company that developed the technology had a line of products used by general surgeons who perform surgery, such as gall bladder removals and colectomies

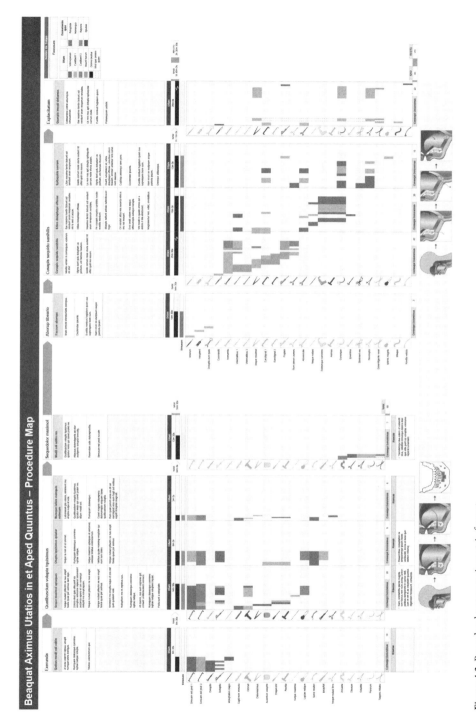

Figure 4.3 Procedural summary in matrix format

Courtesy Design Science.

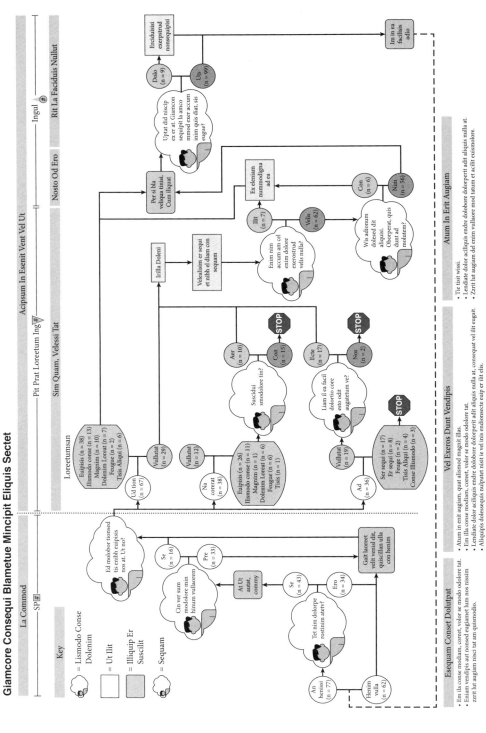

Figure 4.4 Flow chart format to summarize procedures and associated decisions

Courtesy Design Science.

(removal of sections of the intestine). The size reduction suggested that they could potentially create products for more delicate forms of surgery, such as those performed by ear, nose, and throat surgeons (ENTs). The problem the company had is that they didn't know much about ENTs and the procedures they perform.

Thus, they conducted contextual inquiry to understand the new procedures, the new environments of use, and the new users. They contracted with ENT surgeons to observe twenty actual procedures, which happened to be thyroid removals. For each procedure, the designers observed, asked many questions, and collected a video record. This research provided a wealth of information about ENTs (e.g., their preferences for small instruments), their procedures (e.g., use of instruments that involve delicate finger movements rather than arm movement, like general surgeons), and the use environment (e.g., how ENT procedure labs differ from general operating rooms). The information, thus gained, allowed the company to develop a new instrument that fit the various constraints imposed and the various preferences of ENTs. The research dictated the

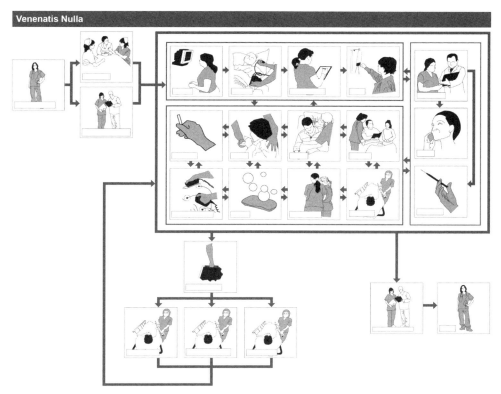

Figure 4.5 Storyboard procedural summary
Courtesy Design Science.

initial design direction for the new product and served as a reference for ongoing design decisions as the project unfolded.

GO DEEPER

Read the following:

- *Doing Design Ethnography* by A. Crabtree, M. Rouncefield, and P. Tolmie.
- *Designing and Conducting Ethnographic Research: An Introduction* by M. LeCompte and J. Schensul.
- "Ethnography as a Product Development Tool" by S. Wilcox in *Appliance Manufacturer*.

REFLECTIONS

- Try carefully observing a friend doing some common task, such as brushing his or her teeth. What are the steps and how many are there? How does your friend decide what the right amount of toothpaste is? How would you communicate the results?
- Go to a retail location and observe. Try to build a model of how people make purchasing decisions. How might you summarize this with a flow chart? With a storyboard? How many alternative decision processes are there?

Critical Questions

- How do you know when you can trust conclusions that you or others draw from observational research? How can you tell if they're wrong?
- What can you do to reduce the likelihood of errors with observational research? What do you do in ordinary life to make sure that your observations are accurate?
- When you fear that you've misperceived something, what do you do? How do misperceptions tend to come about? How common is it?
- What happens when what people say contradicts what you observe? Which do you trust? Why?

Application of Technical Information about Humans

Observational research typically precedes product design. It creates an "informational platform" from which the design team can work. Applying technical information requires at least some preliminary design work in order to generate the questions that the researcher can answer. As the design unfolds, there are all sorts of decisions that have to be made, decisions that have to do with product users:

- What types of controls (e.g., thumbwheels, hard buttons, softkeys, touchscreen objects, etc.) are best for controlling what types of functions?
- For a given type of control, how much force should be required to operate it? How large should it be? How far should it travel?
- What information should be conveyed to users and what's the best way to display it?
- What sorts of errors should be expected and can they be minimized?
- What can be done to make it as easy as possible to learn how to use a given product?

However, few or none of these questions emerge until there is some sort of design. You can't worry about grip span (the width to which a person can open his or her hand) until you know that a whole-hand grip will be used with a given control. You can't know what types of errors to mitigate until you know, at least in general terms, how a device will be used.

A large amount of literature is available that contains answers to questions of this type. It can be found in journals, such as *Human Factors* or *Applied Ergonomics*; technical reports that are generated by researchers (e.g., conducting grant-funded studies); and reference books. However, one complication is that relevant information is not restricted to the area of human factors or design research, per se, but it can also be found in the literature of a variety of disciplines (e.g., psychology, sociology, anthropology, or medicine).

Here are a couple of examples: If you're developing a mechanical hand tool, like a pair of shears, you have to determine dimensions, such as those indicated in Figure 4.6. The dimensions relate to the shape and size of the hand: There has to be enough clearance for the thumb (a); you need to know the width of the largest thumb in order to make the "thumb hole" larger than that so all thumbs will fit. You also have to make sure that all users can open the shears, so the grip span (b) has to be smaller than that of the smallest user; otherwise the users with small hands won't be able to open the shears all the way. Dimensions such as these (thumb width and grip span) are given in

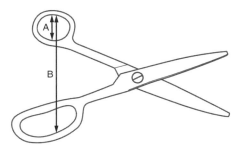

Figure 4.6 Dimensions of shears that relate to hand anthropometry
Courtesy Design Science.

anthropometry books or other documents (e.g., NASA 1978; Peebles & Norris 1998; Pheasant & Haslegrave 2005). As mentioned above, anthropometry is the study of the shape and size of the human body. The data (length of the forearm, width of the foot, overall height, etc.) are provided as percentiles. So, to address the shears, you might look at the thumb width of the ninety-fifth percentile man (the thumb width that is larger than all but the largest 5% of men) and the grip span of the fifth percentile woman (i.e., the largest thumb and the smallest grip span). These data become important design input to determine the relevant dimensions of the shears.

As another example, imagine designing a graphic user interface (GUI) for a product, say, the touch-screen interface for a point-of-sale system (today's cash registers). You have to decide if the menu goes at the top, bottom, or side; how data and text will be entered; what the color palette should be; what fonts the text will be; how large the text and the icons should be; and so on. These types of decisions do not have to be made in a vacuum, since a great deal of research has been done to empirically determine what works best—what is easier to learn and more efficient to use.

Finding relevant information can be challenging, although search engines have made it easier. What's harder is to digest what is actually relevant and present it in a way that product designers can use—that has clear implications for design decisions. In fact, a good heuristic for the design researcher is to ask him- or herself what the design implication of a given bit of information is. If the answer isn't clear, then perhaps the information isn't really relevant or useful.

GO DEEPER

Read the following:

- *Handbook of Human Factors and Ergonomics* by G. Salvendy.
- *The Measure of Man and Woman, Revised Edition: Human Factors in Design* by A. Tilley.
- *Human Factors Design Handbook* by W. Woodson, P. Tillman, and B. Tillman.

REFLECTIONS

- Take a common handheld product that you use and determine if it truly fits your hand. What dimensions would you need to know in order to get it just right? Where would you look to find these dimensions?
- For one of the software products you commonly use, what are the human factors decisions that have to be made? What human characteristics do you need to know to optimize these decisions? Do you regularly make errors with this

product? How could the software be redesigned to eliminate those errors?
- Go to your car and make a list of the control devices. What underlying functions do these control? Why have the controls taken the form that they have? What are the human factors principles that have determined these choices?

Critical Questions

- Given many sources for technical data in this internet age, how do you know what's valid and what isn't?
- Is being published in a peer-reviewed journal still the "gold standard"? Are there ever errors in peer-reviewed journals? Can you trust other sources at all? How do you determine what you can trust and what you can't?
- Given that you always have to extrapolate when using published data (the conditions under which the data were collected never perfectly match the problem you're trying to solve), how do you know which extrapolations are valid and which are not?
- When you find contradictions between multiple published sources, how do you determine which, if either, is correct?

Usability Testing

Whereas observational research and the application of technical information are "proactive" in that they are used to inform design decisions, usability testing is "reactive" in that it involves a type of trial and error. Usability testing involves asking potential product users to perform simulated tasks with a prototype and using the results to improve the design. Perhaps the best way to explain usability testing is to go through the steps involved:

1. Recruiting. Step one is to determine who the potential users are and to create a "participant screener" to recruit a representative sample. The screener specifies the recruiting criteria, which typically include demographic variables like age, as well as more behavioral criteria, such as ownership of a particular existing product (see Figure 4.7, which is a page taken from a recruiting screener). It is typical to use a professional recruiter to obtain participants. Sample sizes, of course, vary, but fifteen or twenty is fairly typical.

2. Creating a research protocol. The protocol specifies the procedure that will be used for the testing as well as the specific questions that will be asked. It is typical to ask questions about preferences and "likes/dislikes" following behavioral tasks. Figures 4.8 and 4.9 show some representative pages from usability testing research protocols—one from the behavioral section and one from the interview section. A full protocol often runs twenty to thirty pages.

3. Conducting the testing. Testing is generally conducted one-on-one with each participant, one at a time. The participant is given a series of tasks to perform with some form of prototype. The testing is typically conducted in a facility that has a testing room adjacent to a viewing room with a one-way window in between, so that the testing can be observed by members of the design team (see Figures 4.10a and 4.10b). The testing is usually documented via video. It is common for there to be a two-person team, one member of which administers the protocol while the other enters the resulting data. Sessions last anywhere from thirty minutes to a few hours. The key data collected include errors, procedural difficulties, the time it takes to perform tasks, and the responses to interviews.

4. Data analysis. The most important data are normally errors. The mistakes that the participants make provide important information about what needs to be changed. Other useful forms of information include spontaneous comments and the opinions obtained from interviews.

5. Reporting. The audience for usability testing reports are those who will make design decisions for the product. The key information that they need to know is what needs to be changed and the data that underlie the recommended changes. It can be useful to include video links in reports in order to convey the nature of key errors that are made.

A representative example is a new cell phone. The design of the screen might be tested via prototypes that are simulated early in the program on a computer screen. Representative phone users would be asked to come in and "use" the prototype in simulated form—performing a series of representative tasks

Screening Questions

Have you been diagnosed by a physician as having diabetes? Which type?

[ ] Yes, Type 1   RECRUIT 7

[ ] Yes, Type 2   RECRUIT 7

[ ] No   TERMINATE

Do you currently take insulin as part of your treatment for diabetes?

[ ] Yes   CONTINUE

[ ] No   TERMINATE

How do you currently take your insulin?

[ ] Disposable Pen   RECRUIT MIX

[ ] Syringe and Vial   RECRUIT MIX

[ ] Pump   TERMINATE

[ ] Other   TERMINATE

If injecting with 'Disposable Pen' or 'Syringe and Vial': Do you inject your insulin, or does someone do it for you?

[ ] I do it myself   CONTINUE

[ ] Someone else injects me   TERMINATE

How long have you been diagnosed as having diabetes? **[RECRUIT MIX]**

[Record response] _____

How old are you?

[Record response] _____

Sample—Participant Screener | July 2, 2014 (V.3) | Page 4 of 8

Figure 4.7 A page from a participant screener
Courtesy Design Science.

Date: ___/___/____   **Injection**:   [ ] 1   [ ] 2   [ ] 3 (if needed)
Participant #: ____   **Hands**:   [ ] Gloves   [ ] No Gloves
Case Report Form   **Music Distraction**: [ ] Yes   [ ] No

Tasks	*Outcome*
Remove Cap *If not removed after 2 minutes, check Not Removed.*	Remove Safety Cap ☐ Easily ☐ With effort ☐ NOT removed ☐ Assisted
Attach pen needle	☐ Used Outer Shield to place needle onto cartridge holder ☐ Screwed on until secure ☐ Removed Outer Shield and saved for needle disposal
Set the dose properly	☐ Yes ☐ No
Select proper location	☐ Correct ☐ With effort ☐ Incorrect [ ] Left [ ] Right [ ] Thigh [ ] Arm [ ] Abdomen
Hold device properly for injection	☐ Needle towards body ☐ Needle away from body ☐ Approx 90° to body ☐ Other, record: _____

Inject entire dose
(no premature lift)
	☐ Needle fully straight
	                    ☐ Needle inserted at an angle
	☐ Continuous motion
	                    ☐ Discontinuous motion
	                    ☐ Potential for / actual needle-stick
	Device held at injection site (injection pad) for:
	☐ > 5 sec. ☐ 2-5 sec. ☐ 1-2 ☐ < 1 sec.

Detach pen needle from pen	☐ Place Outer Shield back on needle ☐ Unscrew needle ☐ Discard needle and Outer Shield in sharps container ☐ No potential for needle-stick ☐ Potential for needle-stick
Inspect and interpret dosage window Ask: "Do you believe you gave a full injection? How do you know?"	☐ Yes, because: [ ] Button fully depressed [ ] Held for 10 sec. [ ] Other: _____ ☐ Unsure: _____ ☐ No: _____

Figure 4.8 A page from a research protocol relating to behavioral task
Courtesy Design Science.

Post Use Questions (following each trial)

Injection: [ ] 1   [ ] 2   [ ] 3 (if needed)

1. Do you recall committing any use errors – making any mistakes – while pretending to inject? *[If yes]* Describe the use errors that occurred when you interacted with the device.

   _____

   _____

2. Do you recall any "close calls," meaning times when you came close to committing a use error? *[If yes]* Describe any close calls you experienced.

   _____

   _____

3. Do you recall any "operational difficulties," meaning times when you experienced difficulty, inefficiency, or frustration? *[If yes]* Describe any operational difficulties you experienced.

   _____

   _____

Follow-up Questions

1. Overall, what do you like about the device you used today? Why?

   _____

   _____

2. Overall, what do you dislike about this device? Why?

   _____

   _____

3. Is there anything that you would like to change about this device? Why?

   _____

   _____

4. Do you have any additional questions or comments about anything you've seen here today?

   _____

   _____

Sample—Formative Usability Testing │ April 20, 2014 (V.5) │ Page 23 of 35

Figure 4.9 A page from a protocol relating to interview questions
Courtesy Design Science.

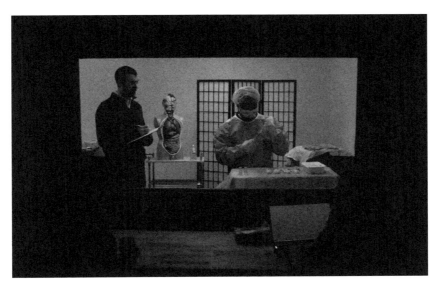

Figure 4.10a Usability testing room
Courtesy Design Science.

Figure 4.10b Usability testing room
Courtesy Design Science.

and answering questions about what they liked, disliked, and so on.

Later in the program, once an actual working prototype is available, the hardware and the software can be tested via usability testing. Now it can be verified that the phone is comfortable in the hand, etc., as well as that it can be used properly without error. Once the product is developed, testing might be performed with the actual product to provide data for marketing claims—to show that texts can be created faster than on a competitor's device, for example. For regulated industries, such as the medical arena, such testing may be required to establish that the new product meets regulatory requirements.

GO DEEPER

Read the following:

- *A Practical Guide to Usability Testing* by A. Dumas and J. Redish.
- *Usability Engineering* by J. Nielsen.

REFLECTIONS

- Imagine testing a product you regularly use for usability. Who would you test it with? What tasks would you incorporate into the testing? What would you record? How would you report the results?
- Choose another product that you use. Do you think that usability testing was part of its development? Why or why not?
- What questions would you ask in the course of a usability test? When would you ask them?
- How might you test the usability of a service? For example, what could

a usability test for a pizza delivery process look like? Or an online-dating site?

Critical Questions

- Given that you only have a short amount of time with participants who have never seen your prototype before, how do you find the potential for problems that will emerge only with extensive use (e.g., those caused by boredom or inattention)?
- How do you distinguish ease of learning from ease of use?
- How do you determine sample size for usability tests? What considerations relate to sample size?
- How do you determine who should participate in a usability test? What are the considerations?

Participatory Design

One final type of design research is to have potential product users participate in the design process (i.e., ***participatory design***). Participatory design takes a number of forms (cf., Sanders 2002), all driven by the fact that the target participants are assumed not to have technical design skills. Participants may be simply asked to periodically sit in on design reviews in which the team looks at drawings and/or models. The participants are asked to give their responses to the design artifacts in question and to make suggestions. This helps to assure that user needs, biases, and preferences are adequately met.

There are also methods that involve providing tools to make people into "artificial designers"—what Sanders (2002) calls "Make Tools." Examples include:

- Providing images to people and asking them to make collages to express the "feel" that a new product should achieve.
- Asking people to keep diaries in order to obtain access to ideas that people may not think of in a particular scheduled session.
- Soliciting drawings of maps, diagrams, and so forth, to obtain information about how users see things.
- Providing three-dimensional "building blocks" and asking participants to create their version of what a product should be.

What all these tools have in common is that they provide participants with the ability to express their wants and needs for a particular product in various visual ways—by going beyond what they can express verbally. Sanders advocates providing both "cognitive toolkits" that involve maps, models, diagrams, and so on, and "emotional toolkits" that involve collages or diaries. As Sanders (2002) puts it:

Every artifact tells a story and so we typically ask the creator of the artifact to tell us that story. The stories associated with the artifacts from the emotional toolkits tell of feelings, dreams, fears, and aspirations. The stories associated with the artifacts of the cognitive toolkits tell us how people understand and misunderstand

things, events and places. The cognitive toolkits can also reveal the intuitive relationships between system components (5).

GO DEEPER

Read the following:
- "Participatory Design: Issues and Concerns" by F. Kensing and J. Blomberg
- *Participatory Design: Principles and Practice*s by D. Schuler and A. Namioka

REFLECTIONS
- Imagine a common product or service. How might its design change if users were part of the design team? Do you think they were?
- With the products you imagined above, what types of user representatives should have been part of the design process? What roles would they play?
- What would you say to the designer of your toothbrush about how you would change it? Your coffee cup? The line at your favorite coffee house?

Critical Questions
- What is the role of the designer, the design researcher, and the user/participant in participatory design? Should you take the user/participant's ideas at face value?
- Why is there a need for a designer? A design researcher? Why can't the user design his or her own product?
- Is there a potential problem that a user who works with a design team will quickly become an atypical user? How can this be mitigated?

Design Research Vignettes

What follows are the answers of various design researchers who were asked to describe a design research project that was "particularly noteworthy or interesting." The first one is my own.

Stephen Wilcox, Principal, Design Science

I think my favorite project was in the early 1980s, shortly after I joined Herbst LaZar Bell. We were retained by Raytheon Medical to redesign a mammography X-ray system. In those days, industrial designers would begin a new project by getting a brief (and they were brief) and immediately start to sketch. We approached the project differently by first going into hospitals and studying the process of taking breast X-rays. From our observations, we made a list of problems to solve—the time required for the tech to walk several times between the patient and the control panel, the awkwardness of placing the patient up against a wall of sheet metal, et cetera—which the designers used to completely revolutionize mammography. It was easy in those days in that there was a lot of "low-hanging fruit."

Elizabeth Sanders, Associate Professor, Design Department, The Ohio State University

This is a memorable project from the 1980s. I was asked to determine the color palette for an educational product for preschoolers. It was not a toy and therefore could not be offered in different colors for boys and girls, which was the usual thing to do at the time for the preschool market. So I contacted a local preschool where I spent three days conducting a range of very short activities with the children, either individually or in small groups. In one activity, they colored in a drawing of the product. In another activity, they chose their favorite product from a set of six that we had painted ahead of time. I had favorite color conversations with the children who were verbal, and I took photos of the children and what they were wearing. At the end of the three days, one of the preschool teachers asked me what the results were. At that time, I didn't know since I had yet to analyze the data. She decided that she would guess. A week later, I could see that she was right! After that, when working with small children, I always started the design research process with their caregivers! This project also marked my initial steps toward participatory design—before I knew that the approach was already going on in Scandinavia.

Will Reese, Principal, Ethno

It's hard to work in design research without encountering the word "strategy." I always wonder what it means. As often as not, people just use the word "strategy" in order to make what is otherwise just a plan sound more important. But eventually I have come around to a usage that might mean something practical for design. I think strategy is about being holistic. A project that helped me appreciate this more than others was one I did at Ziba Design for the Li Ning sports company, in China. Li Ning was the biggest domestic athletic apparel manufacturer in the country at the time, but they were hemorrhaging market share to Nike and

Adidas. So we had to come up with a group of unifying principles to help Li Ning create new products, retail stores, and communications materials that all made sense together. Everybody had to get on the same page: consumer insights and trends, brand, communication design, retail, and product design. We iterated principles over and over again until we found a structure that all the different design and marketing functions could use. Those principles that we eventually arrived at were very sharp, not watered down, not lowest-common denominator, and yet they held something that each of the disciplinary silos could act on and design to. It solidified a definition of strategy in my mind: the more holistic, the more strategic.

Graham Pullin, Course Director of Digital Interaction and Product Design, University of Dundee

In the speech technology used by many people who cannot speak, a lack of expressive tone of voice can lead to misunderstandings and even a false impression of social ineptitude. But how to include people with complex communication needs in discussions about what is needed, given that even phoneticians find nuanced tone of voice difficult to describe? We addressed this issue by creating a collection called *Six Speaking Chairs* to provoke new conversations about tone of voice in everyday conversation, using design not to solve a problem directly but to explore an issue. The research has progressed to the design of a kit with which speech and language therapists can conduct experimental research, in order to direct future developments in speech technology.

Chris Conley, Cofounder, Gravity Tank

A favorite project happened very early in my career. We were designing baby strollers, and the client was intent on doing focus groups. I suggested we have the mothers bring their babies and strollers, and we set up a few real world scenarios they could try. This was met with grand objections of difficulty and compromising the research, since it wasn't a proven approach. We had the focus facility remove all the furniture, and we did a stand up and demo focus group. Mothers went from extolling the virtues of the wonderful strollers they had selected and purchased to cursing them as they tried to show people how they fold, fit in a trunk, and carry baby supplies and mom's bags. The idea of observing real behavior to understand a person's experience was permanently etched in my professional approach.

Charles Mauro, President/Founder, MauroNewMedia

One of our projects involved designing and executing a complex study to determine the effectiveness of the pedestrian warning system known as the LOOK! campaign, funded by NYC Department of Transportation. The study utilized existing and updated observational methods and mental models of pedestrian behavior to determine whether or not the proposed graphic warning system was effective. The study produced robust insights into NYC pedestrian behaviors as a function of the LOOK! solution and other factors. This research was funded by

MauroNewMedia in conjunction with the New School for Social Research.

Rama Gheerawo, Deputy Director, Helen Hamlyn Centre for Design, Royal College of Art

We did a memorable project with Samsung between 2008 and 2009 that involved cell phones. This showed the strategic importance of including customers in the design process. A group of sixty- to eighty-year-olds in Norway, UK, and Italy helped us challenge the original brief and cocreate ideas that sought analog ways to solve digital discord—namely, the struggle in learning to use a new digital device. We focused on the out-of- box experience and redesigned the throwaway manual into a hardcover book to be kept on a shelf and referred to throughout the life of the phone. Turning the pages revealed step-by-step advice with graphical and text-based instructions pointing to the actual device and accessories encased within the book. Centering research on people led us toward unexpected, innovative solutions.

Uday Dandavate, Cofounder and CEO, SonicRim

Design research is not just about delivering reports anymore. It's more about becoming an integral part of the client team and serving as a catalyst of a shared process of discovery, synthesis, and innovation. One of our clients, Michigan-based Johnson Controls (JCI), is a perfect example of a company rooted in an engineering culture but recognizing the value of generative research, synthesis, and storytelling in inspiring a vision of opportunities for innovation across an entire industry. We have done several projects with JCI over the past eight years, where the design research objectives were not just to give directions to JCI designers to design a new product but also to craft scenarios of the future and develop specific frameworks that can shift automotive-industry focus from product features to experiences of the future. A more recent project with JCI involved identifying metaphors dormant in people's relationships with their vehicles and using those metaphors to inspire criteria for creating new experiences in the design of vehicle interiors. JCI has been sharing the findings of this study with its several customers in the automotive industry. Such a unique and inspiring storytelling process positions JCI as a visionary company rather than as a mere supplier of components. This work is a good example of co-creation, which embeds design research deeply into the design process.

Conclusion

Design research is a field that has its roots in the mid-twentieth century, but that really only picked up steam in the 1980s, making it only roughly thirty years old. However, in that time, it has gone from an interesting or even exotic curiosity to a crucial part of the design process. At least in product design, the first step used to be described as "conceptual design." Now the first step is universally identified as "research."

The field continues to grow and to innovate. It will be interesting to see what happens in the next thirty years.

Acknowledgments

The author would like to thank Lindsay A. Carrabine and Christina Stefan who created the visual content for this chapter.

References

Crabtree, A., M. Rouncefield, and P. Tolmie (2012), *Doing Design Ethnography*, London: Springer-Verlag.

Cross, N., ed. (1984), *Developments in Design Methodology*, Chichester, UK: John Wiley & Sons.

Dumas, A. and J. Redish (1999), *A Practical Guide to Usability Testing, Revised Edition*, Chicago: University of Chicago Press.

Jones, J. and D. Thornley, eds. (1963), *Conference on Design Methods*, Oxford, UK: Pergamon Press.

Kensing, F. and J. Blomberg (1998), "Participatory Design: Issues and Concerns," *Computer Supported Cooperative Work*, 7: 167.

LeCompte, M. and J. Schensul (2010), *Designing and Conducting Ethnographic Research: An Introduction*, 2nd edn, Plymouth, UK: AltaMira Press.

NASA (1978), *Anthropometric Source Book. Volume 1: Anthropometry for Designers*, NASA Reference Publication 1024, Webb Associates (ed.), Houston, TX: National Aeronautics and Space Administration Scientific and Technical Information Office.

Nielsen, J. (1993), *Usability Engineering*, Cambridge, MA: Academic Press.

Peebles, L. and B. Norris (1998), *Adultdata: The Handbook of Adult Anthropometric Data and Strength Measurements*, London: UK Department of Trade and Industry.

Pheasant, S. and E. Haslegrave (2005), *Bodyspace: Anthropometry, Ergonomics and the Design of Work*, 3rd edn, Boca Raton, FL: CRC Press/Taylor & Francis.

Salvendy, G., ed. (2006), *Handbook of Human Factors and Ergonomics*, 3rd edn, New York: John Wiley & Sons.

Sanders, E. (2002), "From User-Centered to Participatory Design Approaches," in J. Frascara (ed.), *Design and the Social Sciences: Making Social Connections*, 1–8, Boca Raton, FL: Taylor & Francis.

Schuler, D. and A. Namioka, eds. (1998), *Participatory Design: Principles and Practices*, Hillsdale, NJ: Lawrence Erlbaum.

Squires, S. and B. Byrne, eds. (2002), *Creating Breakthrough Ideas: The Collaboration of Anthropologists and Designers in the Product Development Industry*, Westport, CT: Praeger.

Tilley, A. (2002), *The Measure of Man and Woman, Revised Edition: Human Factors in Design*, New York: John Wiley & Sons.

Tufte, E. (2001), *The Visual Display of Quantitative Information*, Cheshire, CT: Graphics Press.

Wilcox, S. (2001), "Ethnography as a Product Development Tool," *Appliance Manufacturer*, July: 58.

Wilcox, S. (2012), "Design Research Has Come a Long Way," *Innovation*, Winter: 18–19.

Woodson, W., P. Tillman, and B. Tillman (1992), *Human Factors Design Handbook*, 2nd edn, New York: McGraw-Hill.

Cindy Tripp (president, Cindy Tripp & Company, LLC) is a consultant integrating the empathy and imagination of design with the practicalities of business to deliver results. Her in-depth understanding of insights, branding, and design thinking integrates into her unique approach to innovation and strategy. Cindy is an alum of Procter & Gamble Co. and an adjunct professor at the University of Cincinnati.

Cindy Tripp

Focusing Question: What are design-thinking tools, and how might we leverage them to solve strategic design opportunities?

This chapter explores how to leverage the tools of design thinking to solve strategic design opportunities.

This chapter explores the key questions:

- How do you frame a business opportunity for innovative solutions?

- How do you build empathy so that you see new opportunities?

- How do you leverage visualization and play to bring your opportunities to life?

Tools of Strategic Design

Strategic design helps problem solvers to sustain innovation over time. Strategic design requires choice and is enabled by leveraging the tools and mind-sets of design thinking. It is not complicated, but it is challenging to do. Why? First, people don't like to choose. But in fact, to deliver strategic design, you must decide what to do and more importantly, what you will *not* do. Second, people often approach a problem too narrowly and don't see the larger system in which it lives, so that they are not appropriately addressing the real systemic opportunity. Design-thinking tools can help you avoid these pitfalls because design, at its very essence, is choice and context. That's why business is enticed by design thinking. It has broad application for business, not only in innovative products, services, and experiences but also in the very nature of strategic choice itself.

When you are thinking about strategic design, there are a couple of critical questions to answer (see Figure 5.1). First, what is the nature of the opportunity or challenge you are solving? Are you working on a problem that has been framed correctly? Half the

Strategic Design Power Questions

Here are some simple questions that can help you be open to possibilities of Strategic Design.

1. Am I working on the right opportunity?
   - How else might I consider framing this challenge?

2. Do I have sufficient empathy for key stakeholders (customer, suppliers, employees, users) in this system?
   - How might I deepen empathy?

3. Are we stuck and spinning? What else is needed to drive engagement?
   - Have we visualized it yet?
   - Do we need a play break?

Figure 5.1 Strategic design power questions
Cindy Tripp & Company, LLC.

battle of innovating or solving a problem is knowing which problem to solve. Second, it is important to ask, how does this opportunity fit in the context of the people and processes that exist today? To do this, you have to build empathy for key stakeholders and understand their larger story. Clearly framing the problem, developing an empathetic stance and story, and setting up the right team will create a meaningful difference through strategic design.

You have heard people say, "It's all in how you look at it." It's true. We all have our default way of looking at things, and yet there are many possible ways to consider them. While it may initially feel as if there

is only one way, if you can override that default tendency, you can see possibilities. Structured tools can help you navigate this challenging terrain. And the simplest one is asking yourself "how else might I consider this?" Still, this can be very difficult, even with high self-awareness of your own paradigms and defaults. A tool box can help. Here are some tools that might just jog your thought process out of its default mind mapping.

There are several tools that stem from the field of design thinking that are useful for strategic design. First, above all else, are the framing tools, which help you define the real opportunity space. If you do nothing else in strategic design, it is essential that the true question be revealed. Once this is understood, the other tools of empathy, story, visualization, patterning, and play are highly effective at advancing your team toward insightful strategic design. Let's take each one in turn.

Framing Tools

"Some people see the glass half full. Others see it half empty. I see a glass that's twice as big as it needs to be."

—George Carlin

The Situation

What problem are you trying to solve? Often, the first attempt is too simplistic and self-serving to lead to a real innovative solution. In my work with a company on female retention, executives believed their issue was that they had the wrong portfolio of flexible, part-time working options and simply wanted to "refresh" the options. Through framing the issues from many perspectives, they discovered that they had an entirely different issue, one that was growing in importance to both men and women: life integration and a risk of burnout. As a globally connected business, each role and person had unique flexibility requirements. For example, if your role requires that you be on conference calls every night with China until midnight, do you really need to have a nine-to-five in-office expectation? The solution of tying flexibility to the role's requirements and the person's goals would not have been discovered had they not first looked at the issue from multiple points of view. In this instance, they talked to men and women within the company, as well as women who had recently left the company.

Four Corners Problem Definition

In the **four corners** exercise (see Figure 5.2a), you force yourself to consider alternative perspectives from those in different positions in the ecosystem in which you are operating. First, in the center of the page, write how you would describe the challenge. Then in each corner of the page, consider another person's perspective and how he or she might articulate it. Perhaps the upper-left corner is your customer or consumer's take on the issue from his or her point of view; the upper-right is a key partner in delivering your business, such as a retailer, agent, or supplier; the lower-right is a key competitor's take on the issue; and finally, the lower-left is an external view of how to address the problem (how another industry or mentor brand would

define this challenge). The discipline to write down the challenge from these various perspectives is essential to opening up your mind to what the real issue may be. When you see these various frames, you see a wider array of possible creative solutions.

Once the four corners have reframed the questions, you can begin to imagine specific solutions for each one. Compare opportunities across these different frames. What do you see that you did not see before? Is there another solution trajectory beyond the initial one suggested by your original problem frame? The answer is typically yes.

Circle the Problem

Another way to explore the nature of the challenge to be framed and solved is to **circle the problem** (see Figure 5.2b). Simply put, our tendency is to define a problem in very concrete terms and to do so in a way that severely limits the opportunity space to be explored for solutions. You can again push outside this default by taking a tangible step to circle the problem. In this tool, you are not switching points of view of different stakeholders as much as you are changing your vantage point on the challenge, taking various perspectives, for example, up close, at a distance, or from 10,000 feet. Each of these offers another view of the problem and offers new solution spaces.

First, write the problem statement in the center of the page. Circle it. Now consider a broader, more contextual definition of it and write it around the first definition and circle it. Do this one to two more times, each time getting more contextual and abstract as it relates to the original problem definition.

Figure 5.2a Four corners problem definition
Cindy Tripp & Company; graphics: Troy Woolery

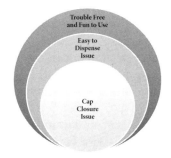

Figure 5.2b Circle the problem definition
Cindy Tripp & Company; graphics: Troy Woolery.

For example, perhaps your team is working on a liquid detergent bottle with a faulty cap issue, where liquid is escaping and creating a mess. You might define the problem as a "cap closure issue." Write that in the center and circle it. That is a highly concrete problem definition, and one that is easily solved, but the solution set to this problem is probably very evolutionary and boring. Now write a more contextual problem definition, perhaps it is an "easy to dispense issue." Circle it and offer a third level of abstraction: the challenge is "trouble free and fun to use." Again each of these definitions gets you a different solution set, with the last one perhaps being the open space that yields an innovation such as Pods for dispensing.

Ambitions and Ambiguity

Part of strategic design is being candid with yourself and others about what you are really seeking out of an innovation effort. Too often teams are sent off to reinvent or reimagine without clarity on what is truly the real purpose and need. Teams

return from this exciting quest with breakthrough ideas that require investment and have a risk profile that is higher than the requesting leader intended. What a waste for everyone. A thirty-minute conversation could have saved time and money, and yet we forget to have this conversation upfront as part of our problem framing. The questions to explore might include:

- What is the nature of the solution we want? Disruptive or sustaining? Do I need a sure thing?
- Do we need it yesterday or tomorrow?
- Have I committed to the commensurate resources for the challenge I am commissioning?

Slow down and have this discussion. I have found Clayton Christensen's (1997) concept of disruptive versus sustaining innovation helpful here. **Disruptive innovation** is something new and previously not experienced, whereas **sustaining innovation** is newly improved innovation in an existing category of benefits (see Figure 5.3). And, of course, there are efforts every day to continuously improve what we deliver. Each of these changes could be desired on a variety of time horizons. The type of change you desire, and the timing you seek, affect how you approach it.

For instance, if a leader does want disruptive innovation on "as soon as possible" timing, then it is critical to have the conversation on resources, people, and money required to identify it and to nurture it to market. This simple conversation is important for establishing the boundaries of your strategy. Without it, you can expend hours of effort unnecessarily. While it may not be a conversation that people are asking for upfront, ultimately, it is most important and highly appreciated by leadership and the people tasked with the challenge.

Alien Eyes

Edie Weiner coined the term "alien eyes" in her book *FutureThink: How to Think Clearly in a Time of Change* (2005) to represent the approach of trying to consider a situation through the eyes of an alien, so you see potential other realities. Similar to this, I think it helps to have someone outside the system, who is alien to the challenge at hand, to provide how he or she might see it. Going to someone not vested in the outcome or familiar with the business can be so enlightening. This person has fresh, naive eyes and will see things differently from you and ask good questions. A coffee or conversation with someone outside the system is powerful for opening up your mind to where the opportunity is. Sometimes, it is even helpful to seek out people with whom

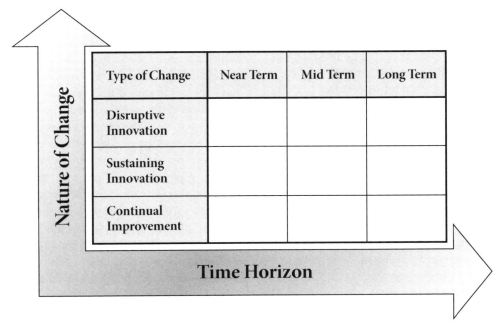

Figure 5.3 Ambitions and ambiguity matrix
Derived from Clayton Christensen's work of disruptive versus sustaining innovation; Cindy Tripp & Company; graphics: Troy Woolery.

you usually don't see eye to eye. Hear how they assess the situation. Yes, you have something valuable to offer, but it is also important to realize you might have something valuable to learn. Being open to hearing from those with a different perspective from you can help you get to the heart of the matter.

GO DEEPER

Read the following:

- *The Innovator's Dilemma: When New Technologies Cause Great Firms to Fail* by C. M. Christensen.
- *The Design of Business* by R. Martin.
- *FutureThink: How to Think Clearly in a Time of Change* by E. Weiner.

REFLECTIONS

- Next time you approach a challenge, stop and reflect on your framing of the challenge. What assumptions are you making? Name them and make it explicit.
- Now, try on another framing of the problem. What opportunities reveal themselves when you look at the problem from another frame?

Empathy

Having empathy for someone is part of the capacity of being human. Yet, it can be incapacitated by power dynamics. If a person has or perceives he or she have power, that person can be less empathetic. In several recent studies exploring empathy, it is clear we are wired to empathize but conditions, such as relative power, can hinder that natural response (Hogeveen et al. 2013). Even

our daily routine can hinder our ability to see and feel how another person experiences something. There are tools and techniques that can help us build back our capacity to empathize. And, of course, the simplest of actions, such as listening, eye contact, focus, and attention, can help you build empathy.

"When people talk, listen completely. Most people never listen."

—Ernest Hemmingway

The Situation

"We have tried everything. The data says we should be winning. We have a better product and better distribution and yet, we are losing share year after year. What is going on?" When all the facts don't add up, perhaps there are data you are ignoring.

In this case, there was a missing link, the human data. Yes, the business had analyzed all the facts gathered and research conducted, but it failed to listen to its stakeholders to see how they were viewing the situation. So, we did some empathy work, spending time with category buyers on their terms to learn about their lives. Getting shoulder to shoulder with our buyers made it happen: that aha moment when the picture came into view for the business. Through ethnography, we saw the product was being used by the consumer in a way that inhibited its benefit and the brand's message was not resonating either.

The leaders stopped looking at the data through their own lens and tried on the eyes of their stakeholder to realize that it all made sense. By trying on an empathetic stance, they now had a plan of action to reverse the business trends (see Figure 5.4).

Path to Empathy

Pathway	Your Stance
Reframe your view from research mode (target) to human mode (person)	Watch your language. If you focus on targets you will spend energy aiming arrows at them
Focus on a few people and really get to know them, be open to listening to "extremes" of your potential user base	Enter into her life versus expecting her to enter your world
Understand her hopes and dreams in the broader context of her life	Be curious, without judging
Imagine her story and what looks like help to her	For now, don't consider feasibility issues

Figure 5.4 Path to empathy
Cindy Tripp & Company, LLC.

Empathy enables strategic design by helping you see the larger system in which an opportunity is living. Empathy tools, in many ways, are additional methods of framing, as they get you out of your worldview and into another's. The number of tools to help you get to empathy are numerous and they are evolving every day as necessity breeds invention in this space. The key is that the tool help you let go of your worldview and see another's.

Side-By-Side/Participant Observation

The greatest way to empathize is to "walk a mile" in someone else's shoes. This is the underlying thought in the side-by-side approach (see Figure 5.5). The essence here is to shadow someone in his or her day-to-day activities that include an area of interest to you. For instance, helping in the home on laundry day or working alongside a key supplier for a day are examples where one is working side by side. You don't replace users or simply observe them; you join them.

The side-by-side approach is participatory and is one approach of ethnography, which is the study of complex human systems and cultures by detailed observation in the subject's natural environment. By getting involved in helping with the laundry, perhaps under the instruction of the homemaker, you do real work in partnership with your stakeholders and have the casual, natural conversation that occurs by doing so. You see their system from their perspective. The idea is to blend in so this is not a time for direct questions, but rather using wide eyes and ears to observe and listen. Of course, as part of the follow-up conversation you ask clarifying questions. This can be challenging: You need to keep your participation contextually relevant and engage on a topic much broader than perhaps your specific

Figure 5.5 Inspirational design target (IDT) empathy map
Graphics: Troy Woolery; Cindy Tripp & Company.

business interest. How do you let go of egocentric needs to see the world through her or his eyes and to learn how you might fit in? If you can release your project deadlines and deliverables for a day or two it can be an inspiring exercise.

Typically, you will need the assistance of a research firm, such as a market research firm or a design research firm, which employs professionally trained anthropologists to recruit the people you will shadow. While there are a number of ways you might recruit, it is advisable to recruit for articulate respondents to enable connection and communication; also try not to default to a representative audience but rather recruit people who are inspiring and out of the norm.

Extremities: An Inspirational Design Target

You might think that the safe way to build empathy is to pick people to explore who are in the norm, or **representative consumers** (see Figure 5.6). This is troublesome in getting to strategic design, as representative consumers rarely teach us anything we don't already know. It is the outliers, the extreme users or nonusers, who are inspiring. I like to think of extreme users as our *inspirational design target* (IDT). Developing empathy for them is much more productive for innovation work than a more comfortable representative user. Go outside your comfort zone when you do empathy work, and you will learn much more.

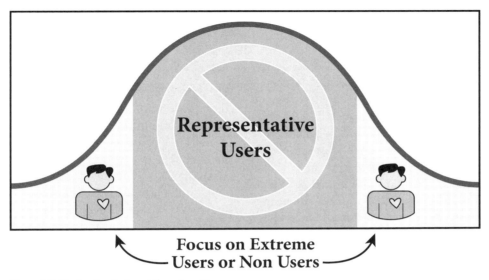

Figure 5.6 Finding inspiration at the extremities
Cindy Tripp & Company; graphics: Troy Woolery.

Once you are engaging with IDTs and considering the world from their perspective, it is important to go deeper than just what is on the surface of what they say and do. Assess their body language and emotions in order to consider what they are thinking and feeling. Full engagement and tuning into their subtle signals will provide this pathway. We are wired to be able to do this, as neuro-research has revealed that we have "mirror neurons" in our brains, which give us our capacity to empathize (Marsh 2012). When we are focused on someone else, we can literally feel what they are feeling in our own brain. By paying attention, we can know what they are doing and how they are feeling. Now, we can begin to articulate this in a description that goes well beyond facts and figures. It is helpful to visualize this in a sketch picture of this IDT.

It is important that at the early phase of discovery you work in the context of clearly defined individual IDTs rather than a summation persona. You want their uniqueness and quirkiness to stand out and to help you see opportunities. They should not be representative but rather inspirational.

Picture Swap

"Take a picture of the experience." These words can mean very different things to people depending on their perspective. For a business leader, taking pictures of an experience that includes his product can result in photo after photo of product shots. However, for a potential customer, it might be just the opposite. It might be of her kids helping with laundry or of her hairdresser and the salon environment. A powerful tool is to make these different perspectives real for a team about to embark on strategic design by capturing them in a picture.

The key to this method is to not overtly direct the photography subject. Provide a broad scope that is inclusive of the topic you wish to study and ask the stakeholder to photograph that experience (twenty-five to forty pictures), as it relates to his or her life. In today's world of smartphones, this approach is usually readily available for your IDT. If not, you can provide a phone for his or her use during the research. If you are working in the beauty category, it might be "photograph getting ready for a date." For a household cleaning product, it might be "photograph what it means to care for your home." For a reorganization project, it might be "photograph times where you feel like you are doing meaningful work vs. times when you are not." Then have the stakeholders bring in their photos and share their stories. For fun, you might have the business team do the same exercise on themselves or even side by side with a stakeholder, such as a coworker or consumer. How do the pictures compare between the team members' and the other stakeholders' perspective? The photographs can be dramatically different, and this difference can be insightful and inspiring for strategic design innovation.

Letters

Writing letters may be old-fashioned and falling out of social favor, but letter writing can help a team understand a person much more clearly. It is simple really: Have stakeholders put their thoughts into a letter and then later read it to you and explain what they were thinking. There are several ways

you might leverage letter writing, and you can craft the right approach for your challenge; however, here are a few examples you can ask your IDTs to complete:

- Have the IDTs write love letters to their favorite companies explaining why they love them. This will help you understand what matters to your IDTs in a brand.
- Have the IDTs write a letter about a daily routine (perhaps getting ready for work). Ask the IDTs to have a close friend or family member (partner, spouse, etc.) write a letter about this same routine. Ask the IDTs not to read the letters before the next meeting. Then, have each IDT read both letters and comment on them to help expose some of the invisible, automatic things done. This can be a great way to glean insights during a time of day or context when it is tough to observe, such as a morning ritual of getting ready for work.
- Ask the IDTs to write a "Dear John" letter firing a brand, product, service, or boss that has let them down. This will help you understand the emotion of the failure and the opportunities for turnaround.

This exercise helps increase your capacity to empathize with a person's life and to understand what he or she values. The key to these letter writing exercises is that the topic not be too narrow or prescribed in order to build full empathy. The letters need to be contextually relevant for the area being explored but not so specific as to force an unnatural articulation of how a product, brand, service, or person might fit.

Story: A Hero's Journey

Story can be applied in a number of ways in a design process, and one great use is to incorporate it as part of the empathy suite of tools discussed thus far in this chapter. With story, you are looking through your IDTs' lenses and considering their life stories, where they are the hero.

This is an application that builds upon the understanding of human myth and story as explored by Joseph Campbell, who recognized a recurring pattern in history, literature, and storytelling: the hero's journey. The ***hero's journey*** (see Figure 5.7) is when an ordinary person is called forward to an adventure that is bigger than just himself. He must cross a threshold of tests and challenges. He perseveres and returns back to his ordinary world transformed with an elixir (Campbell 2008). It can be quite useful to apply this model to our stakeholders. What if the people we want as customers are on their own hero's journey? What is it that they seek that is bigger than themselves? What do they need that we might be able to help with? It can be challenging for results-oriented and time-crunched business people to want to do this work, as it feels irrelevant and not action oriented. It is definitely uncomfortable as you must delay the gratification of moving straight to solutions that benefit your business. It can also be quite a reframe for those businesses

Figure 5.7 The hero's journey as inspiration
Derived from work by Joseph Campbell; graphics: Troy Woolery.

where typically the consumer is never thought of as the hero, the product is. Considering your IDTs as the hero in the quests of their own lives can be quite inspiring to seeing with new eyes the opportunities obscured previously. Avoid focusing on your product or service category, or even your objectives for a while, and simply seek to see a life in context.

Once you have that picture, now you can consider your interests. How does your product or service fit? What could you do to help him on his journey, even in some small way? Perhaps a new product or service that would enable a larger systemic change? For example, understanding the larger dream of mothers wanting their kids to have a brighter future can help you see many avenues for growth, beyond even product performance. Ideas typically start flowing at this point about things you never considered before. You can have a higher purpose in the stakeholder's world. Pampers cares for baby development, not just in the dryness and fit of the diaper, but also through a good night's sleep, the parenting support online, the immunization program for developing countries, even in creating employment opportunities in villages for families. Executives who have experienced story in this context are always thrilled afterward because they see new avenues of growth, or strategic spaces they need to cultivate. These spaces have a natural connection baked in with their stakeholders; they are more meaningful to their future customer. An empathic story can unlock a higher brand purpose that connects with people and fosters great business results (Stengel 2011).

GO DEEPER
Read the following:
- *Mirroring People: The Science of Empathy and How We Connect to Others* by M. Icoboni.
- *The Empathic Brain* by C. Keysers.
- *Wired to Care* by D. Patnaik.
- *How to Be an Explorer of the World* by K. Smith.

IDEO on human-centered design principles. Available online: http://www.designkit.org/

REFLECTIONS
- Pay attention differently for one morning or afternoon. To help you break your normal routine, get a copy of *How to Be an Explorer of the World* by Keri Smith and try a few of the observational exercises.
- Reflect on your industry. List all the automatic assumptions that you make in a given week. Imagine how another person might interpret these? What would he or she notice about your business?

Visualization

If a picture is worth a 1,000 words, a prototype is worth a 1,000 pictures.

The Situation

Words can be deceiving and can obscure opportunities, leaving participants discouraged in the strategic design process. One department going through a redesign was convinced there was not any opportunity to increase productivity. Regulations had grown over the years and compliance activity was increasing workloads. Yet, employees were being asked to do more with less. The team members tried visualizing their point, creating a mobile of all the work they had to do, color-coded by work type. The mobile became several mobiles, one for global, one for regional, and another for corporate. That's when they saw it—the amount of duplicating work happening on each mobile. This visual unlocked where the productivity could be found. Work was happening multiple places, and it was also causing many time-consuming debates on whose work was the right approach to follow, which was a major frustration to the team. It also caused people to feel as if their work was not as meaningful, since so many people were duplicating efforts. With this insight, the team was able to reassess where the work should be done in order for it to provide the best guidance. The result was a streamlined, redesigned organization with meaningful work.

Often the space of strategy is one filled with bullet-point lists and debate. Still, teams often resist visualizing because working in the tangible land of prototypes and visualizations feels tactical not strategic. It is a false objection. Imagining things tangibly can help inform strategy. By looking at the patterns, one can see themes that cross the tangible expressions. These themes are the reinforcing rods, which can be harnessed strategically by a business. Here are some ways to overcome this debate and use visualization to inform strategic choice.

Visualize Your Strategy

This is a powerful technique that is not as easy as it sounds. Most organizations have a written strategy and assume that people understand it. However, ask people to visualize their strategy, and you will see how clear and purposeful the strategy is or is not. Try these steps on a clear wall space:

1. Using large paper plates or large sticky notes, post up the major strategic choices made.
2. Using smaller sticky notes, post up the supporting choices made.
3. Congregate and connect the smaller sticky notes to the larger choices to which they closely relate via arrows, tape, or string.

Step back and consider the picture that has emerged on your wall. What do you notice about the picture? Is it cluttered? Are things well connected? Is there something not well integrated into the overall picture? What does the picture tell you about this strategy?

As simple as this exercise appears, consultants have seen teams disintegrate with this work.

In Figure 5.8, strategic choices 1, 3, and 4 are well integrated and connected, but strategic choice 2 is not. Given a picture like this, you can consider important strategic implications. In addition, it is important to consider any new data that is relevant; perhaps trends, market shifts or reframes, or consumer insight that might suggest the strategy is incomplete or needs to be evolved. Visualize these trends and implications through prototypes that show possible adjustments to the current visualized strategy or by creation of a new prototyped strategy, which can be compared to the current picture. What must be stopped, started, or continued to create a relevant

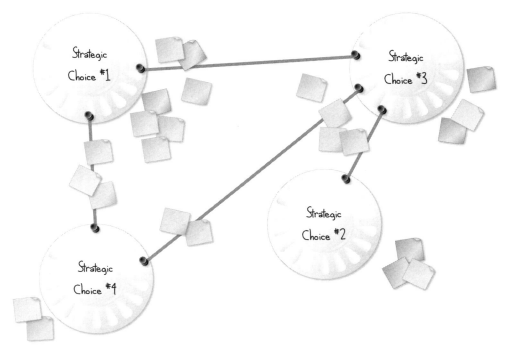

Figure 5.8 Visualizing strategic choice
Cindy Tripp & Company; graphics: Troy Woolery.

strategy in this new scenario? Pictures help point out what is often overlooked in words alone. They require time to create, but visual imagery can be accelerators to understanding and progress.

Storyboarding & Skits
Sometimes it is difficult to develop a physical prototype of what you are exploring. Perhaps it is an experience redesign that lends itself to another type of tangible, visual exploration. In these situations, visualizing the experience or story in the old versus new world can be helpful. To use the storyboarding approach, we return to our story model of hero, goal, and obstacle

to overcome. To storyboard you first set the context and introduce the hero and his goal in one or two simple visual sketches. Then you visualize how he was able to overcome that challenge (the resolution) and the resulting benefit. In three to six frames you can give the essence of the challenge to which someone can react (see Figure 5.9).

In the example provided by Intuit, this was a quick sketch done by Joseph O'Sullivan at Intuit, pre-Uber, to explore a similar idea and to demonstrate how a very low resolution storyboard can evoke great learning on a new idea.

You can take this to the next level by turning the storyboard into a skit that you

Figure 5.9 Storyboard courtesy of Joseph O'Sullivan, Intuit

act out live for others. Physically bringing the storyboard to life is powerful because people acting it out bring emotion and subtle cues to it that paper alone does not. Also, skits develop team building because skits require shared risk in order to demonstrate ideas.

Prototype & Generalize

Another way to start this work is to begin with new understanding, such as empathy (previously discussed) or emerging market trends. Ideally, you will have multiple iterations of prototypes exploring product ideas, strategies, services, or organizational designs. A variety of prototypes helps you to identify common themes. You can then ask, "Does this prototype fit a strategic choice?"; "If this were a strategic choice, how would it map to the current strategy? Or does it represent an entirely new area to explore?"

Patterning: Visualizing the Data

Throughout any design process, there is much data generated in the form of observations, insights, prototypes, and so on. It is important to keep this data in a visually flexible format. Using sticky notes to capture data and being disciplined to put one idea per sticky note is important to enable this critical step of strategic design, patterning in new ways. The reality is that as data is created, we are naturally patterning it by current, default frame of reference, and the insights that emerge are typically as expected. By writing a single idea per Post-it, a team is equipped to try re-patterning the data from a variety of perspectives, to try on different views and to see where it might lead them. There are several ways to approach patterning, such as the ones that follow: a day in the life, four corners framing pattern, opposites, and concept mapping.

A Day in the Life/Flow

In the **day in the life** approach, you reconfigure the data you have about your stakeholder to the flow of a typical day. (Note: this can also be done by mapping to a process or procedure.) This is similar to a customer journey map, which typically just looks at the customer's decision journey relative to a product choice. In the day in the life tool, however, you think much more expansively about the stakeholders. You look at their entire life cycle, mapping a typical day. Then you pattern the insights and needs of your stakeholder, or any product insights, to that flow. Which moments are the most populated and which are least? What does this tell you about the opportunity space?

Four Corners Framing Pattern

In this approach, you build upon your four corners framing exercise earlier in this chapter, where you considered your challenge from four other possible vantage points. First, you return to these reframed challenges and brainstorm ideas for each frame individually. Second, step back and look at all the ideas generated across the four reframes, and pattern all the brainstormed data generated across all frames by grouping ideas together that seem to be related. Third, create a headline sticky note that captures the essence of what grouped ideas have in common. What do you see? What emerges that is new? Are there new headlines emerging? Are there key themes emerging across the patterns created? What else is sparked by this view of the data (you might brainstorm a bit more based upon what you are seeing)?

Opposites Patterning

In this approach, you pattern the data across opposites. Here are some to try:

- tangible/intangible
- wild/safe
- emotional/rational
- today/tomorrow
- champagne/beer
- wildcard (feel free to make up your own)

Essentially you create a continuum with your opposites creating the polar extremes. You then sort your sticky notes along that continuum, perhaps with ideas that are tangible on one side and intangible on another and perhaps a few fall in between the poles (see Figure 5.10). After each patterning pair, what do you see and learn? What are the implications for your business? Where are the ideas naturally congregating? Try two or three rounds of opposite patterning to learn about what

Figure 5.10 Patterning ideas via four corners framing
Cindy Tripp & Company; graphics: Troy Woolery.

you are creating. Consider exploring more ideas for the less populated spaces in your patterns by doing an impromptu brainstorming to create additional ideas.

In one case, a team patterned the data along a continuum of ketchup versus mayonnaise. The team initially protested because they wanted to overthink the labels on a continuum. I encouraged them to just try it and see if anything emerged. Turns out, once sorted, they saw some interesting patterns about how the data was grouped that had not appeared in the more rational groupings. It sparked a new insight that led to a new solution set.

Concept Mapping

In the **concept mapping** approach, you pattern the data you have generated in your brainstorming in its relationship to one another using sticky notes. A great place to start is to first map how the data relates in the current state. What do you notice about the data profile? Now prototype an alternative picture. How does the data map compare? What pattern emerges?

You can use this process to map from a variety of perspectives. For instance, you can map the essence of a concept, idea, or body of knowledge by breaking it down into its parts and putting each sticky note in its relative position and hierarchy within the knowledge set. Essentially, this is a mind map of how you see an area. You can also do mind maps for how others see a topic, perhaps mapping the mind of a stakeholder who has been interviewed to understand the interconnections within his system.

Design Audit: What are the Invisible Patterns?

In this approach, you are using data from what you publish and make public, looking for clues of what you are actually communicating in aggregate to stakeholders. A simple way to do this is to commandeer a conference room so that you can post all your materials on the walls (advertising, promotions, packages, PR efforts, web pages, customer marketing collaborations, etc.) and step back. Peruse the wall of artifacts with open eyes. What do you see? Does the picture make coherent sense? Where are the outliers that disconnect from the overall picture?

Once the work is up and people have taken it all in individually, it is important to have a conversation considering what you see. Are you communicating what you thought you were? What are the key patterns emerging? How does this public pattern connect with the data patterns we see emerging in our other insight work, if applicable? Are they complementary or not? What do we need to do to align today and tomorrow?

This is a crucial conversation to have and to have it in the context of all the artifacts surrounding you. It can lead to new awareness that can unlock solutions previously missed. It is an incredible torture test of how well your strategy is being executed and how clear the choices are within the strategy. Sometimes, you need to see your strategy in action to know where it is failing and to realize its full impact.

GO DEEPER

Read the following:
- *Exposing the Magic of Design* by J. Kolko.
- *Design Thinking for Strategic Innovation* by I. Mootee.
- *Visual Meetings* by D. Sibbet.
- *Disrupt Together: How Teams Consistently Innovate* by S. Spinelli and H. McGowan.

REFLECTIONS

- Next time you are stuck on an issue at work, try visualizing the problem, using simple sketches, or create Post-its of dimensions of the challenge and pattern them.
- Reflect on how your organization communicates. Is its default mode visual or verbal? What are the implications of that preference?

Play

"The creation of something new is not accomplished by the intellect but by the play instinct."

—Carl Jung

The Situation

The team's energy was dropping fast, and the creative ideas were nowhere to be found. The team was hitting the wall and it had yet to discover something that would deliver the breakthrough it needed. It is at this moment one has to resist the effort to "try harder" and disengage from the task to try a little play, which is what was done. The team members took a break, played an energizing clapping game, began to laugh, and their muscles loosened. When they returned to their task, the energy returned and ideas began to flow again. Suddenly, like magic, they were onto something.

Playfulness is a helpful energizer in the strategic design process. It can be used to motivate a group, stimulate creative juices, or build a sense of camaraderie. Play, alone, is not that productive a concept in strategic design, unless it's woven into the fabric of the other tools, where it can be powerful. Playful games should be used with intention, rather than randomly. To set up a brainstorming and creative exercise, play accept-and-add games. To get people back together and present, there are point-of-focus games. And, there are games to drive a sense of team or to help drive integration of learning. All of them raise energy because they cause us to goof up and laugh at ourselves with others. Playful activities must be good-natured, allow the participants to opt in by free choice, and represent a reasonable risk.

Play is a form of teaming activity and helps by getting the group to become united in effort, while still maintaining people's uniqueness. The goal is to bring people together so they can collaborate more effectively.

For teams just starting on their journey, the games and activities should incorporate less risk. The more advanced the team, the more risk that can be introduced into the game. The point is to open people up and not to close them down. Meet them where they are and move them forward. Forcing doesn't work and can backfire. Play is an ingredient, not the main point of a strategic design effort.

Accept-and-Add Games

There are a host of games built on the concepts of improvisational theater. Concepts such as "accept what you are given and build on it" or "never make your partner look bad" are powerful approaches that help us to override our judging function and "go with it." And, in a brainstorming, you need to be able to join the flow and move with it.

The simplest approach to achieving this flow is to warm it up with a "Yes! And …" exercise. With a team in a circle, one person steps into the circle and offers a wild idea; another joins in the circle and offers to build upon the wild idea with a "Yes! And …" idea. Then the original person steps out and another steps in to offer another "Yes! And …" idea. This continues for several rounds and a few laughs. At the end, it can be interesting to have the originator step back in and remind people of how far the wild idea took the team.

Another approach to the same goal, but perhaps a bit riskier, is to do this in the context of building a picture, or a "human living sculpture." With the team in a circle, someone steps into the circle and strikes a pose, naming what she is (e.g., "I'm a tree."). Another joins her and adds to the picture, striking his pose, "I'm a bird in the tree." A third person joins and adds more, "I'm the nest for the bird," striking her pose. Laughter usually erupts. After three or four people create a picture, they return to the circle and another one is begun. Again, people must work with what they are given and build upon it in a good-natured way.

Another great exercise is the storytelling circle. People stand in a circle and have to create a story as a collective group, one word (or sometime three words) at a time. The rules are simple but difficult. You must work together to build a coherent story (hero overcomes obstacles to achieve a goal), and you must build upon the word or words you just received from your neighbor. Someone starts with a word like "Once" or "There." The person to the first person's right must add the next word (e.g., "upon," "is," etc.). You must accept that you wanted to take the story one direction, but if the word your neighbor provided takes you in a new direction, you must build upon his or her direction. Build upon what you are given, not what you want. This is much harder than it sounds. To do this well, you have to stay present, focused, and flexible. It usually takes a couple of times around the circle before the story comes to a logical conclusion. At that point the facilitator can bring it to a close.

Placement of this storytelling activity can heighten its usefulness. It can be just a game to drive accept-and-add behavior, or it can also be used to drive integration of learning. Using the storytelling circle after empathy work can help a team integrate its insights into a story of the stakeholder. As members work together around the circle to tell the story of the stakeholder they are studying, they deepen their understanding. This type of storytelling is more

difficult to do because in addition to staying present, you also need to share the story of a specific stakeholder in a way that is true to what you have learned. It's not just storytelling for fun; it is storytelling with purpose.

Point-of-Focus Games

There are times when the process becomes scattered in a team. Perhaps everyone in the room is not mentally focused or engaged. **Point-of-focus** games are simple exercises to make everyone present. Two examples are the Clap Game and the Blind Counting Game.

Clap Game

Everyone forms a circle with hands free and ready to clap. One person starts the game by making eye contact with someone in the circle and then clapping in his or her direction. The person receiving the clap then makes eye contact with someone else and claps to that person. The key is eye contact first so the person you are sending the clap to knows it is coming to her. In the beginning, things are awkward and slow, but then things pick up speed and you hear "clap, clap, clap, clap" with no hesitation. The advanced version of this game is to make eye contact and then clap simultaneously with the person receiving. Then he makes eye contact and claps simultaneously with his partner. Typically, there is good-natured failing with this game as well. But again, with a little time, people pick up speed and get in sync. It is always interesting to play this game early in a team's collaborative work together and then again later, as you typically see how far the team members have come through their ability to do this task.

Blind Counting Game

Everyone circles up tightly, with heads down and eyes closed. The goal is to count to twenty as a team, without looking at one another or speaking at the same time and without going in a circle or pre-established pattern. In the beginning, it is difficult to even count to five without two or more people saying "five" at the same time. If that happens, you start over at "one." The team has to use sensing skills to pay attention to when there is space to add a number. Teams struggle, but they can do it, and once completed they are present for the next conversation.

The point of these games is that by doing an activity that requires focus, team members warm up for conversation. It is amazing to see how something so simple can make such an impact. If a team is distracted, try one of these exercises and then reengage in the conversation.

Charades and the Power of Pantomiming

Charades is another approach that requires focus and helps a group get warmed up for creative work. For a quick primer for any creative work you have, again you circle up as a team. Someone introduces the imaginary ball of clay that can be formed into anything. Silently he or she forms the clay into something and starts pantomiming its use while the rest of the team guesses. The one who correctly guesses receives the imaginary ball of clay and begins to form another imaginary object and to act it out in his or her charade. A twist on this, done in silence, is that only the person next to you can guess the object. This is a more difficult version, requiring keen focus of the receiving individual. She demonstrates she knows what you have when she starts shadowing your pantomime. Once you are sure she has it, you stop and she reforms the clay into the ball and then into her object and the person to her right shadows her pantomime, and so on, until the circle is complete.

The Impossible Knot Game (Works Best for Teams of Five to Eight)

Circle up. Each person reaches into the circle and grabs the hands of two separate work colleagues randomly, creating a big human knot. Silently, the team must untangle the knot and form a single circle without breaking hands. It might take a few tries and teams who struggle with it often believe it is not possible. It works, and it's always amazing to them that they were able to do something together that looked impossible. A couple of tips: Sometimes groups of eight or more actually form two concentric circles, and everyone may or may not face the same direction of the circle when it is all untangled.

GO DEEPER

Read the following:

- *Thinkertoys: A Handbook of Creative Thinking Techniques* by M. Michalko.
- *The Big Book of Team-Motivating Games* by M. Scannell and E. Scannell.

REFLECTIONS

- When is the last time you and your team had fun together at work? How did that impact the team's productivity?
- Consider trying a game from *The Big Book of Team-Motivating Games* by Mary Scannell and Edward Scannell at an upcoming team meeting.

Conclusion

Strategic design is about systemic solutions. It is enabled by design-thinking methods, which, at times, operate in a very local way. Yet, the tools can unlock seeing the broader system with new eyes. The keys to this understanding are being able to frame the challenge from many perspectives, building empathy for stakeholders, withholding judgment, and leveraging visualization techniques to see the patterns emerge. These tools are further enhanced by managing team energy and connectedness by tapping into good-natured play. Simple tools like these lead to profound insights and ideas. Once your eyes are able to see the system from a variety of perspectives, you see new paths to how you can design your strategy.

While these tools are complementary and ideally leveraged together, you can choose to use only one or two as part of your strategic design process. The key is to start leveraging them even before you are completely comfortable with them. In design thinking, it is critical to "do to learn." The tools of design thinking are powerful, simple stimuli and teach us that the key to great strategic design is being open to learning and paying attention. With that as your guide, you are on your way.

Acknowledgments

Thanks to my business partners over the years who helped me gain wisdom on how imagination and discipline work together to make great things happen, especially Claudia Kotchka, Phil Duncan, Roger Martin, my friends at Stanford dSchool and the Clay Street Project. And, thanks to my family and friends who encourage my dream to make a positive difference in the world.

References

Campbell, J. (2008), *The Hero with a Thousand Faces*, Novato, CA: New World Library.

Christensen, C. (1997), *The Innovator's Dilemma: When New Technologies Cause Great Firms to Fail*, Cambridge, MA: Harvard Press.

Hogeveen, J., Inzlicht, M., & Obhi, S. S. (2014), *Power Changes How the Brain Responds to Others*. Journal of Experimental Psychology: General, 143(2): 755–762.

Icoboni, M. (2009), *Mirroring People: The Science of Empathy and How We Connect to Others*, New York: Picador.

Keysers, C. (2011), *The Empathic Brain*, Netherlands: Social Brain Press.

Kolko, J. (2011), *Exposing the Magic of Design: A Practitioner's Guide to the Methods and Theory of Synthesis (Human Technology Interaction Series)*, Oxford: Oxford University Press.

Marsh, J. (2012), "Do Mirror Neurons Give Us Empathy?", Greater Good—The Science of A Meaningful Life. Available online: http://greatergood.berkeley.edu/article/item/do_mirror_neurons_give_empathy

Martin, R. (2009), *The Design of Business: Why Design Thinking Is the Next Competitive Advantage,* 3rd edn, Cambridge, MA: Harvard Business Review Press.

Michalko, M. (2006), *Thinkertoys: A Handbook of Creative Thinking Techniques*, Berkeley, CA: Ten Speed Press.

Mootee, I. (2013), *Design Thinking for Strategic Innovation: What They Can't Teach You at Business or Design School*, Hoboken, NJ: Wiley Publishers.

Patnaik, D. (2009), *Wired to Care: How Companies Prosper When They Create Widespread Empathy*, Upper Saddle River, NJ: FT Press.

Scannell. M. and E. Scannell (2009), *The Big Book of Team-Motivating Games: Spirit-Building, Problem-Solving and Communication Games for Every Group*, New York: McGraw Hill.

Sibbet, D. (2010), *Visual Meetings: How Graphics, Sticky Notes and Idea Mapping Can Transform Group Productivity*, Hoboken, NJ: Wiley Publishers.

Smith, K. (2008), *How to Be an Explorer of the World*, New York: Perigee Books.

Spinelli, S. and H. McGowan (2013), *Disrupt Together: How Teams Consistently Innovate*, Upper Saddle River, NJ: Pearson FT Press.

Stengel, J. (2011), *Grow: How Ideals Power Growth and Profit at the World's Greatest Companies*, New York: Crown Business.

Weiner, E. (2005), *FutureThink: How to Think Clearly in a Time of Change*, Upper Saddle River, NJ: FT Press.

6 Models & Frameworks: The Impact of Strategic Design on How Organizations Innovate
Michelle Miller

Michelle Miller (of 2nd Road) works at the frontier of strategic design in business. Across diverse industries like telecommunications, media, insurance, and consumer products, she helps teams design the future—from strategy to value propositions and innovation engines.

Michelle Miller

Focusing Question: How might we understand innovation in organizations by exploring strategic design methods?

This chapter explores the key questions:

· What frameworks and processes might we use?

· How do you tap into the power of networks?

· What individual capabilities are required?

How Strategic Design Impacts Organizations

This chapter focuses on the effects that strategic design has on organizational innovation. In discussing innovation, we are talking less about inventions (the ideas) and more about the process of developing ideas into outcomes. This chapter will detail some of the most significant impacts that strategic design can have on organizational innovation, including:

· creating a whole new business model
· giving diverse individuals a shared process for working together

· changing who is involved and how they contribute to innovation
· building strategic, creative, and intuitive skills

To explain these impacts, this chapter will look at organizations in terms of three forms of assets: organizational, social, and human.

Definitions

By changing our methods, we can change entire organizations. For this reason, when we implement strategic design, we need to address each of these three assets— organizational, human, and social (see

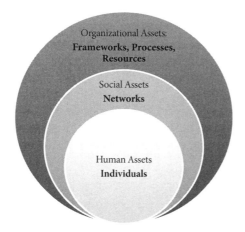

Figure 6.1 Assets impacted by strategic design
Michelle Miller

Figure 6.1)—so that we can make innovation a reality as well as get change to "stick."

Section 1: The Impact on Organizational Assets— Frameworks, Processes, and Resources

The first way we will look at the impact of strategic design on organizational innovation is in terms of **organizational assets:** the collective frameworks, systems, processes, and resources that structure the way we perform our work to produce value. This includes the strategy, identity, and value proposition of an organization. It also refers to the collective property of an organization, including intellectual property, patents, legal and financial assets, real estate, and so on.

A strategic design process should help a business to ask fundamental questions, including:

> Does our business model serve our markets and our customers optimally?

Could we offer a different mix of services and products?

Could we be serving other markets and customers?

Do our processes produce the greatest value possible?

This is part of the practical usefulness of strategic design. In this chapter, we will look at three powerful organizational asset tools:

1. Design process
2. Business Model Canvas
3. AcdB™ strategic conversation

Design Process

The central element of strategic design is the **design process** itself, also referred to as design thinking. In strategic design, the medium is people—their ideas, personalities, and capabilities, as opposed to raw materials, manufacturing processes, colors, and finishes. We define design thinking as the combination of "empathy for the context of a problem, creativity in the generation of insights and solutions, and rationality in analyzing and fitting various solutions to the problem context" (Wikipedia, "Design Thinking").

At its heart, the design process is a learning process. In order to create something new, to innovate, we must see differently, think differently, and interpret differently so that we gain the fresh insight it takes to make something that has never existed before.

There are many ways of describing the strategic design process. The IDEO model is the most well-known. In work with nongovernmental organizations (NGOs) and social enterprises, as part of their Human-Centered Design toolkit, they describe it as Hear—Create—Deliver (IDEO 2009). As another example, consider this version: Understand—Observe—Define—Ideate—Prototype—Test (Stanford dSchool 2011). Like any discipline, the further you dig into it, the more nuanced it becomes.

In the simplest way, the design process boils down to three major types of activity: discovery, creation, and testing. The most basic goal of design is to tap into insight so that we can fuel new action. Insight is new understanding that reveals the essence or nature of something. Insight is the cornerstone of disruptive innovation, breakthrough thinking, and fresh solutions. Insight moves us forward. Insight can be as simple as realizing that if you provide a more comfortable handle and then turn the blade of an apple peeler at an angle, it is more natural to use and less painful for arthritic hands, as Oxo and Smart Design discovered when designing the now iconic Good Grips peeler (Smart Design 2015). Insight enables you to develop a solution that works—because if you already understood what you needed to do and how to do it, then you wouldn't need to design a solution. To begin the process of generating insight, the first step is to learn to see with new eyes: We seek to discover what we do not know or to see what is hiding in plain sight. Often the most fundamental and powerful insights are the ones that are so obvious that we overlook them every day. Building upon what we learned in discovery, we then seek to create solutions.

It is important in this phase to really stretch our thinking and creativity. Looking at many options, applying design criteria to those options, and seeking to build out and prototype those solutions will help us generate insight into what ideas are most appropriate. With a range of solutions in hand, we move into testing. We need feedback, in many forms and at all stages of the process, to help us improve our ideas. Testing gives us insight into how well our solutions work. We proceed through these three activities in iterations until we've developed a solution that meets needs and satisfies our objectives. Ideally, the design process delivers solutions that just work: They relieve pain points, bring delight, inspire more ideas, and so on. Figure 6.2 shows the core elements of the design process.

Discover—Looking with new eyes
- Frame the challenge—Context, parameters, objectives
- Conduct research—For instance, ethnography, bodystorming, data collection
- Define the problem or opportunity—Synthesize what you have learned

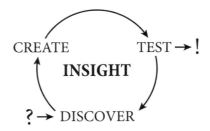

Figure 6.2 The design process
Michelle Miller

Create—Bring solutions to life

- Set the vision—Dream a big dream, redefine what's possible, restate what's desirable, connect to meaning
- Generate ideas—Unleash a storm of creativity. From mild to wild, explore all angles and really push the thinking
- Refine ideas—Eliminate, combine, and hone ideas until you have a solid set of vibrant options that do justice to your thinking
- Build prototypes—Enable people to experience the key elements of the ideas

Test—Get feedback

- Design tests—Figure out how to get the answers you need
- Find test subjects—Chose people who can give you real feedback
- Conduct tests—Use a repeatable, scientific method
- Explore the feedback—Identify what you have learned
- Reframe the problem—Allow insight to change how you see

It is worthwhile to note that strategic design works well in combination with other frameworks, such as agile and lean start-up because it establishes an overall flow for activity, into which agile and lean practices can be integrated.

While strategic design is a critical tool for the "fuzzy front end" of initiatives, strategic design is not limited to the research and ideation phases of a project. It is beneficial to view implementation as

another cycle of designing because creativity, experimentation, and new ideas are needed at every step. Here is an example of how a series of design cycles comprised a service design project for an insurance company. In each of the phases described below, conceptual design, detailed design, and implementation, we undertook the discover—create—test design cycle with different goals each time:

Conceptual Design: "Effortless Communication"
Following research prompted by unexpected customer complaints, we identified several surprising issues. One issue we wanted to fix immediately was that over 40 percent of phone calls were not reaching the right service agent on the first try. We wanted to eliminate complaints that customers can never reach the service agent they need and to give them a great experience when they called. We envisioned what "effortless communication" could mean for both customers and employees and got input on that concept with our stakeholders.

Detailed Design: Replace the Phone Tree with Operators
In detailed design, we looked at our options: (a) simplify the phone tree; (b) provide increased training to help employees route calls if customers rang through to the wrong agent; and (c) remove the interaction with the phone tree altogether. We chose to replace the phone tree with an operator because all other solutions still put our internal complexity onto the customer. We prototyped what an operator model might look like and worked through ideas of how we could move to that model.

Implementation: Implement the Operator Model

As we moved through implementation, each task required its own design process. How many operators could handle the call volume? Where and how should they be located, physically? What tools and resources would they need? How could we train them (and other staff) effectively? What should the customer's experience be like? What were the service measures and protocols? How could we implement the change smoothly, with no disruption? This work helped us to ensure a smooth launch.

Now, if companies are not using a design process, then what are they using?

Waterfall—Organizations that use a waterfall or similar process are commonly in highly regulated, slow-changing industries. This can be a problem when the best solution—or even the need for the solution—is unclear. Have you ever heard anyone refer to "a solution looking for a problem"?

Agile—Agile can help you avoid over-building, speed time to market, and respond as requirements change. But, again, if you've got the wrong overall solution, teams may not be equipped to address the issue. It requires leadership with the guts to make the "No Go" decision once you've gone too far. A five million dollar spend on a sales system that doesn't help the sales staff is a painful mistake—no matter how much money you pour into fixing defects.

Nothing—Most technology organizations have a process, such as Agile or Scrum. Project managers often use project management methodologies, such as PRINCE2 or PMBOK. But if you've never worked on a project before, then more than likely you don't have a "way of working." Consider an insurance firm: people come from a wide variety of backgrounds—lawyers, nurses, physical therapists, brokers, teachers, retail sales, and so on. They occupy roles as diverse as underwriting, relationship management, claims, learning and development, and risk management. When these people must execute a project together, how do they go about working together?

These examples point to three of the key benefits of using a design process:

1. Give people a chance to think creatively and strategically. Many people find it refreshing, fun, and challenging to participate in strategic design projects.
2. Solve the right problem. The design process helps teams hone their skills at framing problems and asking questions. Asking the right question is an art, and the first step to making sure you are asking the right question (and therefore solving the right problem) is to invite people to question from the very beginning.
3. Establish a shared way of working. Because anyone can use strategic design, it gives people across an organization a shared language and approach to projects.

If you seek to implement strategic design, you may encounter a number of concerns. You may be adding work to the front-end of projects that was not done previously. Leaders may be concerned that design will blow out project timelines or that, because you begin research not knowing what you will find, design will delay projects interminably. It is true that project plans need to be adjusted accordingly. But organizations also need to shift how they define project success. "On time and under budget" shouldn't be rewarded if millions of dollars are spent on a project that failed its mission.

Designing strategies, services, and business models can involve a lot of conversation, which can lead people to think that design is all talk and no action. Design processes must be crafted so that participants get a sense of progress and understand where they're going. It helps to involve them in creating and testing prototypes. Designers should also scale design efforts proportionately to the need. Many projects don't call for a full-blown design process that includes ethnography, cross-functional invention workshops, and weeks of user testing. It takes creativity to find ways to engage customers, ideate fully and test ideas within tight timelines and budgets. In one organization, the marketing team built a small panel of friends, family, and loyal customers (rotated every few months or so) that could be emailed with concept comparison surveys and who would respond within twenty-four to forty-eight hours. Active participants got free product swag.

If you are building strategic design as an organizational capability, consider the following:

- Commitment—Leaders must lead. Not only must they show commitment in terms of their actions and how organizational resources will be invested, but they also need to develop new skills to lead design.

- Long-term Strategy—Position design in terms of your overall strategy. Set horizons for near-, medium-, and long-term goals, and align expectations to those horizons. Don't expect results overnight.

- Investment—This requires funding, people, and space. Make sure that design is adequately resourced. Having dedicated design spaces is a great way to get attention, as well as create the inclusiveness that is desired in design processes.

- Capability Building—Invest in building skills. Start first with leadership and key talent. Leading design is different from doing design, and capability development must address both.

- Select Projects—Designate at least one or a small handful of projects that are meant to use design. Give them extra time and space to take the learning journey. Consider making them highly visible as well.

- Get help—Enlist external experts and consultants to help coach you through initial projects. Consider bringing in experts for the medium-term to help you get momentum and signal commitment.

- Treat it as change—Treat implementing design as if you were implementing a new organizational reporting structure or some other major shift—it requires a change process like anything else. Build a change plan, communicate what's happening, and get input.

It is also important to determine how design will operate within your structure: Each model has its advantages. Shifting between models as organizational capability grows is part of the iterative process.

Project-based—The organization may want to develop a small cadre of resources that are capable of executing design initiatives. These may be consultants or staff to be pulled from substantive roles when the need arises, potentially supplemented with outside support. This model can set the organization up for large-scale and highly visible successes. The downside may be that the capability is not retained within the broader organization and evaporates when the project concludes. Organizations may begin here, or they may use this case by case once capability exists.

Separate structure—Like a classic R&D department, this could take the form of an innovation or design center. This is a group that sits apart in the structure and is responsible for leading and executing projects or facilitating projects and helping to build capability. One pro is that it protects the function as it matures. One con is that it will be seen as a separate entity that adds to overhead costs. This may be a good place for organizations to begin building long-term capability.

Embedded in the structure—Most organizations have teams working across the organization who are responsible for improving their area. Building capability in these teams allows design to be targeted at local problems and to grow organically. However, this decentralized approach may constrict the size of problems that design can address, create different notions of design, and lack the support needed to mature. This model may work best once a baseline of capability is built.

Organic—This model requires a level of comprehension of the role and usefulness of design, discernment as to who needs capability, and shared understanding around when design should be employed. It relies upon a thriving ecosystem of training, capability development, and project opportunities. This model is for organizations that have a fairly mature design practice, have made investment in design over the course of many years, and have the expectation that design is how they work.

Business Model Canvas

One of the most powerful tools for strategic design that has emerged recently is the Business Model Canvas, developed by Alexander Osterwalder and Yves Pigneur (2010).

Figure 6.3 shows a visual map of key business drivers in designing a business model. The significance of this innovation is that it takes what used to get lost in a business plan and turns it into an easy-to-read visual, which then allows teams to play freely with new strategies and

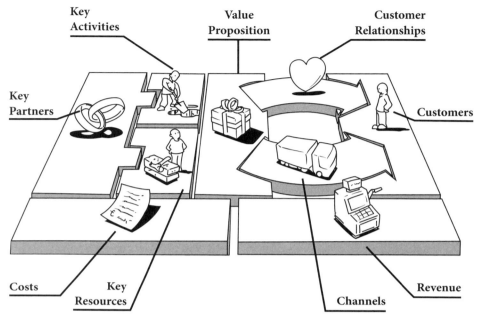

Figure 6.3 The Business Model Canvas by Alexander Osterwalder and Yves Pigneur
(Source: Osterwalder & Pigneur 2010: 18–19)

anticipate the implications of alternative business models. It also lends itself well to inclusiveness.

A strategy is the way your business will win. It "describes how the ends (goals) will be achieved by the [limited] means (resources)" available (Wikipedia, "Strategy"). Previously, strategy was the domain of people who worked in the "ivory tower." For most of the twentieth century, business models didn't need to change. As a result, executives didn't get the chance to substantially experiment with their business model all that often. Instead, when a new business idea was created (such as the automobile), businesses found a way to make it profitable and then they optimized

it for efficiency. It has been common for major strategic changes, such as mergers, acquisitions, and new market plays, to be instigated at the hands of new private equity management or the board. New business models often arose when entrepreneurs exploited technology to disrupt existing industries.

With the increasing pace of change and industry disruption, organizations have to revisit their fundamentals more frequently. For the first time in history, not only do we need the capability to design business at the board, executive, and strategy levels, but we also need the capability to design business embedded throughout the entire organization. Technology can be an impetus for change, but nothing drives substantive innovation and industry disruption more than a distinctly different business model.

Because the Business Model Canvas is complex, it may be helpful to begin a project with an alternate tool, like Ash Maurya's Lean Canvas (Figure 6.4), which can be used as part of a design brief for strategic design.

Maurya created the Lean Canvas to: "[capture] business model hypotheses on a single page," "[make] it as actionable as possible while staying entrepreneur-focused," and "enable more learning versus pitching conversations" (Maurya 2012). Also, whereas a Business Model Canvas lays out most of the components of a strategy, it doesn't necessarily represent the strategy itself. First, it does not provide a narrative—a way to quickly summarize the components. It also does not provision for classic elements of the strategy, such as vision, mission, and values. Nor does it provide any sort of process to guide you through the development of a new business model or link your desired business model to plans to enact that business

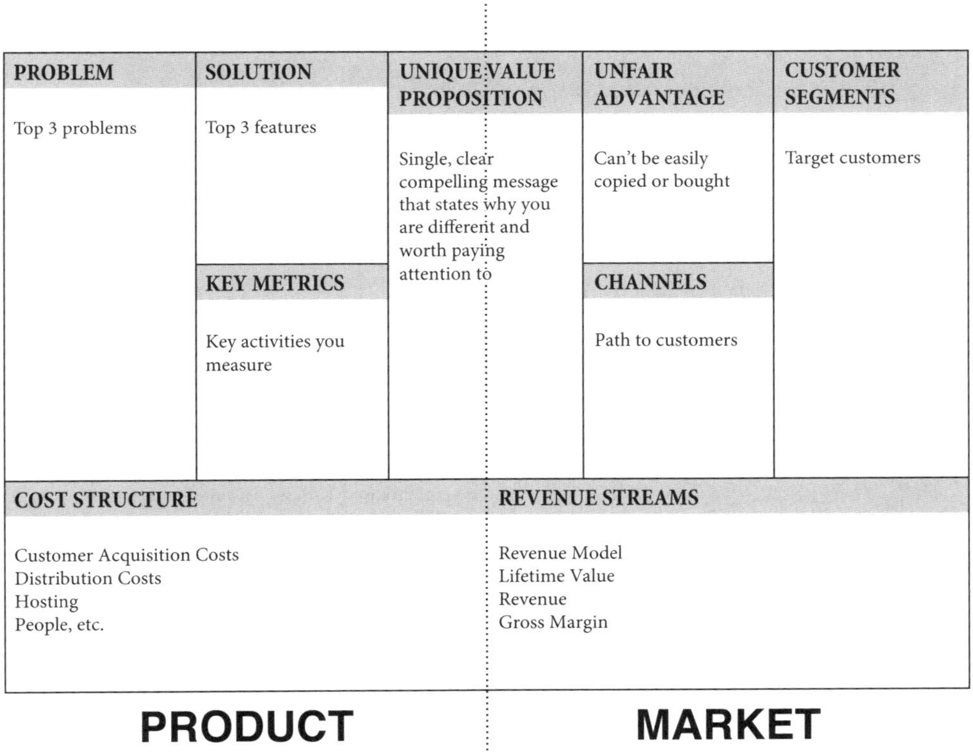

PROBLEM	SOLUTION	UNIQUE VALUE PROPOSITION		UNFAIR ADVANTAGE	CUSTOMER SEGMENTS
Top 3 problems	Top 3 features	Single, clear compelling message that states why you are different and worth paying attention to		Can't be easily copied or bought	Target customers
	KEY METRICS			**CHANNELS**	
	Key activities you measure			Path to customers	
COST STRUCTURE			**REVENUE STREAMS**		
Customer Acquisition Costs Distribution Costs Hosting People, etc.			Revenue Model Lifetime Value Revenue Gross Margin		

PRODUCT   MARKET

Figure 6.4 Ash Maurya's Lean Canvas

Lean Canvas is adapted from The Business Model Canvas (http://www.businessmodelgeneration.com) and is licensed under the Creative Commons Attribution-Share Alike 3.0 Un-ported License. Source: Maurya 2012.

model. For reasons such as these, when seeking to develop a new business model and actually make changes to your business model, it is helpful to use the Business Model Canvas as a tool in the context of a strategic conversation.

AcdB™ Strategic Conversation

While both the design process and the Business Model Canvas can help deliver the innovation that sits at the heart of a strategy, neither will directly yield a strategy—an articulation of how the organization will win—or a strategic plan. 2nd Road has developed a dialogue-based framework, called the AcdB™ (Golsby-Smith 2001), for helping organizations come together to develop a strategy and a plan (see Figure 6.5). The process helps teams navigate complex and highly uncertain environments together. Since the AcdB model is a broad framework, other tools can be used in conjunction to inform the strategy: a customer-based design process; the Business Model Canvas; scenario planning; analytic tools,

such as SWOT, PESTEL, or PROFIT; creative tools, such as narratives, role playing, and metaphor; and so on.

The tool has four key conversation spaces, and each one frames a different kind of inquiry:

A—"Where are we now?" The "A-space" is the initial conversation concerned with building a shared understanding of the current situation, including the internal and external environment, the system in focus, and key challenges facing the group. This conversation space builds agreement as to the "burning platform" for change. In terms of a design process, this is the time for discovering, sharing, and converging upon the problems and opportunities that an organization is facing. This is a time to understand customer and market needs, assess the current environment, and recognize the issues at hand. The "A-space" requires perception, insight, and honesty.

B—"Where are we going?" The "B-space" is concerned with creating a picture of success. It captures the firm's vision, mission, values, and goals. Above all, it articulates an organization's noble purpose: its reason for being and the value it brings society. In terms of a design process, this is the point at which a team will imagine what is possible and set the design criteria for success. A productive "B-space" conversation relies on imagination and will.

C—"Building Blocks." The "C-space" is an assessment of the gap between

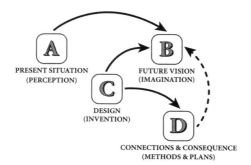

Figure 6.5 2nd Road AcdB strategic conversation framework

the current state and the desired future state so that the team can identify the building blocks and key themes for strategic action. This is a creative time for designing solutions and identifying the hypotheses that need to be tested. The "C-space" is where invention lives.

D—"Detailed Plans." The "D-space" is where plans are drawn up to actualize the building blocks. This includes responsibilities, resource allocations, accountabilities, and so on. The "D-space" is where an organization commits to doing work.

These four conversation spaces can be run sequentially as a single conversation among a leadership team over the course of three to five days for an iterative progression of existing strategy, or as a series of conversations over the course of several months, with intensive engagement inside and outside the organization, in order to pave the way for a disruptive strategy, initiate significant change, or address wicked problems. Bringing together a strategic conversation requires a number of skills, including strategic facilitation, conversation design, business design, creative visualization, change expertise, senior-level stakeholder management, cross-functional engagement, communication, coordination, and event planning.

Another strategic design approach worthy of mention is Theory U (Scharmer 2009). Theory U is appropriate for large-scale social change initiatives in multi-stakeholder, highly complex, and uncertain environments, where the future is emerging and much of what is required is a change within ourselves and in how we engage.

Benefits of Using Strategic Design Methods

When used inclusively, at scale, strategic design helps improve ideas, manage risk, and generate substantial innovation for business. It helps you access diverse expertise. It helps you see anew, visualize possibilities, and play with ideas. It helps you look at options and solve the right problem, decreasing risk. It gives people an effective way to work together creatively.

Try it yourself:

- AcdB: With a group of colleagues, put four sheets of flip chart paper side by side on the wall. Label each A—B—C—D. Talk through your organization's current strategy. How much do you know? Where are you having to guess? What questions remain? The gaps that you note are opportunities for leaders to either clarify or work with teams to build out the strategy and plans.
- Business Model Canvas: From there, on another wall, put up three to four sheets of flip chart paper side by side. Draw out the sections of the Business Model Canvas. Through conversation, deconstruct your organization's business model. Again, how much do you know? What elements of the Business Model Canvas are least familiar to you? Areas where you have little knowledge are opportunities for greater cross-functional interaction and potentially development. Do you see any opportunities for innovation?

- Reflect: What did you learn? What is a logical next step? How can you involve others? How might you use the AcdB and Business Model Canvas as tools to make a case for change?
- Download: IDEO's Human-Centered Design (HCD) toolkit is available online: http://www.ideo.com/work/human-centered-design-toolkit/. Think of a social change you'd like to see in your community. Using the process illustrated in the HCD toolkit, how might you go about bringing people together to create new solutions?

GO DEEPER

Read the following:
- *Solving Problems with Design Thinking* by J. Liedtka, A. King, and K. Bennett.
- *Business Model Generation* by A. Osterwalder and Y. Pigneur.
- *The Lean Startup* by E. Ries.

REFLECTIONS
- What strategic design method is most appropriate to the challenge you are facing right now?
- Consider how these business models have disrupted different industries: iTunes and music/media; Amazon—bookselling, as well as retail; and Airbnb for hospitality.
- Map out your organization's business model. What opportunities for innovation do you see?

- How might you make a strategic design process as provocative, creative, and engaging as possible? For instance, in a case study documented in the book *Solving Problems with Design Thinking* (Liedtka, King, & Bennett 2013: 35–36), 2nd Road used metaphor to help two recently merged organizations create a shared future.

Section 2: The Impact on Social Assets: Networks

The second way we will look at the impact of strategic design on organizational innovation is in terms of **social assets**. We have defined social assets as the relationships, ties, linkages, and connections that form intangible but very real networks of people and ideas that lead to cooperation and collaboration between individuals and groups for the purpose of creating value. This includes interdependencies for mutual benefit, which may be both internal and external to the organization. Networks may be composed of relationships formed among teams, former team members and colleagues, suppliers, partnerships, and even customers.

Although many factors are driving us toward networked interactivity (including technology), organizations are not necessarily accustomed to it—internally, externally, across organizational boundaries, and even within teams. There are a number of common barriers to collaboration and cooperation, including silos; command-and-control power structures; lack of skills and tools; fear of taking risks or "sticking your neck out"; policies, taboos, and biases that prevent cross-pollination; lack of communication; "them or us" mentality between leaders and team members or organizations and their customers; processes that favor speed over inclusiveness … The list goes on and on.

Throughout this chapter we have referred to the concept of inclusiveness. Network strength is built through a habit of inclusiveness. Networks are an important source of innovative ideas, and are increasingly the means through which innovation is delivered. In order to show how we can shift organizational practices to be more inclusive, so as to tap into the real potential of networks, we will explore the practice of stakeholder management. During the course of any project, teams need to manage stakeholders. For the initiative to be as successful as possible, and in order to build design capability across the organization, it is important to engage stakeholders in an inclusive, collaborative manner.

Inclusive Stakeholder Management

Stakeholder management is the process of "[identifying] both internal and external stakeholders in order to determine the project requirements and expectations of all parties involved" while "[managing] the influence of the various stakeholders in relation to the project requirements to ensure a successful outcome" (Project Management Institute 2013: 248–49). The process includes:

- Analysis—Identifying stakeholders and developing a stakeholder register
- Mapping—Grouping stakeholders, using a stakeholder map (also a matrix or grid)

- Strategy—Generating a management strategy for each stakeholder group
- Planning—Aligning communication and engagement to the initiative plan

Stakeholder management is vital because:

- Unsatisfied stakeholders can railroad initiatives
- To effect change, stakeholders need to participate in the journey
- In contexts such as government, it is unacceptable not to engage stakeholders
- Employees, customers, citizens, and so on, increasingly expect to have a say
- To get innovative outcomes, you need diverse ideas, expertise, and experience

In Figure 6.6, you will find the collaboration circle stakeholder map that is designed specifically for strategic design projects, inclusiveness, and codesign (Miller 2013).

The collaboration circle stakeholder map is based on three main ideas that help us represent the whole system, include every voice, and clearly establish a role for every stakeholder:

1. The traditional symbol of the whole system, a circle, indicates the (permeable) boundaries of the system.
2. The stakeholders of a system are the people able to help answer these questions:
   - Why are we doing this?
   - What are we doing?
   - How will we do it?
   - What's possible?
   - What's going on in reality?
3. These questions create a set of "voices," which have very different roles in an initiative:

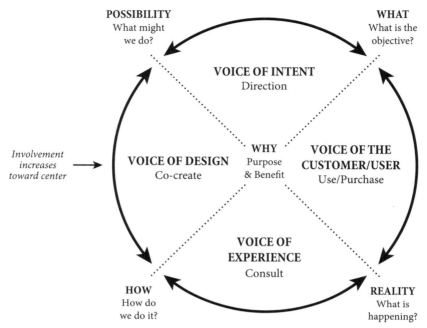

Figure 6.6 Collaboration circle stakeholder map
Michelle Miller, 2013

- Voice of intent—Circumscribes "What's possible for this initiative?" and "What is the overall objective?"
- Voice of customer/user (or citizen, client, etc.)—Informs "What are the specific objectives?" and "What are the issues in reality?"
- Voice of experience—Surfaces "What patterns do we see happening in reality?" and "How do we make things happen in this system?"
- Voice of design—Imagines "What are the possible solutions?" and "How do we make the solutions work?"

Figure 6.7 shows how the tool was used for a service design project aimed at fixing a number of customer experience issues.

Each stakeholder group was critical to the long-term success of the project.

Voice of Intent

CEO—The CEO flagged known issues, requested the project, and set the overall objective.

Sponsor—The sponsor reported directly to the CEO and was the primary advocate for securing funding and resources, removing barriers, and ensuring progress.

Steering committee—Comprising a set of executives who reported directly to the CEO, the steering committee shaped the overall project direction and made high-level decisions. Prior to critical meetings, we walked through our

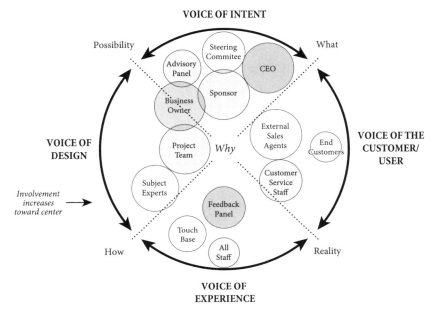

Figure 6.7 Example of the collaboration circle stakeholder map in use
Michelle Miller, 2013

progress with each individual so they could ask questions and arrive prepared.

Advisory panel—Because we were using a design-based approach that was fairly new to the organization, we consulted with a small, informal group on how to set up the project and work effectively with stakeholders. The group included the strategy executive, the strategy manager, and an external consultant.

Voice of Experience

Feedback panel—We regularly delivered project updates and sought feedback from a cross-functional group of service leaders and customer relationship representatives impacted by poor service performance. We depended on the group to validate our results and represent the "voice of the customer."

Touch base—Some stakeholders, such as Risk, Legal, HR, and other colleagues, needed to be informed, were curious about the project, and could help flag risks, but they had little desire to be more involved beyond an initial meeting and informal catch-ups.

All staff—We worked with the internal communications team to make sure that everyone across the organization had access to basic information about the situation, knew the steps we were taking, and could channel feedback appropriately.

Voice of Design

Business owner—For day-to-day guidance, a mid-level manager from the service team was dedicated to us for roughly 50 percent of her time. She worked with us to determine how we engaged stakeholders, presented findings and articulated recommendations.

Project team—The project team structure and level of resourcing flexed as required. Viewing the project team as stakeholders, we conducted an immersive induction process and maintained transparent and proactive involvement, collaboration, and communication.

Subject experts—From time to time, we drew upon the expertise of service leaders, customer relationship managers, underwriters, analytics experts, marketers, customer design specialists, and technology leads.

Voice of the Customer/User

External sales agents—Improving the external sales and service agents' experience was our primary goal. Whereas an end customer may have one single experience with the business over the course of several years, sales and service agents work with the service team daily and are thus significantly impacted by poor service.

Customer service staff—Our service staff also sat at the heart of this challenge. Despite much hard work, our service teams weren't succeeding. In order to understand what was happening, we used design ethnography to listen to customer calls, observe service staff in action, and document what we learned. It was important that they did not take our research personally, and they knew

we were not auditing performance. Progress was dependent upon fair representation of their perspective.

End customers—Although our customers were not as significantly impacted as our external sales and service agents, they were impacted nonetheless. We monitored their feedback and ensured that decisions made for the benefit of the agents would also benefit the customer.

Benefits of an Inclusive Process

Diverse Perspectives

Diverse ideas and cross-pollination of information set our brains in motion and spark creativity. When you bring together the whole system and look at a problem from every angle, you give the team a chance to see the situation in its entirety, form new insight, take all needs into account, and create a solution that is truly useful, usable, and desirable.

Creative Tension

Inclusiveness generates creative tension, and creative tension is a critical ingredient of creativity. Managing creative tension (or tension of any sort) is a delicate balance—too much is detrimental and not enough leaves value on the table.

Synergy

When people are excited about something, the energy they generate is phenomenal. Inclusiveness taps into this, building synergy—the presence of spontaneous, serendipitous activity among the network of people, information, and ideas. Inclusiveness sets up relationships for tomorrow, and this important because social capital—as well as trust—builds organically over time.

Alignment

Inclusiveness builds buy-in, aids the change process, and speeds communication. All of these create alignment, which increases efficiency and effectiveness. This makes the transformation that innovation requires possible.

Meaningfulness

When stakeholders come together around a challenge, they create a shared purpose, tap into their own passions, and find community and connection that may not have existed previously. The effect of inclusiveness is that people often come away with a heightened sense of meaningfulness.

Considerations When Using Inclusive Processes

Inclusiveness, stakeholder management, and change management can make or break the success of a strategic design project—as well as determine the limits of innovation. Organizations, leaders, and individuals unaccustomed to inclusiveness and collaboration can find it confronting to work this way. It changes how power is used. Leaders are not expected to have the answer, and this changes the paradigm of leadership. Using an inclusive process can also increase the scope and scale of stakeholder engagement, which will add to the perception that the process will take longer. We have to remind ourselves that change can't be measured by the beginning and ending of projects. When we engage more people earlier, we actually bring the change process forward—giving people space and time to work through change productively.

GO DEEPER

Read the following:
- *Managing Transitions* by W. Bridges.
- *Influencer* by J. Grenny, K. Patterson, D. Maxfield, and R. McMillan.
- "Everyone Has a Role: Whole System Engagement Maximizes Collaboration" by M. Miller. Available online: http://bit.ly/19tq51P

REFLECTIONS
- Reflect on a difficult project. Can you identify any stakeholder engagement issues?
- Map out the stakeholders of a project using the collaboration stakeholder map. Are all the needed roles present and clearly defined?
- Conduct a project review for a completed project. Ask each stakeholder about the project process and how you could have pushed the level of innovation. What do you learn when you compare stakeholder perspectives?
- Map Stakeholders. At the kickoff for a project with multiple stakeholders, have everyone in the room brainstorm potential stakeholders—by name where possible. As the list grows, group stakeholders that will be engaged together or in the same way. Write the name of each stakeholder group onto sticky

notes—one group per sticky note. In the case of executives, it may be a group of one. Draw the collaboration circle stakeholder map across a couple of flip chart pages placed side by side on the wall. Explain the concept. One sticky note at a time, have everyone agree on where to place each stakeholder group. If stakeholders need to be aggregated again, or disaggregated, then do so. Discuss the implications of the different roles that each quadrant plays in the overall project.

- Reflect. Where do you have gaps? Is the voice of the customer/user adequately represented? Are there a lot of stakeholder groups in one category? What will be your stakeholder engagement challenges? Are you comfortable sharing this map with stakeholders who are not in the room to assess whether or not they agree with their role? How does everyone feel about the roles that they have been assigned?

Section 3: The Impact on Human Assets: Individuals

The third and final way we will look at the impact of strategic design on organizational innovation is in terms of **human assets**. We have defined human assets as the human competencies, including creative and cognitive abilities, knowledge base, social proclivities, and personality attributes that are embodied in the ability of individuals to perform work so as to produce value. Human assets also include the degree of alignment between the talent in an organization, how well their roles suit their skills, and how well the organization invokes their passions.

Strategic design and innovation can be an emotional journey. The process of diverging (generating new ideas and options) can be exciting when the team is cranking out ideas. It can be stymying when the team runs into dead ends. The process of converging and editing can be difficult when you're not certain, or it can be freeing when you're excited to pounce on an incredible idea. As you go through prototyping and things just aren't flowing, the team can get frustrated. When the solution starts to work, the excitement is contagious. The journey is never the same, and you have to develop a feeling for the ebb and flow. Building a few key meta-skills can help us manage strategic design, as well as use our emotions as a pathway to creativity and intuition:

Dialogue—The process of conversation between two or more people for the purpose of exchanging information, ideas, and opinions to solve problems and/or come to an agreement. Not only do we use strategic design to help us gain insight that will lead to innovative new ideas, but we also use strategic design to help us have a productive conversation about the future we want and how we get there.

Critical thinking—"The mental process of actively and skillfully conceptualizing, applying, analyzing, synthesizing, and evaluating information to reach an answer or conclusion" (Dictionary.com, "Critical Thinking"). With design, we must be able to think critically about both objective and subjective concepts. To think critically involves not only identifying and evaluating existing options and choices, but also identifying and evaluating options that don't yet exist in the world.

Design rationale—The better able we are to explain our design rationale—the decisions we make during the process—the better we are able to help others see our ideas, understand their options, and have informed dialogue. It's a designer's job to enable the client to think about her options—not to try to persuade her. It's the client's job to evaluate ideas and select the solution that best fits her objectives. In order to empower others to do their part of the critical thinking, we have to hone our articulation of design rationale.

Giving and receiving feedback—Every day, when people are working on projects, an email, a presentation, and so on, they seek feedback on their work. We do it so often that we don't always realize that there are skills involved—or that we can improve those skills. Designers call this a design critique, a critique, or just a crit. It can be emotionally challenging for both the person requesting feedback and the person giving feedback. Learning how to translate our emotional cues into productive feedback is a critical component of providing direction and enabling creativity.

Dialogue

Dialogue is at the core of each of the tools discussed in this chapter. The act of dialogue helps us to see ourselves and one another, build trust, refine our ability to frame questions, and move forward together. Open and honest dialogue processes can help us deal with disagreements, pressure, and failure. When we engage in dialogue, we increase our capacity to sit with uncertainty, complexity, ambiguity, and fresh insight. We gain tolerance for diversity, enable ourselves to loosen our grip on our own ideas, and provide an arena to refocus a team on shared challenges and meaning. When teams are uncomfortable or unskilled with dialogue, it can be helpful to:

- Build facilitation and conversation design skills.
- Address "safety" before engaging in dialogue. Safety refers to comfort in sharing ideas without fear of negative consequences. Although the dialogue process helps build trust, it can require some trust for people to be willing to begin dialogue. Once safety is established, it is a facilitator's role, working in conjunction with the leader or convener, to "hold space"—that is, to create a container in which vulnerability can be risked and conversations can unfold.
- Interview attendees, customers, and other stakeholders to provide an overview of the perspectives in a pre-read prior to meetings. This helps people come expecting the intended discussion.

- Use visual facilitation to track the conversation visibly, so that people do not have to defend their own positions and can see what the conversation reveals.
- Use structured, facilitated dialogue activities to increase comfort and skill levels. Give people a chance to articulate their thinking and exchange ideas before sharing with the broader group. For activities, refer to the Liberating Structures website (http://www.liberatingstructures.com/).
- Model the behavior of reacting with curiosity and questions, as opposed to defending positions and battling opinions.
- Where it is not culturally appropriate for ideas and differing opinions to be shared among all attendees, structure activities and dialogue processes to work within these bounds: respect authority and help people save face—while surfacing the variety of perspectives.

Critical Thinking

Thinking critically is vital precisely because strategic design and innovation decisions involve subjective decision making. It helps us keep from battling over opinions. Here are a few common techniques:

Focusing question: Used to converge a team around the project or team ambition, it is a question typically stated in the format "How might we _____ so that we _____?"

It should cover the following: What is the action that is taken; who is doing the action; what is the method of action and the quality of that action; who is the beneficiary of the action; what is the purpose of the action; and what is the tension inherent in the challenge. It should not prescribe the solution, but rather it should mark the territory for exploration. One example might be: "How might our company improve our customer experience so that we become the first choice in the external sales agents' consideration set—with customers we desire—five years from now?"

Design criteria—Building upon the focusing question, list out the qualities of a successful solution. Return to these criteria relentlessly to judge decisions, or to determine whether goals need to be modified. Do not shy away from criteria that seem to be in conflict—setting this challenge stimulates creativity. For the service design project presented earlier, here are some of the design criteria:

- Be bold.
- Focus on a few things that will make a difference.
- Prioritize customer impacting activity and eliminate pain points first.
- Address root causes—no "Band-Aids."
- Reinforce proactive behavior and completion of customer service.
- Build a collaborative approach and skills.
- Create transparency into the experience and organizational performance.

Multiple concepts—Identifying several viable solutions enables the critical thinking needed to evaluate options and make well-informed decisions. As a rule of thumb, designers often try to present no fewer than three solutions or directions, and generally they present an odd number. It is also common to create a "mild-to-wild" range of solutions. Teams endeavor to offer only solutions they are happy with and that solve the challenge well. Looking at multiple solutions prevents us from jumping onto the first solution that comes to mind—often this is not the best or even the right solution. For example, consider the case of a growing strategic communications firm. Their business operated roughly in two halves: medical illustration and communications design. It would have been easy for them to simply increase staffing on the design side. But we looked at their strategic options. As it turned out, they had many options—from pursuing an agency model to building out their technology-based capabilities. They realized that there were more exciting and potentially more profitable avenues for growth that made better use of the whole team than what originally seemed the natural solution. If they had not allowed themselves to suspend reality and entertain multiple options, they likely would not have reached this insight.

Variety of prototypes—From sketches to bodystorming to pilot runs, there is a huge variety of prototypes that can be used throughout the design process. For ideas on how to prototype, try Bill Buxton's book, *Sketching User Experiences* (2007). As with an MVP (Minimum Viable Product) in lean start-up, prototypes can only help you test portions of the entire concept. Select the right prototype for the question at hand. In prototyping, you also have to learn to suspend judgment and to play. This can be uncomfortable, but it's well worth it. In the example of launching the telephone operator team mentioned earlier in this chapter, there was a risk that the operator team would launch with too few resources. What a nightmare that would have been! Can you imagine the debacle: On the first day of proudly launching live operators nationwide, the service fails because there aren't enough operators to handle the volume of calls. We avoided that with prototyping. Early on in the setup of the team, the designer sat down with the project manager to simulate calls. The designer had spent time listening to calls, documenting the queries, and cataloging the scenarios, and so took on the role of caller. The project manager had been working on the design of the phone tree to help operators route calls as quickly as possible, and so took on the role of the operator. With these tools and a stopwatch, the designer and project manager quickly realized that calls were more likely to take ninety seconds or more, versus the thirty to sixty seconds initially estimated. As a result of this prototyping, the team increased their staffing levels. This, and a lot of subsequent work in prototyping and training through simulations, ensured that the launch went smoothly.

The process of critical thinking not only helps us make better decisions, it also helps drive creativity. It pushes our thinking, questioning, and ingenuity further to address constraints, so we work past our existing mentality. This takes us into new territory—the domain of innovation.

Communicating Ideas: Preparing Your Design Rationale

In preparing to present work, even informally, take the time to articulate your design rationale. We like to think that our work will speak for itself, but it doesn't. People need guidance to understand what they're looking at and what you're asking them for. Think of it like giving a tour.

1. Put yourself in their shoes. Think about your audience. What are their priorities and concerns? Try to anticipate the questions they will ask.
2. Revisit the design criteria. (What were you asked to do and why? Have you solved the problem? If not, how far away are you?) Use the design criteria to explain the merits of each option.
3. Identify your design choices. At what points did you need to make decisions? What were the choices you faced? Why did you make those choices?
4. Spell out the options. For each concept, describe it, list out the features and their uses, and describe your considerations, pros and cons, of each. What influenced you, and what questions arise from each concept?

The process of articulating your design rationale helps people better understand your ideas, think critically about options, and give useful feedback. Another less obvious but important benefit is that you often catch something you've forgotten or see new ideas, which leads you to improve the work.

Giving and Receiving Feedback: Participating in a Design Critique

A leader or a client's job is to set direction. What does it mean to set direction? Day to day, setting direction is all about providing feedback. But people can struggle with giving feedback, often because their emotions get in the way. We all have experienced the stress of seeking feedback: "Have I missed something big? Is the work good? Am I going to have to start over?" Or if giving feedback: "Will they get it? There's a lot of pressure to get this right. What if my feedback is poorly received?" All of these concerns can create anxiety during the critique process. People are vulnerable, and we don't often behave well when we're vulnerable. It is easy for emotions to escalate and relationships to sour. So how do we manage this so that we can move innovation forward?

When Giving Feedback: Use the Critique Process

Start at the high level or "big picture": Are we even in the ballpark? If a piece of work doesn't satisfy the highest objectives, resolve that before moving forward. Does it reflect the design criteria and vision of success? Does it meet your expectations? What's missing? What details should we pay attention to? What is and isn't working? Be wary of "That will never work" or "We've tried that already." Put it in perspective—how significant is the feedback? Bring it back to intent—orient everyone around the overall purpose.

Mind Your Emotions

Keep an open mind. Always ask: What are we trying to achieve? Consider what you expected to see. Be prepared to be surprised. Take on new ideas. Keep your intent in mind, and ask yourself if it needs to evolve. Pay attention to your thoughts, feelings, and physical sensations. Are you uncomfortable? Sweaty palms? Clenched stomach? Dry mouth? Locate the source of your concern. Conversely, if the work creates energy, pinpoint what accomplishes this.

When Receiving Feedback: Don't Take It Personally

Represent your work and thinking faithfully, fairly, and respectfully, then ask questions and listen. Separate the comments made about the work from your ego and self-esteem. It's not about you. Evaluate your own ideas based on whether they achieve the desired result.

Lean on the design criteria to help judge objectively. Identify your emotions: Fear? Anger? Defensiveness? Anxiety? Excitement? All these at once? Examine your reaction. Help people understand your reaction and what you're hearing.

As you seek to build these skills, consider the following:

- These are tacit skills; learn by doing.
- Emotions are a sensitive subject; it is not always acceptable to discuss them openly.
- People think they already do this; to help bring awareness to behavior, set ground rules, repeat the ground rules regularly, model the behavior you want to see, and be willing to jump in and work through situations in the moment

How are emotions related to innovation? They're really important. Building the skills of critical thinking, communicating design rationale, and giving and receiving feedback helps increase our command over our soft skills, such as imagination, creativity, emotion, and intuition. By watching our emotions, we can get better at spotting misunderstanding, identifying differing expectations, and hearing our intuition. Sometimes intuition is a whisper. Sometimes it's a light bulb. And sometimes it's a cold sweat, clenched stomach, and uneven breathing. Intuition is the heartbeat of creativity, innovation, and risk taking. The more we learn to listen to it, the more we can tap into this powerful source of insight. And it takes practice to really harness intuition—practice every day. Everyone involved in a design process (designer, client, leader, and anyone giving feedback) needs to build these skills. The more an organization nurtures these skills, the higher the potential for innovation.

GO DEEPER

Try the following exercises:
- *Sketching User Experiences* by B. Buxton.
- Use the Group Works pattern language card deck to help you design your next workshops. Available online: http://groupworksdeck.org/
- Experiment with a different way to run meetings and workshops using the ideas at Liberating Structures. Available online: http://www.liberatingstructures.com/
- At the next opportunity to give people feedback on work, don't jump immediately to suggestions. At the beginning, ask them to do the following: (1) Summarize the task that they were given, (2) list the challenges they came up against, (3) explain the rationale behind the decisions they made, and (4) provide pros and cons for the solution they have developed (ideally there are multiple solutions). After doing the above steps, they should then describe what point they are at in the process, and clarify what feedback they would like from you.
- Then proceed with your feedback. Summarize what you have heard. State the extent to which you feel the solution is hitting the mark. Describe what you feel is working and is not working. Avoid suggesting explicit changes, but rather provide three goals that you think still need to be met. If these are not clear, provide related examples of what you

mean. Leave room for them to solve the problem themselves. Recap how close you feel they are to the solution. Ask them for questions. Leave it open for them to come back to you after they have reflected more. Agree whether or not they will seek your feedback again before proceeding to the next step.

REFLECTIONS
- Reflect on a conversation where you gave someone feedback on his work. Was he able to take onboard your feedback? Why? How might you have given feedback differently?
- Think about conversations you have seen that have stifled innovation. What could have been done differently to give the ideas a chance?
- At your next opportunity to provide a solution, generate many options and set up a conversation to review those options. How does this change the dialogue you have?

Chapter Summary

Looking through the frame of three assets, organizational assets (frameworks, processes, and resources), social assets (networks), and human assets (individuals), we have explored how strategic design methods alter the way organizations innovate. When we implement strategic design, we must address each of these three assets to be successful:

What builds organizational assets (frameworks, processes, and resources)?
- The design process helps build a shared language and way of working

across an organization. When used at the beginning of initiatives, it helps you solve the right problem.

- Business Model Canvas democratizes innovation and allows you to play with the building blocks of a business. Disruptive innovation comes from new business models, which often also leverage technology in a fresh way.
- AcdB strategic conversation provides a framework for an organization to design a strategy together.

What increases social assets (networks)?

- Inclusive stakeholder management productively uses diversity, harnesses creative tension, enables synergy, builds alignment, aids the change process, and creates a sense of meaning.

What strengthens human assets (individuals)?

- Dialogue helps you see differently, exchange insight, and improve ideas.
- Critical thinking pushes the bounds of your current mind-set, ensuring that solutions are robust and strategic.
- Design rationale gives you a framework to articulate the decisions you made during the design process so that others can understand your work and have a basis from which to evaluate your ideas.
- Design critiques puts best practice in place to help people give and receive feedback so that you can manage emotions and proceed constructively.

Tips for Using Strategic Design

These tips can keep a strategic design process moving:

Getting started

1. Acknowledge that you are kicking off a change and transition process—agreeing to a problem is the first step in letting go of current solutions. For information about organizational transitions, refer to William Bridges, *Managing Transitions* (2009).
2. Agree to the parameters of the initiative and set expectations of the process—get buy-in to push ideas from "mild to wild."
3. Begin with a design brief or a Lean Canvas.
4. Take the time to really understand the problem. Use ethnography or other tools to see for yourself what your customer is experiencing. This forms the heart and soul of your new business model, while galvanizing the "burning platform" people will need for change.
5. Find ways to make the whole process as creative, visual, interactive, and inclusive as possible.

Designing

1. Treat the design process as the second phase of a transition process—the "Neutral Zone." It can be overwhelming and disorienting. Engaging people in creating the future empowers them to work through uncertainty and complexity.

2. Equip people with the skills and capabilities they will need to participate.
3. Use facilitation techniques, coaching, and mentoring to help people let go of existing paradigms.
4. Explore multiple ideas and bring inspiration from diverse sources.
5. Push teams to strive for a truly different value proposition, bold strategy, and noble purpose.

Implementing
1. Treat the implementation process as the third phase of transition so there is a new beginning.
2. Communicate, communicate, communicate.
3. Enable people to solve problems. The design process will not have covered every detail. Set a clear intention and then provide a structured framework that empowers people to design their own solutions.
4. Constantly monitor and respond to feedback.

So What? What Impact Does Strategic Design Have on Organizational Innovation?

Strategic design processes generate new ideas with disruptive potential. By looking at opportunities differently, whether from the perspective of the customer/user or by playing with the building blocks of our business in low-risk experiments, we push ourselves out of our current frame of thinking. Once we have moved past the bounds of our current paradigm, we begin to create the fuel for innovation.

Dialogue, diversity, and inclusiveness enrich insight and aid change. By moving strategy and innovation outside of the ivory towers of the strategy team or the R&D department, strategic design gives us the chance to tap into our collective expertise, increase cross-pollination, and ease the change process.

Critical thinking, articulating design rationale, and critique builds intellectual rigor, intuition, and creativity. By bringing discipline to our minds and our emotions, we hone intuition and creativity, so that we are better equipped to push boundaries.

The discipline of strategic design equips us to deal with subjectivity so we can deliver innovation. Taking the risk to innovate depends on subjective decision making. Strategic design brings discipline to help us see the rationale in our creativity and intuition, link insight to ideas, and have productive conversations about something that doesn't exist yet—the future.

Acknowledgments

I am thrilled to share the AcdB, thanks to 2nd Road, Tim Golsby-Smith, and Tim Fife. Many thanks to Bartley Hassall, Marie-Claire Grady, Richard Rawling, Manuhuia Barcham, S. Fisher Qua, Christopher Allen, and Pyxis for feedback on the collaboration circle. Much gratitude to my mother, Noreen Wedman, for enduring support!

References

Bridges, W. (2009), *Managing Transitions—Making the Most of Change*, Boston: Da Capo Lifelong Books.

Buxton, B. (2007), *Sketching User Experiences: Getting the Design Right and the Right Design*, 1st edn, Burlington, MA: Morgan Kaufmann Publishers.

Dictionary.com, "Critical Thinking." Available online: http://dictionary.reference.com/browse/critical+thinking?s=t (accessed July 14, 2015).

Golsby-Smith, T. (2001), "Pursing the Art of Strategic Conversations: An Investigation of the Role of the Liberal Arts of Rhetoric and Poetry in the Business World," PhD diss., University of Western Sydney.

Grenny, J., K. Patterson, D. Maxfield, and R. McMillan (2013), *Influencer—The New Science of Leading Change*, New York: McGraw Hill.

IDEO (2009), "Design Kit: The Field Guide to Human-Centered Design." Available online: http://www.ideo.com/work/human-centered-design-toolkit/

Liberating Structures (2014), http://www.liberatingstructures.com/

Liedtka, J., A. King, and K. Bennett (2013), *Solving Problems with Design Thinking—Ten Stories of What Works*, New York: Columbia University Press.

Maurya, A. (2012), "Why Lean Canvas vs Business Model Canvas?" LeanStack.com. Available online: http://practicetrumpstheory.com/2012/02/why-lean-canvas/

Miller, M. (2013), "Everyone Has a Role: Whole System Engagement Maximizes Collaboration," in XXIV ISPIM Conference—Innovating in Global Markets: Challenges for Sustainable Growth, Helsinki, Finland, 16–19 June 2013. Available online: http://bit.ly/19tq51P

Osterwalder, A. and Y. Pigneur (2010), *Business Model Generation*, Hoboken, NJ: John Wiley & Sons.

Osterwalder, A. and Y. Pigneur (2010), "The Business Model Canvas." Available online: http://www.businessmodelgeneration.com/

Project Management Institute (2013), *A Guide to the Project Management Body of Knowledge*, Newtown Square, PA: Project Management Institute.

Ries, E. (2011), *The Lean Startup: How Today's Entrepreneurs Use Continuous Innovation to Create Radically Successful Businesses*, New York: Crown Business.

Scharmer, C. Otto (2009), *Theory U: Leading from the Future as It Emerges—The Social Technology of Presencing*. San Francisco: Berrett-Koehler Publishers.

Smart Design (2015), "Oxo Good Grips." Available online: http://smartdesignworldwide.com/work/oxo-good-grips/

Stanford dSchool (2010), "Bootcamp Bootleg." Available online: http://dschool.stanford.edu/wp-content/uploads/2011/03/BootcampBootleg2010v2SLIM.pdf

Wikipedia, "Design Thinking." Available online: http://en.wikipedia.org/wiki/Design_thinking (last modified July 11, 2015).

Wikipedia, "Strategy." Available online: http://en.wikipedia.org/wiki/Strategy (last modified May 18, 2015).

PART III
The What: Introduction to Part III—Chapters 7, 8, and 9

It is important to remember that, ultimately, the big picture is to make sense of a complex process in totality. Recall the fabled blind man touching the elephant: depending on which part of the elephant he touched, he felt different textures and qualities of the elephant. Similarly, being able to make sense of all components in parts I and II is essential to grasping the full application of strategic design in a broader sense. The final third of this book will expose you to big-picture thinking.

Chapter 7, written by Sarah Brooks—a social innovation designer, founder of Networked Culture, and Presidential Innovation Fellow—is a thorough and creatively written foundational journey into systems thinking, and it successfully contextualizes strategic design thinking in terms of sustainability and what Terry Irwin and Cameron Tonkinwise refer to as "transition design." This chapter is a subdued cautionary tale and wise acknowledgment for us to consider our own limitations and to be holistic in the ways that we design and in the ways that we grow businesses. This chapter will give you an excellent foundation into complexity theory and complex adaptive systems using very accessible language, exercises, and real-world case studies.

Chapter 8 is my contribution to the text, where I explore the bigger picture of strategic design through the lens of service design. I was introduced to service design when I researched The Ritz-Carlton hotel, and I identified the ways that it designed meaningful experiential services for its guests. After exposing you to the theoretical tenets of service design, experience design, and improvisational organizations, I conclude with practical case stories in the health and food sectors.

Chapter 9 is a real treat, written by Manoj Fenelon, director of foresight at PepsiCo. Manoj takes us through a forward-thinking vision of how much better our designed businesses can be if we approach them with the tenets of empathy, story, embracing failure, and holistic systems thinking. It is the perfect way to end this book, as it incorporates elements of each of the preceding chapters and then challenges us to do some serious envisioning work.

We conclude the book leaving you with expansive awareness about what you can do to actualize strategic design—and by extension, strategic design thinking—in your studies, your businesses, and your communities.

7 Transition Design: System Shifting

Sarah B. Brooks

Sarah B. Brooks

Sarah B. Brooks is a designer, researcher, and advocate for social change. For the past fifteen years Sarah has worked with the corporate world, nonprofits, and foundations, leading product development and multidisciplinary creative teams through initiatives across sectors, including food systems, health care, media, education, finance, and civic innovation. In addition to her practice work, Sarah is a frequent speaker, writer, educator, and active design community organizer around the theme of design for social innovation and living systems. Sarah is currently serving as a White House Presidential Innovation fellow at Veterans Affairs, using service design to improve the lives of veterans.

Focusing Question: What are comprehensive, living, and adaptive systems approaches to designing for resilience?

This chapter explores the key questions:

- How does a deeper understanding of systems thinking and complexity change the design process and practice?
- What role do strategic designers have in shaping a more resilient future?
- How can you as a designer participate in strategic design?
- What are some examples of people making meaningful strategic design interventions in systems?

Unintended Consequences

On Midway Atoll, a remote cluster of islands more than 2,000 miles from the nearest continent, nesting albatross chicks are fed lethal quantities of plastic by their parents who mistake floating trash for food as they forage over the vast polluted Pacific Ocean (see Figure 7.1). Their flight path traverses what is called the Great Pacific Garbage Patch, a trash vortex roughly twice the size of Texas. Although dumping of industrial, nuclear, and other waste into the world's oceans was made illegal in the 1970s, it continues today. Nearly 90 percent of the floating marine litter is plastic: polyethylene, polypropylene, Styrofoam, nylon, and saran—all materials that do not biodegrade (Weiss 2006).

Figure 7.1 Image of bird's digestive cavity, from Chris Jordan's photographic essay "Midway: Message from the Gyre."
Courtesy of Chris Jordan.

The fate of a full third of the baby albatross chicks is sealed. These chicks don't make it to maturity because their bellies are so full of plastic that they can't absorb enough nutrients to grow. This sad situation is one direct result of the deep interconnectedness of our global economy and ecology—a negative unintended consequence of industrial production and consumption.

We commonly speak of throwing things away. But where is away? Away is magical thinking, a denial of painful knowledge. How does this magical thinking contribute to the problem of unintended consequences? There is a constant flow of material things into and out of our lives. Many people are increasingly thoughtful about sharing items on a personal and community scale, or buying used items to reduce consumption. On a global scale, some corporations are moving toward design for disassembly and reuse. The most progressive companies are reaching beyond reuse to explore regenerative design materials, which can improve or add nutrients to the biosphere with use. And yet, today, we remain in a predicament where there are millions (if not billions) of manufactured items made with a complex mixture of toxic chemicals that are not easily reusable or biodegradable. Everything that passes through our waste-disposal systems ends up someplace else. Plastics that end up in the ocean get passed gut to gut between sea animals, like the albatross parents who feed debris to their chicks. This happens far away from where most of us will see these effects in our daily lives, but it happens every day. This is the way interconnections work.

Invisible Interconnections

Unintended consequences of our global economy are often invisible in the daily life of the bustling modern world, and often actors that play a role in creating these problems aren't faced with the aftermath of their behaviors. That is, unless we're living in the majority world. The *majority world* is a term advocated by Bangladeshi photographer Shahidul Alam to represent what has formerly been referred to as the "third world" (see Figure 7.2). The majority world, representing most of humankind, reckons with the effects of Western lifestyles from which there are often no easy retreats from polluted and dangerously toxic environments (Alam 2014). The invisibility of the predicament is simply the failure to see the entirety of our systems at work.

Between our knowledge and our everyday actions there are gaps, blind spots, and perverse incentives that keep us ignoring nuanced interconnections, and looping in destructive patterns that put our very existence at risk.

The 2008 financial crisis typifies our society's magical thinking. Financial firms that grew too quickly in the early 2000s were overextended and on the verge of collapse, yet considered "too big to fail," and as such, they received bailouts of government funds raised from US taxpayers. The infusion of money did not solve the root problem; rather than redesign a resilient financial system, we made an investment in a broken system that bolstered banks and relieved them of the repercussions of their actions, while taxpayers, some of whom lost their life savings, were tapped to pay the cost of the consequences.

At this scale, players at one end of the spectrum aren't always tangibly or visibly linked to the consequences of their actions, consequences that ripple across the globe quickly and dangerously. Interconnectedness is experienced from a variety of vantage points: Some see the sources; some see the midpoints; and some see just the end results of these system-wide processes, just as the trash creators who throw their Styrofoam lunch cup into the garbage never see the thousands of baby birds dying from that same trash consumption.

Pioneering systems thinker Dennis Meadows explained, "When you see whole systems, you start noticing where things come from and where they go. You begin to see that there is no 'away' to throw

Figure 7.2 Shahidul Alam
Courtesy of Rahnuma Ahmed/Drik/Majority World.

things to" (Wilkinson 2001). Everything and everyone is connected to everything and everyone else. We live our lives in contexts of overlapping systems that influence and affect one another.

Particular Challenges in Our Overlapping Systems

The story of the albatross bird is one example of an unintended consequence in the biosphere; yet these challenges are also social and economic. Some of these can be organized into larger ***particular challenges***—challenges of population growth, income disparity, the misaligned weight on gross domestic product (GDP) as a measuring device, a failure to hold businesses accountable on the social and ecological level, and a rapidly changing set of energy and climate problems. This list is suggestive and by no means comprehensive; the following particular problems are examples that begin to indicate the scale within which we're working and how interrelated social and environmental systems are:

Population Growth

Exponential global population growth puts intense pressure on natural resources and infrastructure. Felt acutely in cities, where the majority of the world's population lives, urban communities struggle to provide enough affordable housing, sanitation, education, public transportation, and economic opportunities for these waves of new residents. Lacking better options, informal housing and economies spring up and contribute to the growth of the world's largest slums, including Neza-Chalco-Itza in Mexico City, Mexico; Dharavi in Mumbai, India; and Khayelitsha in Cape Town, South Africa (Tovrov 2011). Middle-class people in cities also feel the pinch around educational access, soaring rents, and a lack of affordable housing stock.

Income Disparity

There are deep inequities in the global distribution of wealth: 0.7 percent of the world's adult population control 41 percent of the world's wealth (Credit Suisse 2013). Furthermore, income disparity is on the rise globally, deepening social and political tensions. The majority world lives in poverty, and struggles for access to basic necessities such as education, health care and economic opportunity. The challenge of poverty is complex—no single intervention will solve every related problem; instead, the question becomes how do various policy and design interventions exacerbate or alleviate this issue?

Businesses without Consequences

The twentieth century saw the rise of corporatism and an optimistic attitude about business and government leading progress and serving the social needs of the many. Today, multinational corporations have overwhelming and unprecedented power over governments and are legally mandated to maximize shareholder return every quarter, without any accountability for the consequences of increasing that business's profitability. Problems such as climate change, species extinction, biodiversity loss, and human rights violations are neither part of the metric nor the conversation about the actions or value of institutions; they are considered externalities. As a result, there is not yet a holistic picture—or economic measure—for the socio-ecological cost of doing business.

An Exclusive Focus on Growth (GDP) as the Measure of Economic Health

A country's GDP is intended to show the total activity within an economy; however, when both positive and negative developments are counted in GDP, this metric forms an incomplete and often misleading picture. On the plus side, GDP metrics include health gains from new medical procedures and increases to quality of life in cities from new green spaces. Yet on the negative side, things like paying for more police in dangerous neighborhoods or rebuilding disaster-damaged infrastructure are also seen as net positive behaviors, despite being the result of damaged social and ecological infrastructure. While GDP remains the standard index in the United States, Bhutan's Gross

National Happiness measure (Centre for Bhutan Studies & GNH Research 2010), the Human Development Index (United Nations 2014), and the Social Progress Index (Social Progress Imperative 2014) are examples of newer alternative indicators that attempt to capture a more comprehensive picture of overall well-being.

Energy Needs and Climate Change

As our global population grows exponentially, so does the demand for energy and the imperative to switch to clean renewable-energy sources. The Stern Review on the global economics of climate change in 2006 stated: "Climate change is the greatest market failure the world has ever seen, and it interacts with other market imperfections ... Climate change demands an international response, based on a shared understanding of long-term goals and agreement on frameworks for action" (Stern 2007: viii). Recent data indicate that what was once seen as a future problem has already arrived (Davenport 2014).

Are These Even "Problems"?

The list of global challenges and their personal, community, and global consequences is longer than the short list here. Yet beneath these "problems" lies a mode of thinking—a system—that may inaccurately set the stage for attempting to find one-off solutions. The word "problem" is in itself problematic: It insists on a solution and suggests that we can neatly tidy up and fix each mess in its appropriate corner of the globe.

These deeply interconnected, complex challenges are larger than any one, or even a few solutions. In addition, it's profoundly difficult to understand the root causes of each challenge. At best, we each get a snapshot from the limited vantage point of our particular disciplines, bringing the mindsets, tool sets, and approaches that we've learned from our educational and professional backgrounds.

What is the deeper issue at the heart of our approach to each of these challenges that makes them so persistent despite the very best efforts of many disciplines? Perhaps it isn't rooted in a need to look more closely at the problem; instead, perhaps it is indicative of a biased worldview. Do we rely on a fundamental orientation to the world that prevents us from working more effectively with our challenges and more harmoniously with each other?

GO DEEPER

Read the following:
- *Poor Economics: A Radical Rethinking of the Way to Fight Global Poverty* by A. V. Banerjee and E. Duflo.
- *The Sixth Extinction: An Unnatural History* by E. Kolbert.
- *Oil and Honey: The Education of an Unlikely Activist* by B. McKibben.
- *Development as Freedom* by A. Sen.
- *Stern Review on the Economics of Climate Change* by N. Stern.

REFLECTIONS
- What behaviors are "throw away" behaviors in your own life?

- Have you seen people do things with unanticipated consequences? What were the consequences, and who felt the results of these actions?
- What global challenges affect your daily life?
- How might you expand the frame of a business challenge to include consideration of the broader social and ecological systems that challenge is nested within?
- What do you see as the root cause of the challenge you're most concerned about?
- Do the "5 whys exercise." When looking for a root cause of a system challenge, ask why you think the challenge is so. Ask why of each answer four more times, to peel back successive layers of the challenge.

The Clockwork Universe

"The universe is but a watch on a larger scale."
—Bernard de Fontenelle, 1686

Have you ever wondered why people ask a colleague to "give me the 'download' on your conversation"? Or why we talk about something being "broken"? Underneath this language is a deep metaphor that goes beyond colloquialisms. It has defined entire disciplines and shaped the current systemic crises in which we find ourselves.

For over 300 years, Western worldviews have grown from the metaphor of the clock—an underlying belief that has had a profound effect on design approaches of systems from economics to education,

health care, and governance. The metaphor emerged from the late-seventeenth-century European Age of Enlightenment thought, during the birth of modern science, when René Descartes and Sir Isaac Newton were making observations in fundamental physics.

Prior to the birth of the scientific revolution, early cultures correlated their lives with the solar, lunar, and seasonal rhythms of sun and moon. Evidence of this exists in depictions of sun gods in pre-Columbian art and Celtic stone circles, such as Stonehenge, which are thought to have served as early calendars. Early civilizations realized that the rhythms of the universe gave them insights into wet seasons, herd migrations, and changing temperatures. In short, survival depended upon one's alignment with the rhythms of nature.

Centuries later, natural philosophers, looking for deeper insights into nature, began to describe the universe as a clock. The consistent cycles of the sun and planets reminded them of the repetitious movement of a clock's gears (see Figure 7.3). As the universe became, in their view, a clock, God became the Great Watchmaker.

Rather than transfer nature's characteristics to the clock, natural philosophers transferred the clock's characteristics to nature. The clock was something an engineer could take apart and understand through its constituent parts. Its motions are repetitive and its actions fully predictable. Hence, one can have perfect knowledge about how the clock works, what it can and will do, and what it communicates. Unlike the sun, moon, or any other

Figure 7.3 Face of the famous astrological clock in Prague
Stock photo © Catmacey.

previous measuring device in nature, clocks divide time into precise units. As such, natural philosophers saw all things in the universe as exhibiting regular motion and made of component parts that could be disassembled and reassembled—even fixed.

To see the universe infused with such characteristics was deeply reassuring because it meant the universe was measurable, which meant it was knowable, predictable, and ultimately, controllable. It was not long before great thinkers began seeking these clock characteristics in societies,

economies, businesses, the body, and the psyche. The world and everything in it was a clock—or more generally—a machine.

This worldview framed the ideas, philosophies, and models that led to the Industrial Revolution in the mid-nineteenth century and drove many businessmen, philosophers, and economists to design business processes and theories in the likeness of machinery. In fact, this approach became the basis of neoclassical economic theory, which uses many of the mechanical ideas from physics to inform the shape of economies.

In viewing society or even businesses as a giant machine, people, by extension, were expected to behave like machines and be constantly working to produce revenue and growth. Unfortunately, this idea ignored the reality that nothing in the world can sustain infinite growth. When businesses and the people who are a part of them are viewed only as machines, the magical thinking that they can grow infinitely is possible only because of a lost sense of the limits and interconnections within the system.

As a result, this places people in more competition for resources, while being confronted with the reality that our planet doesn't have the ability to support infinite growth. The adoption of a mechanistic, clockwork worldview has almost completely obscured the vision of interdependency practiced by many indigenous traditions.

Thankfully, people today are waking up to the limitations of the clockwork mind-set, understanding that our frameworks for understanding the world are influencing our ability to address the complexity of the challenges we face. The discipline of systems thinking provides a way forward.

GO DEEPER

Read the following:

- *Predictably Irrational: The Hidden Forces That Shape Our Decisions* by D. Ariely.
- *The Clockwork Universe: Isaac Newton, the Royal Society and the Birth of the Modern World* by E. Dolnick.
- *Thinking, Fast and Slow* by D. Kahneman.

- *History of Western Philosophy* by B. Russell.

REFLECTIONS

- What are some of your world-views, and do you know where they originated?
- Can you see evidence of clockwork thinking within your own life and routine?
- How might you uncover the world-views of colleagues in a business environment? And how might that affect the depth of inquiry on a project you're undertaking?
- What other metaphor(s) would you use to describe the way the world works?

Systems Thinking

In his work *Principia* (1687) Sir Isaac Newton warned that his calculations for the laws of motion only hold up if there are one or two planets orbiting around the sun—not if there are lots of other planets and celestial bodies also in orbit. He recognized that his thinking was limited and only worked in isolation, not with many things interacting together as a larger whole. This is true of all mechanistic thinking. It has limited use when applied to larger, organic systems because it cannot explain the what, how, or why of them.

Systems thinking is a broad discipline concerned with the what, how, and why of individual, interconnected elements interacting with each other together. This process of inquiry emerged in the twentieth century, cutting across many fields, including physics, mathematics, computer science, ecology, sociology, engineering, and management. The most fundamental idea in systems thinking is that everything and everyone is connected to everything and everyone else across all scales and that the system is greater than the sum of its parts. It accounts for the complexity of interrelationships of parts within systems.

System Types: Simple, Complicated, Complex Adaptive, and Chaotic

There are many different types of systems, each with their own dynamics and capabilities required to work effectively within them: simple, complicated, complex adaptive and chaotic.

Simple systems do one thing; for example, a pendulum swings, or a hammer sets a nail into a block of wood.

Complicated systems have clear problems that can be solved with knowable variables. Planning the waste collection for an entire city is complicated. It requires the coordinated action of city bureaus creating a blueprint for how waste will be collected and sorted; it requires the communication of clear schedules and provision of bins to residents and commercial properties. There are many logistical challenges and clear cause and effect relationships. For example, if collectors go on strike, trash accumulates and disrupts the everyday life and activities of the city. The parts and pieces that need to seamlessly interact are known, even though they are many. This does not mean they are immune to failure. The mechanistic mind-set is an appropriate metaphor for understanding processes within complicated systems.

Complex adaptive systems (CAS) are different from simple or complicated systems. They defy a problem/solution orientation. They are predicaments with places for interventions that will have greater or lesser leverage and impact. Examples of CAS at various scales include a cell, a person, a family, a community, the global economy, violence, and poverty. These predicaments have an infinite number of variables that cannot necessarily be known; they have no central controller dictating the actions of those variables and have no clear cause and effect between the variables. These CAS play out against a backdrop of ever-shifting psychological, social, ecological, political, and economic influences.

Working within CAS requires systems thinking: constant learning and adaptation to shifting influences, the ability to hold multiple perspectives simultaneously, the ability to tolerate ambiguity and deal with conflict, an understanding of the individual system elements and the relationships between them, and the ability to identify where there are leverage points to act. Further, working within CAS requires long-term thinking. Effects of interventions may not become clearly evident for years. A common pitfall of working with these types of challenges is pushing the system in the wrong direction and getting more of the same dynamics the interventions were meant to shift.

Chaotic systems are highly sensitive to initial conditions, meaning that a single action in one part of a system causes a chain of events that lead to large-scale phenomena across that system, referred to as the butterfly effect. Complex systems that act predictably for some period of time can shift into a mode of behavior that follows different rules. We can see this chaotic behavior in the stock market shifts between bull and bear markets, but predicting these changes is extremely difficult.

Knowing the type of a system within which you are working helps to understand the types of approaches that may be more or less fruitful for the change you want to make in that system. Perhaps complexity, if better understood, can become a design tool in itself—and provide a set of design principles to address these complex challenges.

GO DEEPER

Read the following:
- *Thinking in Systems* by D. Meadows.
- *Complexity: A Guided Tour* by M. Mitchell.
- *The Fifth Discipline* by P. Senge.
- *The Black Swan* by N. Taleb.

REFLECTIONS
- What type of systems are you most commonly working within? What are the qualities that differentiate them?
- What type of systems are you most interested in exploring further?

- Leverage points in a system are places where a small shift in one thing can produce big changes in everything. See Donella Meadows's essay, "Leverage Points: Places to Intervene in a System," on donellameadows.org, for a full explanation of why this dynamic is so prevalent, and how it works.
- How might you apply an understanding of systems thinking in your work and in your personal growth?
- What other examples can you think of for simple, complicated, complex adaptive, and chaotic systems?

Digging Deeper into Complex Adaptive Systems

The body is a great example of a complex adaptive system. We can observe this in the way healing occurs after a cut or a scrape. We can see this pattern echoed in communities who work together to rebuild after natural disasters. Complex adaptive systems are distinguished by their ability to adapt to the changing environment in ways that increase their survivability—hence their relevance for strategic design and resilience. Since humans, the natural world, and our most vexing challenges are CAS—or living systems—we'll spend some time focusing on them.

Let's look a little more in depth at some of the key properties of CAS.

Self-organizing system components organize themselves to act as a coherent whole, without the benefit of a central or outside controller.

- An ecological example: Schools of fish moving in unison without any leader.
- A social example: A crowd of people at a concert who decide to give the performer a standing ovation. No one tells them to do it, but there is a wave of the same activity among individuals that happens nearly instantaneously.

Feedback mechanisms produce and use information and signals from both their internal and external environments. A feedback loop is composed of a signal from one component of the system, which passes through other elements of the system, and then returns to the original component.

Negative feedback loops send signals that tend to reduce changes and promote stability, while *positive feedback loops* send signals that tend to amplify changes and can create runaway scenarios. The use of the terms "positive" and "negative" do not imply that the consequences of the feedback are either good or bad but rather that there is an increase or decrease of the behavior or outcome.

- An ecological example (negative feedback loops): An increase in predators results in a decrease of prey. The decrease of prey then results in a decrease of predators.
- A social example (negative feedback loops): The amount of money in our bank account each month limits the amount we can spend. If we reach zero dollars, the bank will stop cashing our checks or allowing us to withdraw money from the ATM. If we have limitless access to credit and no incentives

for more mindful spending, we are in danger of getting into a negative feedback loop of debt.
- An ecological example (positive feedback loops): Farmers use pesticides to reduce the presence of insects on crops. Over time, the insects evolve and become resistant to the pesticides, so farmers increases their use of pesticides, which further increases the resistance of the insects and weakens the effectiveness of the pesticides.
- A social example (positive feedback loops): Rents are expensive in the city you live in. It's a fun dynamic place to live, the news is always full of stories about how great it is, and it has excellent career opportunities. People flock there, which drives up the competition between potential renters, often driving up the price of rent.

Emergent phenomena are new occurrences or behaviors that arise within a system.

- An ecological example: The flocking behavior of birds is an emergent property of the birds interacting with each other.
- A social example: In response to the constant stream of information on Twitter, and lack of functionality in the software that would allow people to search and surface information on a particular term, one twitter user, Chris Messina, began using a hashtag symbol preceding a term to increase "findability" through search—for example, #emergence. This behavior caught on within the network, and it is still the

primary mechanism for finding trending topics that reflect the zeitgeist of Twitter on any given day (Edwards 2013).

Networks are a collection of nodes connected by links. The nodes are the individual elements (whether birds, people, or packets of information), and the links are the connection between them: sensory information, social relationships, and communication mechanisms.

- An ecological example: Mycelium are fungi found in and on soil, and they play a vital role in increasing water and nutrient absorption, providing an invertebrate food source, and decomposing plant material. There is a mycelial network in eastern Oregon noted to be the largest organism on earth, with an underground network spanning 2,400 acres.
- A social example: Social networks on the internet connect people's common interests and goals. People use those networks to strengthen their ties.

Nonlinear is when the output of the system is not proportional to the input.

- An ecological example: An avalanche, an earthquake, mudslides, and populations of rabbits all grow exponentially.
- A social example: The outputs in phenomena such as HIV/AIDS and art movements can be far greater than the initial inputs.

Adaptive cycles and thresholds explain how systems behave over time and remain resilient. Thresholds represent transitions between alternate states of systems. When a threshold is crossed, it is called a regime change. Regime changes create lasting effects in a system's structure and function. These can be difficult to reverse and often seem to arise abruptly.

- An ecological example: Global mass extinctions, such as the dinosaurs, or a more localized example, such as the destruction of a coral reef, occur over time.
- A social example: Organizations also follow cycles of growth. Large organizations are less able to move quickly and can find their long-standing market share leapfrogged or made irrelevant by a start-up. Method home-cleaning products, a company started by two Stanford University graduates, disrupted the long-standing dominance of conventional products from larger consumer products companies, causing them to scramble to develop their own more ecologically friendly products.

System resilience depends on *redundancy*—employing multiple system elements to provide the same system functions and prevent the fragility that is created when there is a single point of failure. In a resilient system, if one part fails, other parts can pick up the slack. This is why machines are typically not resilient—they don't have redundancy. If you take out one gear, the machine breaks down.

- An ecological example: Biotic pollination of plants is accomplished by hundreds of types of insects and birds, including bees, bats, butterflies, and hummingbirds.

- A social example: If a community was truly a machine, everyone would have a unique role to play in that machine, and you wouldn't have overlap between people's functions. If you had only one doctor, who would care for the needs of the entire community? If something happened to that person, society would lack health care because no one else would have that knowledge. Having knowledge and skill maintained by numerous individuals in the community makes community health resilient.

Better Design Using Frameworks for Complex Adaptive Systems

The global predicaments outlined earlier in this chapter exist in part because our traditional methods of understanding and addressing intrinsically complex issues are not working. In contrast to a traditional reductionist method that frames neat problems and solutions, in CAS there is no single solution. Instead, the opportunity for action lies in taking small bets to test interventions, observing outcomes, and adjusting accordingly. Systems thinking, and more specifically, grasping the particular dynamics of CAS—from feedback mechanisms to emergent phenomena and how redundancy creates resilience—adds an important skill and tool set to our practice, and better equips designers and businesses for the increasingly complex challenges they are being asked to consider.

Although each of the examples above separate social and ecological phenomena to illustrate particular system dynamics, in reality we need to remember that the social and ecological are deeply and fundamentally integrated. Every intervention we consider has repercussions and effects for the natural world and for society. And everything we do in society is enabled by nature—from the materials we source to the air we breathe while sourcing materials. Fortunately, several designers throughout the past century have illustrated this comprehensive approach to CAS.

GO DEEPER

Read the following:
- *Biomimicry: Innovation Inspired by Nature* by J. Benyus.
- *Predicting the Unpredictable* by E. Bonabeau.
- "The Intelligent Plant" by M. Pollan.
- *Resilience Thinking* by B. Walker and D. Salt.

REFLECTIONS
- The body is one example of a large system with interdependent subsystems, such as the skeletal, muscular, nervous, and respiratory. Choose a system that interests you—food, education, health care, global economy—and map out the various elements, the relationships between those elements, and how they work together as a whole to produce the effects that they do. Check your analysis with various experts within the system and see what kind

of feedback you get. Do people agree on how the system works? If not, note where the key differences are and identify the factors that may be influencing those differences.

- Can you draw your complex adaptive system or make a 3D model of it? What types of insights does it generate to visualize the system in these ways?
- Can you identify leverage points for change within that complex system? What are they, and how would you utilize them?

Comprehensivist Precedents

Where are the precedents for thinking and action that restores the dynamic interplay between socioecological systems, technology, design, and economics? This thinking can be characterized as **comprehensivist**: that which is inclusive. It both complements and aligns the mechanistic worldview with the living system-based worldview in service of human needs and biosphere health.

Three examples of comprehensivists who have deployed efforts to change mindsets and paradigms by expanding society's thinking, decisions, and actions are R. Buckminster Fuller, E. F. Schumacher, and Rachel Carson.

R. Buckminster Fuller was a polymath who worked across the fields of design, architecture, geometry, science, engineering, cartography, and education. Born in 1892 in Massachusetts, he probed the deep underlying patterns of the universe and worked actively and prolifically until his death in 1983.

Known commonly as Bucky, he resisted categorization, instead referring to himself as a "comprehensive anticipatory design scientist," and our planet "spaceship earth" (Fuller & Kuromiya 1992). Deeply distressed about the death of his young daughter from polio, which he felt was caused by their poor living conditions, he became inspired to work on better housing conditions for everyone. This led to much exploration with geometric form, looking for the strongest patterns, and an effort to do more with less. The geodesic dome is his most known exploration in this vein. The dome is shaped from a lattice of interlocking icosahedrons that form a very light and stable sphere.

Fuller understood well the resistance that incumbent systems and the status quo provide when you attempt to shift them. On this point, Fuller was credited to have had this admonition: "You never change things by fighting the existing reality. To change something, build a new model that makes the existing model obsolete." He did not feel that it was necessary for us to escape society, technology, and machinery. He saw the challenge as being one of how we choose to use and deploy these tools. He was an optimist who believed that if we choose to take the technology we created and obey the laws of nature, we would find ourselves able to take care of every human on the planet.

His many contributions continue to inspire and impact generations of designers. The Buckminster Fuller award is an annual international design challenge that grants $100,000 USD to the most comprehensive solution to a pressing global challenge that seeks to make the world work for 100 percent of humanity.

E. F. (Fritz) Schumacher, an economist born in 1911 and working through the mid-twentieth century, was also deeply challenging to the status quo in his field. He advocated for a rebalancing of values and respect for all beings in the creation of our technology and societies. Introduced in his book *Small Is Beautiful* (1973), the idea of "appropriate technology" emphasizes applications that are small-scale, decentralized, energy efficient, environmentally sound, and locally controlled. The root of the idea is credited to Mahatma Gandhi, who advocated for small, local, and village-based technology in India to help villages become self-reliant. Schumacher (1973: 275) argues that in our excitement for science and technology, we built a system of production that is harmful to ecology and culture. And in our prioritization of money over all else, we overlook the importance of nonmaterial values, such as justice, harmony, beauty, or even health—the need for which cannot be erased. He was an early advocate for resisting dependence on the finite resource of fossil fuel.

Schumacher University was founded in 1990 in Devon, England, inspired by E. F. Schumacher's ways of thinking. It teaches whole-systems perspectives to emerging leaders focused on social and environmental challenges through a variety of graduate programs. His notion of appropriate technology continues to ripple through the design community today, exemplified by those focusing on the needs of the majority world.

Rachel Carson, a contemporary of R. Buckminster Fuller, was born in Pennsylvania in 1907. She studied marine biology, zoology, and genetics at Pennsylvania College for Women (now Chatham University). After her start writing for *The Baltimore Sun* and other newspapers, she went on to write a series of influential novels that brought her deep understanding of science to modern readers in a way that was engaging and approachable. Her seminal book *Silent Spring* (1962) explored the dangers of synthetic pesticides in a way that captured public imagination and provoked a national conversation that led to policy change—namely a ban on the agricultural use of DDT by the Kennedy administration. She remained passionately engaged with the issue throughout her life. The book is widely credited with helping to launch the environmental movement in the United States and the establishment of the Environmental Protection Agency.

These comprehensivist thinkers and designers display the type of broad vision, deep empathy, moral courage, and practical exploration that all designers can take inspiration from, particularly if we want to shift systems. Swimming against the stream of "business-as-usual" modalities requires time, patience, and persistence. It also requires a deep level of self-awareness, commitment to personal growth, maturity, and tenacity.

GO DEEPER
Read the following:
- *Buckminster Fuller: Poet of Geometry* by C. Gerst.
- *The Business Solution to Poverty* by P. Polak and M. Warwick.
- *Design for the Other 90%* by C. Smith.
- The Buckminster Fuller Challenge: http://bfi.org/challenge

REFLECTIONS
- Who else would you add to this chapter's list of comprehensivist thinkers?
- Why does that person inspire you? What qualities does s/he bring to their work that you admire?
- What makes design comprehensivist to you?
- What examples of comprehensivist approaches to market-based challenges can you think of?

A Starting Set of Principles

Through an understanding of systems thinking and the qualities of CAS, we can begin to expand our design principles and add approaches and tools that are comprehensive in their approach and use them in service of participatory and inclusive strategic design that strengthens empathy, trust, and relationships.

Can we begin to distill the comprehensivist approach into a set of principles that intentionally designs with interconnectedness and complexity in mind? My colleague David McConville and I assembled a starting set of principles and

first presented them at a SOCAP Europe conference workshop in Malmo, Sweden, in 2012 as a prompt for consideration. These principles synthesize ecological and resilience thinking of many practitioners and take a humanistic stance toward the breadth and scope of these challenges.

Principles of resilient design (Brooks & McConville 2012):

1. Encourage open collaboration across disciplines, embracing multiple perspectives and moving beyond silos of specialization and pillars of power.
2. Consider the implications and limitations of the pursuit of scale, and draw wide enough margins that the failure of one solution does not imply the impossibility of another.
3. Solve for whole systems. Look deeply at the chain of causality from particular actions, and thoughtfully do your best to prevent unwanted consequences.
4. Include voices at the margins and build relationships.
5. Make previously invisible patterns visible and then build on them.
6. Emulate nature's principles and improve the balances, symmetries, and harmonies within a pattern.
7. Design for short feedback loops between prototyping and iterating, making sure failures are useful for learning.
8. Recognize that there is no silver bullet and that searching for one is folly.

9. Look for nuanced solutions that evolve, adapt, and modify.
10. Acknowledge that we can never know it all and reason cannot be our savior.
11. Acknowledge that uncertainty is ever-present, as is ignorance. There are limits to our knowledge.
12. Encourage trust in intuition. A gut instinct is a powerful thing.

We recognize that creating change is difficult. People are reluctant to change even when faced with information that change is warranted. Yet shifting systems requires nudging people who shape these systems to change behaviors, which is where the power of design enters. If we design systems that nudge different, healthier behaviors, people will change their minds to resolve that cognitive dissonance. Behavior change that leads to greater system resilience is grown into existence, not imposed.

GO DEEPER
Read the following:
- *Predictably Irrational: The Hidden Forces That Shape Our Decisions* by D. Ariely.
- *The Unsettling of America: Culture and Agriculture* by W. Berry.
- *Design for the Real World* by V. Papanek.
- Living Building Challenge: http://living-future.org/lbc

REFLECTIONS
- What principles of resilient design would you add to the list?

- Where can you find examples of these principles in your work?
- What is a change in your own behavior you've made recently?
- What old ideas did you have to let go of in order to make that change?
- What are ways in which you might make previously invisible patterns visible and build on them when designing a new service?

The Strategic Design Framework

Knowing that change is difficult, when does a designer decide to take action without being caught in a theoretical merry-go-round? How do we know when and where to intervene or suggest change?

There are multiple pathways for strategic designers across all areas of practice that want to play an explicit role in designing change toward a healthier and more equitable society. No one way is inherently more valuable than another.

The **strategic design framework**, developed by a group of design educators at the 2013 Winterhouse Symposium for Design Education and Social Change, is intended to help practitioners see various possible pathways for designers to engage, create, and affect change within the global set of inter-related and complex challenges—from the scale of small individual interventions all the way to cross-sector efforts (see Figure 7.4).

In the following two case studies, we will look at how designers can create meaningful output within projects aimed at local cultural change, or as part of a larger movement toward global system shifting.

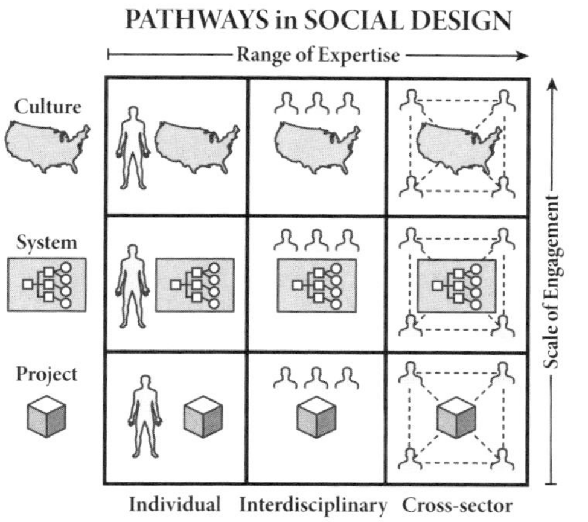

PATHWAYS in SOCIAL DESIGN

Figure 7.4 Pathways in social design
Creative Commons Attribution 3.0 Unported License.

Case Study 1. Individual Culture Change: Theaster Gates, Dorchester Projects

Background

Theaster Gates is a multidisciplinary artist living and working in Chicago (see Figures 7.5 and 7.6). A native of the West side, he has an educational background in urban planning, religion, and pottery, and he is known for fluidly transitioning between the worlds of community interventionist, artifact creator, performance artist, educator, university administrator, and entrepreneur.

Born in 1973, Gates grew up in a large family, attended undergraduate and graduate school at Iowa State, and traveled to South Africa for graduate studies and to Japan for a ceramics fellowship. After several years working for the Chicago Transit Authority as an arts planner, he had his first solo art exhibit at the Hyde Park Art

Center in 2008; he has been on a bullet train of productivity and recognition since. He has had exhibitions at the Whitney Biennial, Punta della Dogana, Venice; Documenta 13, Whitechapel Gallery, London; and Museum of Contemporary Art, Chicago. He has an academic appointment as the director of arts and public life at the University of Chicago. Through his art and exhibitions, he is affecting change at the community and cultural levels.

The Challenge

Gates is concerned with issues of inequality, availability of resources, violence, and self-identity. About his work, he says:

> I was always making art that was asking questions about the city, and why the city functioned the way it did. How does cultural and economic disparity happen? How can we fight it? I was trying to

Figure 7.5 Theaster Gates's Dorchester Projects in Chicago
Courtesy of Theaster Gates; photo by Sara Pooley.

Figure 7.6 Theaster Gates speaks to workshop participants at the Listening House in Chicago
Courtesy of Theaster Gates; photo by Sara Pooley.

present these questions in the form of little abandoned ceramic houses and drawings or performances that spoke to the issue. And I just got tired of pointing a finger at it and wanted to actually do something about it, challenge it in a real way. (Creative States 2013)

Gates wanted to do more than make art that told a story—he wanted to affect change in his neighborhoods and community.

The Intervention: A Group of Renovated Previously Abandoned Homes

Gates lives in the Greater Grand Crossing neighborhood on the South Side of Chicago. Beginning in 2006, he purchased and renovated a series of houses that had been previously abandoned, known as the Dorchester Projects.

The houses include the Listening House, the first house he purchased, which contains a large record collection from the Dr. Wax record shop; the Archive House, which contains 14,000 art, architecture, and design books from the Prairie Avenue bookstore and 60,000 glass slides from the University of Chicago; the Black Cinema House; the Dorchester Arts House collaborative; and a large warehouse Gates will be using as a studio.

Archive House is open on Sundays every other week for anyone who wants to come and look at the books. On the interval weeks, Black Cinema House screens films, and there are a variety of other workshops and programs for the community, which are always free. The youth programming, in particular, is geared toward neighborhood residents.

The Outcome

This is his best-known social practice project. Kate Hadley Williams, Gates's studio manager, notes that part of the impact of the Dorchester Projects is the change in people's perceptions of what the neighborhood is like, and how the project creates an opening for people to come to the neighborhood and interact.

The project has taken abandoned spaces and made them active and beautiful, strengthening community ties in the process. Gates's work at the University of Chicago and his other art practices sit alongside the work in the Dorchester Projects, showing his range of engagement in creative practice. Hadley Williams is struck by Gates's feeling that one doesn't need to define oneself by a singular facet of creativity. Varied experiences can serve each other and are worth pursuing (Brooks & Williams 2014). Gates's work harkens back to that of the artist Joseph Beuys, who created the term "social sculpture" to describe the idea that a work of art can be a practical social action with lasting ripples through culture.

Case Study 2. Interdisciplinary Systems Change: Reos Partners & Rocky Mountain Institute

The Background

Reos is a global social innovation consultancy that organizes, designs, and facilitates multi-stakeholder change processes with business, government, and civil society organizations. Founded in 2007, it has worked on initiatives such as growing mainstream

Figure 7.7 Participants in the eLab at Rocky Mountain Institute use Legos to prototype concepts for research project on redistributing energy resources.
Courtesy of Rocky Mountain Institute. © 2014.

sustainable food chains, reducing child malnutrition in India, supporting aboriginal health in Australia, and envisioning postwar futures in Guatemala.

The Challenge

One of its current projects, the Electricity Innovation Lab (eLab), is a multistakeholder interdisciplinary group that's been convened by the Rocky Mountain Institute (see Figure 7.7). The stakeholders include renewable grid and distributed resource providers, energy customers and investors, advocates, utility companies, regulators, and grid operators. Group members generated three key research questions when they began their work together:

1. How can we understand and effectively communicate the real costs and values of distributed energy resources as part of the electricity system?
2. How can we better align regulatory frameworks, pricing structures, and business models in the electricity sector to enable varied solutions that yield the greatest value to customers and society as a whole?
3. How can we accelerate the pace of economic, distributed resource adaption?

The group is coming together to change how distributed resources, such as solar power and energy efficiency, are developed and integrated into the electricity grid to create a more resilient, affordable, secure, and sustainable electricity system. They know that adversarial and antagonistic positioning between stakeholders on key issues can delay needed changes by decades and that their challenge is one of coordination and collaboration across many players.

The Intervention

They have formed a multiyear social lab where all stakeholders work together on their key questions. They use a variety of methodologies, one of which includes mapping the current situation, via physical modeling with simple materials, and scenario planning in order to envision the possible futures they might create together.

The Outcome

At the end of the first year their outcomes included:

1. A discussion paper exploring the utility business model challenge and suggestions for new models
2. A report exploring the benefits and costs of distributed solar photovoltaic power, to provide a foundation of information to inform new pricing and business model design
3. A collaboration with Fort Collins Utilities that produced a strategy for how the community could reduce its carbon emissions 80 percent by 2030 and also a new proposal for a business model that would allow the utility to help its customers adopt energy efficiency and renewable energies. This

work leveraged net zero energy district work for broader community change
4. A collaboration with the US Navy to identify the value proposition in microgrids

If the lab is successful, this experiment will help to transform the perspectives of the individual players by breaking through emotional and perceptual barriers that will prepare them to work together in ways that were not previously possible. Through experimentation and careful study of all of the stakeholder positions, they can do more than just create new possibilities—they can also shift the way the players perceive each other and work together, resulting in a larger system change.

Using Strategic Design Pathways to Develop Your Career

One of the interesting things recent graduates face when entering the world of work is understanding that both the challenges they want to address—and the type of career they select—are ongoing evolutions. The role of strategic designers is always shifting and changing; likewise, the projects and opportunities a practitioner seeks may not yet be a traditional role. Strategic designers are in the business of finding creative and innovative approaches to an array of challenges, an evolving discipline that is suited to being entrepreneurial and creating one's own niche in a way that is not otherwise readily available. Choosing where to apply your skills and how to become part of the process of change is itself a dynamic process.

GO DEEPER

Read the following:

- *The Social Labs Revolution: A New Approach to Solving our Most Complex Challenges* by Z. Hassan.
- *Transformative Scenario Planning: Working Together to Change the Future* by A. Kahane.
- "Outside the Citadel, Social Practice Art Is Intended to Nurture" by R. Kennedy. Available online: http://nyti.ms/1nnfqsq
- *Getting to Maybe* by F. Westley and M. Patton.

REFLECTIONS

- Are there examples of social practice in your locale?
- How might you engage in a social practice project in your community?
- How might you craft a social practice project with clear business benefit?
- Pick a subject and imagine which players would need to be in attendance to represent all voices of the system?
- What methods do you think could best support your work? Why?
- What other skills could you bring to the mix?

Conclusions: Shifting Systems

We've lived for 400 years with the echo of mechanistic thinking creating the false notion that we can control the natural world. It's now clear that nature cannot be controlled, and in our efforts to do so, we've dilapidated it. The destruction we've wrought is evident around us.

What systems thinking offers is not the comfort of control, but understanding and insight into how nature actually works. By recognizing our place in the larger system of nature, we can appreciate the potential to act in a way that benefits all. If we are to let go of false thinking and false expectations and see the world for what it is, we must think in a bigger way—which we know to be systems thinking.

Rachel Carson started a conversation that awoke us to the shortcomings of our mechanistically designed society. She became a translator for the natural world. It's now time for those with creative and constructive talents to find a joyful dialogue between nature and culture. There is much talk about innovation and collaboration, but really what we need to do the most is *listen*. That is the new design imperative. It is not our duty to invent that which hasn't been invented before. The answers are out there. Nature is constantly telling us what works. It is the lab of innovation. But not enough of us are listening because we think we can do this heroic thing of inventing it ourselves, or together. But that is incorrect. We must listen to nature and collaborate with nature, collectively, for the benefit of all our systems (Figure 7.8).

Samuel Taylor Coleridge, in "The Rime of the Ancient Mariner," bestowed the "bad-luck" image on the albatross. Whomever killed an albatross was doomed. He may have been prescient, but, on the other hand, he may have neglected to consider the adaptability of people—our ability to learn from experience and evidence: The albatross rather than serving as a harbinger of doom may be leading us to our own salvation.

Figure 7.8 An image of what we can preserve if we work collectively with nature: CJ Soaring Albie Midway
Courtesy of Chris Jordan.

Acknowledgments

Thanks to my husband, Freddie Brooks; father, Dr. Leonard Rubin; and friends and colleagues Maggie Hendrie, Leland Maschmeyer, Natalie Nixon, and Sarah Peck, who provided invaluable feedback on drafts of this essay. And to Jeff Barnum, David McConville, and Julie Sammons for conversations that helped shape my perspectives on socioecological systems.

References

Alam, S. (2014), "Shahidul Alam: Photographer/Writer/Curator." Available online: http://www.shahidulalam.com/ (accessed March 17, 2014).

Ariely, D. (2010), *Predictably Irrational: The Hidden Forces That Shape Our Decisions*, New York: Harper Perennial.

Banerjee, A. and E. Duflo (2012), *Poor Economics: A Radical Rethinking of the Way to Fight Global Poverty*, New York: Public Affairs.

Benyus, J. (2002), *Biomimicry: Innovation Inspired by Nature*, New York: Harper Perennial.

Berry, W. (1996), *The Unsettling of America: Culture and Agriculture*, Berkeley, CA: Counterpoint.

Bonabeau, E. (2009), *Predicting the Unpredictable*, Princeton, NJ: Princeton University Press.

Brooks, S. and D. McConville (2012), *Designing Resilience*, SOCAP Europe, June 1, 2012.

Brooks, S., and K. H. Williams (2014), Telephone interview, March 21.

Buckminster Fuller Challenge. Available online: http://bfi.org/challenge

Carson, R. (1962), Silent Spring, Cambridge, MA: Riverside Press.

Creative States (2013), "Theaster Gates: Dorchester Projects," *Creative States: Imagination, Innovation & Inspiration for a Renewed Nation*. Available online: http://www.ourcreativestates.org/articles/gates-redefines-art-of-urban-planning-in-chicago (accessed March 7, 2014).

Credit Suisse (2013), "Global Wealth Databook 2013," Credit Suisse. Available online: https://publications.credit-suisse.com/tasks/render/file/?fileID=1949208D-E59A-F2D9-6D0361266E44A2F8 (accessed March 7, 2014).

Davenport, C. (2014), "Climate Change Deemed Growing Security Threat by Military Researchers," *New York Times*, May 13. Available online: http://nyti.ms/1kiVDL8 (accessed May 19, 2014).

Dolnick, E. (2011), *The Clockwork Universe: Isaac Newton, the Royal Society and the Birth of the Modern World*, New York: Harper.

Edwards, J. (2013), "The Inventor of the Twitter Hashtag Explains Why He Didn't Patent It," *Business Insider*, Nov. 21, 2013. Available online: http://www.businessinsider.com/chris-messina-talks-about-inventing-the-hashtag-on-twitter-2013-11 (accessed July 15, 2015).

Fuller, B. and K. Kuromiya (1992), *Cosmography: A Posthumous Scenario for the Future of Humanity* with Adjuvant Kiyoshi Kuromiya, New York: MacMillan.

Gerst, C. (2013), *Buckminster Fuller: Poet of Geometry*, Portland, OR: Overcup Press.

Centre for Bhutan Studies & GNH Research (2010), "Bhutan Gross National Happiness Index." Available online: http://www.grossnationalhappiness.com/articles/ (accessed May 19, 2014).

Hassan, Z. (2014), *The Social Labs Revolution: A New Approach to Solving Our Most Complex Challenges*, San Francisco: Berrett-Koeler Publishers.

Kahane, A. (2012), *Transformative Scenario Planning: Working Together to Change the Future*, San Francisco: Berrett-Koeler Publishers.

Kahneman, D. (2013), *Thinking, Fast and Slow*, New York: Farrar, Straus and Giroux.

Kennedy, R. (2013), "Outside the Citadel, Social Practice Art Is Intended to Nurture," *New York Times*, March 20, 2013. Available online: http://nyti.ms/1nnfqsq

Kolbert, E. (2015), *The Sixth Extinction: An Unnatural History*, New York: Picador.

Living Building Challenge. Available online: http://living-future.org/lbc

McKibben, B. (2014), *Oil and Honey: The Education of an Unlikely Activist*, New York: St. Martin's Griffin.

Meadows, D. (1997), "Leverage Points: Places to Intervene in a System," www.donellameadows.org. Available online: http://www.donellameadows.org/archives/leverage-points-places-to-intervene-in-a-system/

Meadows, D. (2008), *Thinking in Systems: A Primer*, edited by D. Wright, White River Junction, VT: Chelsea Green Printing.

Mitchell, M. (2011), *Complexity: A Guided Tour*, Oxford: Oxford University Press.

Papanek, V. (2005), *Design for the Real World: Human Ecology and Social Change*, Chicago: Chicago Review Press.

Polak, P. and M. Warwick (2013), *The Business Solution to Poverty*, San Francisco: Berrett-Koeler Publishers.

Pollan, M. (2013), "The Intelligent Plant," *The New Yorker*, December 23, 2013. Available online: http://www.newyorker.com/magazine/2013/12/23/the-intelligent-plant

Russell, B. (1967), *History of Western Philosophy*, New York: Simon & Schuster.

Schumacher, E. F. (1973), *Small Is Beautiful: Economics as If People Mattered*, London: Blond & Briggs.

Sen, A. (2000), *Development as Freedom*, Norwell, MA: Anchor Press.

Senge, P. (1990), *The Fifth Discipline: The Art and Practice of the Learning Organization*, New York: Doubleday Currency.

Smith, C. (2007), *Design for the Other 90%*, New York: Smithsonian, Cooper Hewitt, National Design Museum.

Social Progress Imperative (2014), "Social Progress Index," *The Social Progress Imperative*. Available online: http://www.socialprogressimperative.org/data/spi (accessed May 19, 2014).

Stern, N. (2007), *Stern Review: The Economics of Climate Change*, Cambridge: Cambridge University Press.

Taleb, N. (2007), *The Black Swan: The Impact of the Highly Improbable*, New York: Random House.

Tovrov, D. (2011), "5 Biggest Slums in the World," *International Business Times*, December 9. Available online: http://www.ibtimes.com/5-biggest-slums-world-381338 (accessed February 5, 2014).

United Nations (2014), "Human Development Index," *United Nations Development Programme Human Development Reports*. Available online: http://hdr.undp.org/en/statistics/hdi (accessed May 19, 2014).

Walker, B. and D. Salt (2006), *Resilience Thinking: Sustaining Ecosystems and People in a Changing World*, Washington, DC: Island Press.

Weiss, K. (2006), "Altered Oceans, Part Four: Plague of Plastics Chokes the Seas," *Los Angeles Times*, August 26. Available online: http://www.latimes.com/world/la-me-ocean2aug02-story.html#page=1 (accessed March 17, 2014).

Westley, F. and M. Patton (2006), *Getting to Maybe: How the World Is Changed*, Toronto: Random House Canada.

Wilkinson, R. (2001), "10 Useful Ideas on Systems Thinking," Futurist.com. Available online: http://www.futurist.com/articles-archive/10-useful-ideas-on-systems-thinking/ (accessed March 12, 2014).

Natalie W. Nixon

Natalie is a hybrid thinker, thriving in the space where creativity and strategy are integrated. With a background in anthropology and fashion, she is an associate professor and founding director of the Strategic Design MBA program at Philadelphia University, where she holds the endowed G. Allen Mebane IV '52 Chair for Design Thinkers. She is also a principal at Figure 8 Thinking, LLC (http://figure8thinking.com) and has spoken at TEDx events. Her research and consulting interests are in the role of improvisation and intuition in leadership and organizations, service design, and fashion thinking as a driver of innovation.

Focusing Question: How can design thinking and design methods innovate the ways services are delivered and positively affect the way people experience services?

This chapter explores the key questions:

- What is service design?

- How does service design relate to experience design?

- How can real-world examples from the food and health care sectors shed light on the application of service design?

The Intangible Service

Services evoke meaning through experience. A service is any activity that one party can give to another, but services are intangible and do not result in the ownership of anything. Their production may be tied to a physical product or created by a combination of digital information, products, and people. Services are produced and consumed simultaneously because they are manufactured at the point of consumption, and so there is an immediacy in the ways that customers determine the quality of the service (Langeard et al. 1981; Gronroos 1984; Zeithaml, Parasuranam, & Berry 1985). Consider the following examples: prompt pizza delivery, a dynamic learning experience in a college classroom, or indulging in a spa treatment after a long day of business travel. The diversity of these examples point to service design's complexity.

Service is a system of customer experiences, deployed through touchpoints where multiple elements will change a customer's experience. When a firm incorporates service design, it adds dimension to the way the organization functions beyond the level of the design of a particular product, environment, or interaction. In this additional dimension, management and frontline employees have to consider how customers exist within a system of experiences and ask how all of these elements work together in a dynamic way and in support of one another (Bedford & Lee 2008). By extension, customers move through a system of minimal structures, that is, flexible structures that in the aggregate produce the ultimate experience of the service. For example, when you make the decision to purchase a salad at a new organic food restaurant such as Honeygrow in Philadelphia, the flexible structures that compel you to do so may include a word-of-mouth conversation with a friend, an ad in a local organic food magazine, or the front window visage that you see from the parking lot; the lighting and interior design of the restaurant's space when you enter; the slick user-interface technology designed to easily submit your order at an attractive kiosk; and the smiling faces of the employees that greet you upon handing you your food. Touchpoint analysis is a way to examine all of the points of contact between users and service providers in these flexible structures (Clatworthy 2011).

What Is Service Design?

Service design is multidisciplinary and includes a varied set of perspectives, methodologies, tools, and processes. The marketing of services was first introduced as an independent topic in the 1970s, but the design of services did not exist as a concept until the 1990s (Manzini 1993; Erlhoff, Mager, & Manzini 1997). Service design was not taken seriously when it was first introduced into the academic field; thus, a lot of its definitions overtly assert a scientific method and structured approach in order to make it appear very systematic. Some practitioners consider service design to be the evolutionary extension of industrial design (Koskinen 2009). Service design offers a necessary interpretive framework between business and design, one that focuses on structures for service delivery and that merges contemporary innovation theory with the contributions and models of the user-design driven approach (Hollins 2006).

There are various ways that services can be improved by applying and managing design thinking. For example, techniques to develop a picture of the service offering include customer experience mapping, storyboarding processes, touchpoint analysis, identifying brand language, and attunement to customer perception (see Figure 8.1).

Service design has both tangible and intangible elements, including artifacts, communication, the environment and behaviors—all of which must be consistent, facile, and strategically applied. Jari Koskinen (2009: 21) defined service design as, "designing experiences happening in time and space, which reach people through different touch-points," which is important for its mention of touchpoints—a key part of the service design vernacular. Most definitions of service design borrow from the design

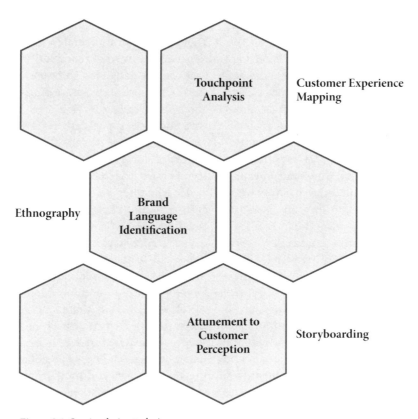

Figure 8.1 Service design techniques
Natalie W. Nixon

tradition and emphasize a user-centered approach (Mager, 2008; Bedford & Lee 2008; Maffei, Mager & Sangiorgi 2005). For example, this definition from Birgit Mager (2008: 355) not only underscores that user-centered approach but also emphasizes efficiency:

> *Service design addresses the functionality and form of services from the perspective of clients. It aims to ensure that service interfaces are useful, usable and desirable from the client's point of view and effective, efficient, and distinctive from the supplier's point of view.*

But this next definition emphasizes idea generation and a functionalist view: "[Service design] consists of the generation of a new idea and its implementation as a new service, leading to the dynamic growth of the enterprise and profit creation" (Taatila et al. 2006: 315). Other definitions contextualize service design as structured around delivering experiences flowing across channels, or touchpoints, over a period of time: "Managing design quality in the service sector is the art of matching people's expectations with an experience that is consistent across all touch-points that make up the service" (Lovlie, Downs, & Reason 2008: 75).

It is this last definition that is relevant to the design of experiential services. An ongoing debate in the service design field is whether service design is about the coordination of human and material interfaces or about the design of experience, where function and emotion are equally accounted for. The latter interpretation is very relevant today at a time when businesses must relate to their users, on emotional as well as functional levels, by delivering meaningful connections. Services pose inherently interesting design problems and contexts for design thinking (Eckersley 2008). Ultimately, service design is rooted in design culture, product design, and interface design and has focused on the interaction between the service dimensions of experience and identity, enabling "the transfer of proven analytical and creative design methods to the world of service" (Mager 2008: 355).

Service design is more relevant in a saturated marketplace because price is no longer the major differentiator; thus, firms must embrace a service model with more human connection. Additionally, as more services have become commoditized (Pine 2004), customer loyalty is developed by establishing an emotional connection underpinning the goods and services that a firm provides. That emotional connection is the vehicle to provide those memorable experiences where memory reflects life experiences and reinforces how we view ourselves (Norman 2004). Service design's increasing relevance has had a direct correlation to the growth of the service sector in industrialized nations. Today, service firms operate within an experience economy where complexity is ubiquitous. Service design is significant to business studies because services are a growth area, and well-designed services can be profitable. Starbucks is popularly referred to as an example of service design's value in the way that its business model shifted the positioning of coffee from a commodity to an experience by adding value through service and customization (Hollins & Mager 2008; Pine & Gilmore 1999). The service sector, referred to as a "tertiary sector," has become the most important sector in the OECD (The Organization for Economic Co-Operation and Development) economies (Hollins 2006). As of 2013, in the United States services accounted for 79.4 percent of the GDP, and they accounted for just over 70 percent of the total employment and value added in both the United States and the European Union (Hollins 2006; Maffei, Mager, & Sangiorgi 2005; Hollins & Mager 2008; Mager 2008; *CIA World Factbook* 2014).

Developing service innovations is a strategic imperative. The growing role of services in market economies is due to a higher demand from customers (both business to business [B2B] and business to consumers [B2C]), growth in franchising, increased outsourcing, deregulation in service markets, technological advances, and the fact that service providers have begun to benefit from economies of scale (Grove, Fisk, & Bitner 1992; Maffei, Mager, & Sangiorgi 2005; Alakoski, Ojasolo, & Pätilä 2007; Hollins & Mager 2008). While this growth is good, some barriers to service innovation include a lack of support for global trade and difficulty in assessing valuation, since services do little to invest in research and development (R&D) and therefore they do not qualify to be recipients of R&D grants from the government or from the private sector.

Much of what is written about service design offers a profusion of tools and practical steps, such as "five fundamentals of good service" and "six elements of service design," rather than consensual frameworks (Saco & Goncalves 2008; Hollins & Mager 2008). This is ironic given that intuition plays a significant role in service development, and the delivery process is not always systematic (Norman 2004). Early attempts to explain service design described it in mechanistic terms, comparing it to total quality management (from the manufacturing sector) and hierarchical control within an organization (Hollins 1993), while the human and emotional connections in a service experience were deemphasized (Eckersley 2008). In other cases the elements listed as being part of service design specifications, "reliability, price, safety, ergonomics, aesthetics and people interaction" were not distinct from product design with the exception of "people interaction" (Hollins 1993)—and even that is arguable, since people's interaction with a product is key. These were proscriptive approaches, emphasizing the linear ways to go about understanding service design. One example of such a helpful, albeit proscriptive approach is SERVQUAL, a method for measuring five dimensions (tangibles, reliability, responsiveness, assurance, and empathy)

of customers' and providers' perceptions of service quality (Parasuraman, Zeithaml, & Berry 1988; Berry, Zeithaml, & Parasuraman 1990; Mangold & Babakus 1991; Koskinen 2009). A more relevant aspect of the SERVQUAL method is that it does account for both the tangible and intangible elements of the design of experiential services. Examples of the tangible elements include the appearance of physical facilities, equipment, and personnel. The intangible elements are exemplified in the way SERVQUAL accounts for empathy, the caring and individualized attention the firm pays to consumers, as well as assurance, the employees' knowledge, and the employees' willingness to convey trust and confidence. What is lacking is that this approach does not account for the turbulence that accompanies rapid change. There is opportunity for service design to influence organizations to become more iterative and fluid, with the capacity to allow for emergent leadership among frontline employees.

It would be great if more businesses used service design to try to capture "the soul of service." There have only been isolated attempts to draw from "art-similar models." For example, service dramaturgy makes reference to a front stage and a backstage (Mager & Evenson 2008; Grove, Fisk, & Bitner 1992). But even these acknowledgments revert to a systematic, sociologico methodology (e.g., service scoring). The performing arts have been used as a source of inspiration and modeling in service design to arrive at innovative forms of organization, notation, and communication (Grove, Fisk, & Bitner 1992). The dynamic and metaphorical structure of stage and theater are used up to a point; for example, the metaphors of the front stage and the backstage have been helpful models for creativity. Creating the best product or service design for your business is a delicate balance between identifying unmet consumer needs and developing a sustainable business model to support those needs in an experiential way. The ARCHe Consumer Model developed by Yamilca Rodriguez and Sabrina Jetton (see Figure 8.2) is a great visualization tool to show the connection between consumer insights and a business model. It helps you to consider new ways to think about relationships between the customer and the business in order to drive new innovation services.

The architectural metaphor (e.g., references to blueprints) is common in service design. For example, "blueprinting service journeys" (Lovlie, Downs, & Reason 2008; Hollins 2006) and other architectural metaphors used to depict transitions between "hotels, lobbies and rooms" to represent web interface touchpoints for global service firms (Gillespie 2008) are present in the academic literature about service design. While it is acknowledged in this literature that the blueprint metaphor could be enhanced by examining the sensory side of the customer's experience, the overall more static, architectural framework of blueprinting is limiting: blueprints rarely account for mistakes. The organizational improvisation view reverses that perspective and views mistakes as opportunities.

GO DEEPER
Read the following:
- *Design for Services*, by A. Meroni and D. Sangiorgi

- "Designing Experiential Services with an Improvisational Stance" by N. W. Nixon.
- Service Design Network website and journal *Touchpoint*: http://www .service-design-network.org

REFLECTIONS
- Examine your own customer journey: Map all of the touchpoints you go through in getting a particular mode of transportation to work or school. Experiment with the shape of the pathways. Are they linear? Circular?
- Observe a group of consumers at a retailer you like—and at one you don't like. Map the customer journeys in the respective stores. Factor in human interaction, signage, digital communication prior to arriving, the physical environment, and the sensorial cues. How do the two journey maps compare?
- Test the ARCHe Consumer Model with a service you enjoy. Which model does it currently employ? Might the service be enhanced if the business experimented with a different consumer scenario within the ARCHe model?

Viewing Service Design through an Improvisational Lens
On the whole, innovation has been poorly applied to the services sector, but organizational improvisation can enhance that. Improvisation in a theater or a jazz context (as metaphors) is a novel way of understanding service design. Additionally, the

ARCHe CONSUMER MODELS can connect the dots between your consumer insights and your business model. Consider new ways to think about relationships between your consumer and your business in oder to drive new innovation services.

Creating the right product or service design for your business is a delicate balance between identifying unmet consumer needs and developing a sustainable busisness model to support those needs in an experiential way.

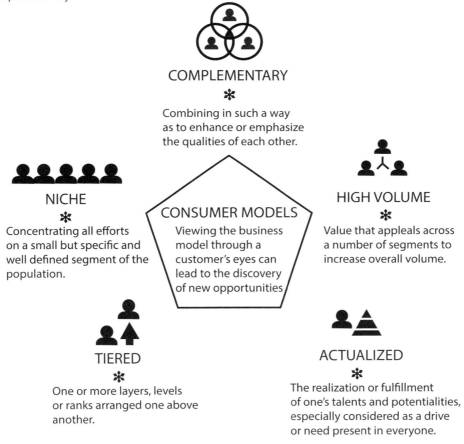

COMPLEMENTARY
✳
Combining in such a way
as to enhance or emphasize
the qualities of each other.

NICHE
✳
Concentrating all efforts
on a small but specific and
well defined segment of the
population.

CONSUMER MODELS
Viewing the business
model through a
customer's eyes can
lead to the discovery
of new opportunities

HIGH VOLUME
✳
Value that appeals across
a number of segments to
increase overall volume.

TIERED
✳
One or more layers, levels
or ranks arranged one above
another.

ACTUALIZED
✳
The realization or fulfillment
of one's talents and potentialities,
especially considered as a drive
or need present in everyone.

Figure 8.2 The ARCHe Consumer Model, developed by Yamilca Rodriguez and Sabrina Jetton

flexibility and fluidity needed in experience-based service design is mirrored in the attributes of the improvisational, specifically jazz improvisation, metaphor. Service design scholars acknowledge that there are other dynamics embedded in the theatrical process related to ideas about performance that could be valuable to the work of service design (Mager 2008: 357), including staff autonomy because it allows for self-organizing and emergent leadership. The improvisational lens amplifies valuable dynamics, such as staff autonomy, self-organization, and emergent leadership (see Figure 8.3).

The literature on organizations presupposes thought, planning, and design first, then action and implementation second. But what happens when the environment is unpredictable and does not allow for such a neat sequence of thought and then action? The improvisational lens supports the unpredictability of long-term outcomes and patterns because it highlights emergent interaction where both intention and spontaneity coexist; thus, the improvisational lens can advance the ways that experiential service design is understood.

Mechanistic approaches to implementing service design do not incorporate how to address services in the context of turbulence and change within an organization, or how to retain an identity while allowing for innovation. In these approaches, innovation is advised only when audits are completed, rather than being integrated in order for the organization to evolve. Many recommendations for service design specifications are reminiscent of blueprint metaphors and assume that the employee can manage and design a static future; this is not part of the postmodern view or the organizational improvisation view, which allows for more fluid considerations.

One dynamic way to understand improvisational organizations is through the heuristic of Frank Barrett—we will refer to it here as "Barrett's 7." In this framework, Barrett outlines seven principles of the ways that jazz musicians innovate musically that

Figure 8.3 Elements of an improvisational organization.
Natalie W. Nixon.

can be applied to innovating organizations. Before applying those seven characteristics, it is first important to remember that there are three key aspects in jazz improvisation. The first is that participants must learn the rules, memorize, and practice. The second is that there is a metaphorical transferring that occurs when recombining elements, producing novel ideas. And the third aspect is the anticipatory nature of improvising: "It is uncertain to what degree improvisers go through unheard, continuous self-editing, an anticipatory, virtual trial and error as they consider different directions and interpretations of the material" (Barrett & Peplowski 1998: 607).

Jazz musicians have only a split second to make choices. This grounding in skills, the rules of engagement, the transference between contexts to produce novel ideas, and the anticipatory nature of improvisation—are themes that can be leveraged in organizations resulting in quite creative and innovative work environments and work products and services.

Here are Barrett's seven characteristics of jazz improvisation that can be applied to the design of more meaningful experiential services in (for example) a hotel, a gas station, a restaurant, a law office, or municipal services.

1. *Provocative competence:* Provocative competence is defined as making deliberate efforts to create disruptions and incremental reorientations; sometimes, competence can actually squelch experimentation.

2. *Embracing errors:* Errors are viewed as an important source of learning, an opportunity to get feedback, and a way for musicians to become familiar with a wider environment. Organizations that embrace errors, treating mistakes as opportunities, end up with more open environments; and where leadership is emergent and more daring, self-organization occurs.

3. *Minimal structures:* These are structures that allow for maximum flexibility. Barrett reminds us that "jazz improvisation is a loosely structured activity in which action is coordinated around songs" (Barrett & Peplowksi 1998: 611). They impose order, create a continuous sense of cohesion and assure everyone that they are oriented toward a common place. Similarly, in an organization, minimal constraints allow staff the freedom to express diversity, transform materials, and intervene in the flow of delivering services. Effective design incorporates the intuiting and experimenting that is part of improvisation.

4. *Distributed task:* In this improvisational element, there is an ongoing give and take between members, where improvisers "enter a flow of ongoing invention" (Barrett & Peplowksi 1998: 613). Musicians speak of those moments when a groove is achieved as flow, a type of autotelic experience and state of transcendence (Csikszentmihalyi 1990). When everything is flowing in an organization, the delivery of experience is far removed from robotic operations delivery, and the ultimate delivery of an amazing experience can have a transcendent effect on clients.

5. *Retrospective sensemaking:* Retrospective sensemaking is about making connections between the old and the new. Here the model of the bricoleur becomes relevant, making usage of whatever is at hand (Lévi-Strauss 1967: 17). Similarly, the organizational member creates new experiences and services by sifting through the resources of personal skill base and talent, knowledge, and organizational memory.

6. *Hanging out:* This refers to membership in communities of practice (Brown & Duguid 1991). Barrett and Peplowski (1998) point out that in jazz, communities of practice are where knowledge is disseminated, communal practicing occurs, and members exchange stories while hanging out. It is critical that organizations develop structures that allow for communities of practice to thrive. Similarly, such structures become vehicles for knowledge dissemination, idea generation, storytelling, and practicing operational skills.

7. *Alternate between soloing and supporting:* This is the practice of taking turns to support each other. In jazz improvisation, this is when leadership rotates. This is an egalitarian idea and one that ensures that each player gets a chance to develop a musical idea, and others create space for this development to occur. In organizations such alternation can occur between management and staff, as well as between colleagues in cross-functional teams.

Organizations can practice Barrett's 7 in order to swiftly and resourcefully adapt to the VUCA (volatile, uncertain, complex, and ambiguous) environment in which businesses must survive. They will ultimately become improvisational organizations, ones that are chaordic and adaptive. A ***chaord*** is an organization that blends characteristics of chaos and order. The word "chaord" evolved out of Dee Hock's (founder of VISA International) observations that self-organizing and adaptive systems in nature were able to emerge on the edge of chaos with just enough coherence and structure to result in order. The chaord is defined as "Any self-organizing, adaptive, non-linear, complex organism, organization or community whether physical, biological or social, the behavior of which harmoniously blends characteristics of chaos and order" (Hock 2005). An improvisational organization is a chaordic system. Improvisation is open to transformation because it borders on the edge of chaos; at that juncture, blueprints are not reliable and improvisation becomes a handier tool.

The chaordic concept is present in improvisation: Spontaneity and intuition (chaos), as well as practice, study, and listening (order), are important dimensions. Intuition is at the core of some definitions of improvisation because it is accepted that intuition is based upon discipline, practice, and experience (Crossan 1998; Stacey 1991, 1992). This has led to thinking about improvisation as a skill that can be practiced. Thus, complexity and CST (chaordic systems thinking) are embedded in principles of organizational improvisation and the improvisational lens can advance how we think about the design of experiential services.

GO DEEPER
Read and watch the following:
- "Luxury Redesigned: How the Ritz-Carlton Uses Experiential Service Design to Position Abundance in Times of Scarcity" by N. W. Nixon and A. Rieple.
- *Yes to the Mess: Surprising Leadership Lessons from Jazz* by F. Barrett.
- "7 Rules for Improvising at Work," TEDx Philadelphia Talk by Natalie Nixon, March 2014. Available online: https://www.youtube.com/watch?v=UTS95OchFOE

REFLECTIONS
Frank Barrett made the following observation:

> Given that many tasks in organizations are indeterminate and people come to them with limited foresight, members often need to apply resourcefulness, cleverness and pragmatism in addressing concerns. They often have to play with various possibilities, re-combining and re-organizing, to find solutions by relating the dilemma they face to the familiar context that preceded it. In spite of the wish for a rational plan of predictable action, they often must take a look around and act without a clear sense of how things will unfold. (Barrett & Peplowski 1998: 615)

- Try applying two of Frank Barrett's seven techniques for improvisational organizations to a service that you use. How does the design and outcome of the service change when the improvisational lens is added?
- How could you play around with recombining the typical way a service is executed to get more resourceful solutions that cater to the end user? Try testing this out on services at a fast-food restaurant, a gas station, or registering for classes at your university.

Experiential Service Design
In experiential services, design is the skin, service is the bones, and meaningful experience is the heart and soul. Having stated that services evoke meaning through experience, in order to explain experiential services, it is important to define **meaning** and to define **experience**. Meaning is defined as our mind's construction of reality (Geertz 1973). It is an asset for understanding complexity and a framework to assess what we value, believe, condone, and desire (Diller, Shedroff, & Rhea 2006). Meaning is what makes experiences valuable. Constructions of shared meaning include artifacts that embody meaning and rituals that transmit meaning. Examples of this would be:

- Amazon.com's Prime membership promising lower cost and higher quality of immediate and consistent service delivery
- Cooking classes at Whole Foods supermarket
- A Zappos customer's one-on-one service that leaves her not only satisfied, but happy

- The stories shared at daily staff meetings at every Ritz-Carlton hotel around the world

The iPhone is an artifact of a community of users; users can build in their own rituals depending on the types of apps uploaded to adapt the experience of the iPhone to their own needs and lives.

Experiences and meaning intersect to create a narrative for an organization. The definitions of *experience* include meaningful interaction that produces a moment of truth (Chase 1981; Heskett, Sasser, & Hart 1990; Heskett, Sasser, & Schlessinger 1997; Roth, Chase, & Voss 1997; Shedroff 1999; Roth & Menor 2003; Bitran, Ferrer, & Oliveira 2008), as well as the sensation of change: "any process we are conscious of and involved in as it happens" (Diller, Shedroff, & Rhea 2006: 18). Madeleine Pullman, and Michael Gross (2004: 553) emphasize the emotional component of experience and define experience as "emotional connections (engendered) through engaging, compelling and consistent context." They elaborate by saying:

> An experience occurs when a customer has any sensation or knowledge acquisition resulting from some level of interaction with different elements of a context created by a service provider. Successful experiences are those that the customer finds unique, memorable and sustainable over time, would want to repeat and build upon, and enthusiastically promotes via word of mouth.

Others have suggested that experience-centric services go beyond evoking emotion to invoking imagination and provoking the senses (Pine & Gilmore 1999; Gupta & Vajic 2000).

Kirtley Fisher is an experience designer with the Business Innovation Factory's education practice. She values experience design because empathy is built into the design process and leads to better outcomes overall. The experience design process also prevents her from following assumptions and instead addresses people's real needs:

> I was part of a team at the Business Innovation Factory (BIF) that developed and piloted Teachers Design for Education (www.TD4Ed.com)—a design thinking curriculum for educators to tackle challenges together in the education system. We saw teachers in just six weeks turn frustrating problems into meaningful solutions. They felt confident and empowered in the end, which was the outcome we had designed for! (Interview, Nixon & Fisher 2014)

Similarly, Amy Kates, a managing partner at the organization design consultancy Kates Kesler, introduces clients to design thinking as a way to help them collectively imagine new organizational options:

> We can't expect employees to deliver a unique service experience to customers if we don't give them an organization that supports the desired behaviors. The best way to create a culture change is to use the organization design process itself to model the outcomes we want. (Interview, Nixon and Kates 2014)

Given that organizations are very real, but essentially invisible, three-dimensional constructs, business leaders who have to work together to create alternatives often find the tools of organization charts and work flow diagrams lacking as a way to articulate their ideas. By having clients focus on what type of experience they want employees and managers to have and deliver to customers, they can design an organization that makes it easy for people to exhibit the right behaviors. For example, a major restaurant chain wanted to encourage customer service innovation among field managers that were traditionally very operationally and efficiency focused. Kates Kesler had them work collaboratively to first assess the current organization and then articulate—through words and pictures—what would need to change in the environment to foster appropriate experimentation, upward feedback, idea sharing, rapid prototyping, and open adoption of ideas. The company's leaders realized that in order to generate the ideas that would change the customer experience, they first had to change the experience of how their managers worked together and used the design process to mirror the behaviors they wanted to drive, including inclusion, candor, and evaluation of ideas based on merit rather than hierarchy. By bringing design thinking into the organization change process, they were able to more quickly change not just the structures, roles, and processes needed to foster innovation, but more importantly the mind-set and culture of the organization.

Experience is crucial to constructing an understanding about the world and functioning within it; through experiences, individuals confront beliefs and rethink possibilities. Experience creators think about how to exceed the expectations of the audience. There are three critical components to defining an experience: (1) experience first requires an attraction, initiated via the senses; (2) then an engagement, the experience itself; and (3) finally a conclusion, the resolution provided through meaning (Shedroff 2001). Meaning is derived from experiences, and memories are the packaged takeaways of experiences; the distinction of memorable experiences is that they are transformative.

GO DEEPER

Read or try the following:

- *The Experience Economy* by J. Pine and J. Gilmore.
- *Lovemarks* by K. Roberts.
- "15 Meanings": http://www. makingmeaning.org/meanings.html
- Design & Emotion Society: http:// www.designandemotion.org
- Teachers Design for Education: http:// td4ed.businessinnovationfactory.com
- Find and listen to an audio interview or report on National Public Radio or Planet Money about a meaningful service.

REFLECTIONS

- Write a one-page reflection about an exemplary service business based upon the type of experience it allows its users to have. What did you find unique, memorable, or sustainable about the service experience?
- What retailers come to mind who are excellent at delivering meaningful

experiences for their users? How do they do that? Do some primary background research by visiting the retailer, observing, and then following up with an interview of an employee and of a customer.

- The authors of *Making Meaning* state that three critical components to defining a memorable experience are that it (a) attracts via the senses; (b) engages the user; and (c) there is some sort of resolution provided through meaning (Diller, Shedroff, & Rhea 2006). Think of a disappointing experiential service, and identify how you could convert it to a memorable and meaningful one.

Case Stories

In this section we explore case stories of practitioners in the health care and food space, who design services.

Case Story: Kaiser Permanente— Integrating Design Research into a Health Care System

The following insights are based on a conversation with Christi Zuber in July 2014. Christi Zuber is the director of the Innovation Consultancy at Kaiser Permanente (KP), one of the United States' largest not-for-profit health plans with headquarters in California. As director Christi gets to experiment with delivering meaningful health care services in the most human-centered ways. Harking to Simon Sinek's "Golden Circle" and "Start with Why" frameworks (see Chapter 3), the "Why" of Christi's service design work is to help break through what is possible through

deeper insights and to try solutions that may otherwise not be considered. Ultimately, her team wants measurable, impactful solutions. "Physicians and nurses tend to be risk averse—they take very good care of being very safe and effective and not making mistakes—they are wired to practice in that way." So with a service design practice in the midst of a large organization like KP, they are introducing an abductive mind-set, as an alternative to the deductive mind-set that physicians and nurses have been trained to develop. Christi asserts that, "I don't want people to change that—but I do want to give them another way of looking at challenges."

Christi realizes that the start of her work in designing services began when she practiced as a registered nurse. Christi's background is in home health and hospital administration and consulting; as a nurse, she did a lot of co-creation, making educational tools, so that patients could help themselves heal and integrate their families in that process. Even as a health care administrator at a children's hospital, she experimented with user-driven ethnography by giving the children and their parents disposable cameras to take pictures, bring them back to clinicians, and use those pictures to tell their stories in order to develop empathy and "So that we could think about it through *their* eyes." Patient-centered care has become particularly important for children and the elderly. That's the start of where she got interested—but the design-thinking language wasn't being used.

Fast-forward to Christi being recruited to work at KP. A year and half into the journey, Marilyn Chow, vice president of patient care services, and a few other executives at Kaiser viewed the IDEO *Nightline* supermarket segment of 2003. They asked Christi to create a team to learn and apply those approaches at Kaiser. Christi eventually put together this team of four: a group of curious-natured, energetic, and humble relationship builders. Paired up with IDEO for over eighteen months, the team essentially apprenticed with IDEO. To this day, they still exchange ideas with IDEO.

In a 2014 interview with the author, Christi had important insights about how to deliver meaningful services in practical ways. For example:

- "It is about human-centered design— so be respectful of the people with whom you interact."

- "There are a range of stakeholders: some projects are more hospital based, others are around the transition to home, and still others are community based or clinic based, and all involve a range of solutions from new processes, to technologies to new space designs. This diversity requires multidisciplinary teams."

- "As part of an internal team within a large organization, doing service design can get very personal—you are observing people's jobs and suggesting how to make them better. You are not just cranking out the work—the people are not a means to the end, they are part of that end, and as such, you must be respectful of that journey." (See Figures 8.4 and 8.5.)

- "My team likes to do projects that surface some universal truths or

Figure 8.4 Kaiser Permanente perinatal journey map workshop—starting with "Getting Pregnant," moving through "Ultrasound," and culminating with "Delivery"
Christi Zuber, Kaiser Permanente

PERINATAL JOURNEY MAPPING
Preliminary Journey Map: Patient experience - across continuum

The first visit with PNC/TAC is a complex encounter that requires significant time and interpersonal skills to:
- Assess the patient's attitude towards the pregnancy.
- Record factual, sometimes sensitive health history.
- Set expectations for the perinatal care process.
- Assess the patients psychosocial needs.

How might we design a process that streamlines the accurate transfer of personal information into the medical record whi assessing and addressing the unique psychosocial needs and expectations of each of our patients?

How might we make the information gathered at this first co actionable for the MD/NP prior to or at their visit?

The process of initiating and proceeding with ongoing car inherently clear to patients when the discover they are pre

How might we better educate patients about what to expect the pregnancy process so that they do not have to figure it ou the way?

Patients' expectations and feelings toward their pregnancy are uniquely shaped by their own previous experiences, as well as those of the people close to them.

How might we assess patients' expectations and bias up-front to better prepare their providers to address their needs in an efficient and satisfying way?

Many patients don't know what to expect as a "normal" length of time to try and get pregnant and rely on their OB to confirm if their experience is "normal."

Planning/getting pregnant

First contact: PNC/TAV, other

First visit with MD

Fertility services

The referral process is not seamless or immediately clear to referring providers and can cause inefficiencies or inconsistencies in the care we provide patients.

It is not inherently clear to patients when and how fertility services would be appropriate and available for them, or if their plan would cover them.

The first pregnancy visit with a provider represents a shift to a more complex relationship with them, that c hold different expectations.

How might we make it more inherently clear to both provider and patient what their new relationship will lo and feel like?

Tension:
Patients' complex emotional needs > < Constraints of 0:30 visit

Patients come to the first visit with diverse expectatio and needs, and there are few tools that help providers quickly assess those needs and expectations if they do not have a previous relationship with the patient.

How might we enable providers to address the uniquely complex needs of each patient both within and outside o the initial :30 visit?

Patients often feel they must "push" to get what they want because of previous experiences where they did not feel heard, or their needs were not met.

How might we make it easier for providers to know if th patients feel heard of feel their needs have been met?

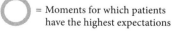
Key

◯ = Moments for which patients have the highest expectations

◯ = Moments that hold the highest emotional salience with patients

Figure 8.5 Kaiser Permanente perinatal journey map final version
Christi Zuber, Kaiser Permanente

Information gives patients a sense of control when the begin to feel a loss of control and power as their pregnancy progresses.

Many patients come to this visit understanding that the results can change the course of their pregnancy, but they do not feel information provided to them in a way that matches their understanding.

There is inconsistency in how ultrasounds are conducted by technicians and providers.
This includes:
- Attitudes, enthusiasm in communicating information to the patient.
- Amount and depth of information provided to patient during the process.
- Whether photos/videos and printed ultrasound pictures are allowed.

How might we provide patients with the right amount of information for them, in the right format and right time to process and understand it completely?

Places where patients spend extended time or have repeated visits present opportunities for bonding with staff and enabling their trust in the system.

What might we learn from these interactions to build trust and rapport between providers and patients throughout the process?

Patients can approach their facility tour with a discerning point of view, and their decision can be based on many subjective factors, ranging from who is providing the tour to the facility's c-section rate.

20 week visit

NST

Antepartum/ Pre-term labor

Choosing where to deliver

Prenatal visits with provider

Over nine months, providers have sometimes built up familiarity with patients - visits can become more conversational and congenial.

Patients can feel the most out of control during their third trimester and may need an increase in emotional/psychological support.

How might we prepare patients and their families for identifying and dealing with the emotional challengers that may happen during their pregnancy?

Inconsistency in providers' approach to care is to be expected - the areas where it should be addressed are where it creates inequity in access to care - such as inconsistent promotion of resources like websites, groups, classes.

How might we identify and provider consistent care for the touchpoints/phases that most significantly impact care equality?

Patients are looking to resources outside of Kaiser for education about the perinatal process, and we do not have any formalized, consistent point of view about which of these resources we trust and recommend for them.

How might we continuously and consistently bridge the divide between Kaiser and non-Kaiser patient-facing resources?

Professional rapport and familiarity - when providers know each other's expertise, interests, and ways of communicating - can help facilitate timely, productive patient care.

How might we build this rapport for new/less experienced staff/providers?

create solutions with minimum specs that can be scaled across multiple regions. Some projects have to do with insights; others are about rapid prototyping."

- "Service design is more than conversation—it is part of a real ecosystem. Though it may be intangible, it is not invisible. You just have to be creative in the ways you try out your ideas."

A great way of understanding what that ecosystem looks like is their "Exercise as Medicine" project, where the Kaiser Permanente Innovation team looked at exercise as a vital sign. The primary determinant of health is your own behavior—not what the medical community determines. In attempting to change patients' behavior (with a focus on exercise, food, sleep, and alcohol consumption), they realized that the behavior of the KP clinicians also had to change! The challenge was that clinicians were trained in medicine—not in behavior change—and all the processes around them were created to support that type of interaction. So it was a struggle for them to have conversations with patients about the questions "What are your barriers to becoming active?" Thus, in designing solutions, Christi's team and her partners at Kaiser had to engage not only patients and clinicians but also internal experts on nutrition who started projects marrying farmers' markets and healthy recipes. Now, on the KP medical-centered campuses, they have local farmers' markets. These farmers' markets act as

reinforcements for good behaviors. The KP team asked questions such as: "How are our buildings built to encourage people to take stairs? Do we have trails? Are there visual triggers in the lobby to bring back *play*?"

KP has the largest private electronic medical record in the world. That asset was used to capture all of this data and develop a tool that would help to connect patients and providers with resources. "[We used] our electronic medical records in a way so that it triggered to help the physician to have those conversations ... By bringing the clinicians' voices into that—they could see themselves in the process." This—the connecting of the farmers' markets to the physicians to the electronic medical records systems—is an example of the larger ecosystem for whom Christi's team designs.

Christi values the ways that the service design process leads to innovation. It allows for trial and error when the team doesn't actually know what the problem is, and allows them to really dig in deep and define the problem (see Figures 8.6 and 8.7). Ultimately, they have been able to create impactful and measurable value for the KP organization on the whole. Nimble and creative thinking is the means to the end of "helping people to think differently so they bring a new competency into their work." Christi believes that the value of service design is that it allows the organization to be more nimble in their thinking and bring the heart into challenges (see Figure 8.8). She doesn't view service design as the end all, be all—it has its place, just as Six Sigma has a place:

Figure 8.6 This kit supplies prompts to help patients and practitioners be self-reflective about their healthcare experience and contribute to the service design process.
Christi Zuber, Kaiser Permanente

This service design approach has brought that voice to the forefront with intelligence—and really truly understanding the emotions that go on behind it. We are looking at the patient and clinician experience differently than before—now we have language for it. The projects and efforts that have come out are great—taking place with tens of thousands of people each year—but doing it in a valuable and meaningful way, with heart.

Figure 8.7 Kaiser Permanente cultural probe kit in action

It has connected people to the reasons why they got into medicine in the first place. (Interview, Nixon & Zuber 2014)

In order to, for example, make health care services affordable, the voice of the people being served has to be in the forefront of

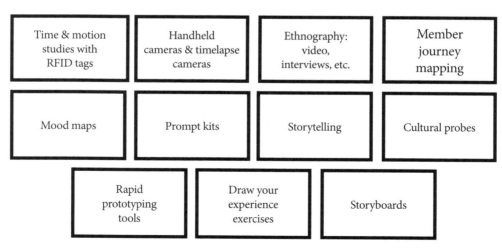

Time & motion studies with RFID tags	Handheld cameras & timelapse cameras	Ethnography: video, interviews, etc.	Member journey mapping
Mood maps	Prompt kits	Storytelling	Cultural probes
Rapid prototyping tools	Draw your experience exercises	Storyboards	

Figure 8.8 Tools used in service design at Kaiser Permanente
Christi Zuber, Kaiser Permanente

decision making. Additionally, the emotion behind those voices must be acknowledged and understood. Service design provides a language to understand experiences.

GO DEEPER

Review the following:

- B. J. Fogg (a researcher in psychology and innovation) has work on persuasion and innovation: http://www.bjfogg.com
- Gravity Tank's Six Principles for Working Differently: http://www.gravitytank.com/education/overview
- IDEO Shopping Cart Project on ABCion/overview video—an oldie but goodie: https://www.youtube.com/watch?v=taJOV-YCieI
- IDEO's Design for Social Impact Workbook: http://www.ideo.com/work/design-for-social-impact-workbook-and-toolkit
- More examples of Kaiser Permanente projects:
- http://hbr.org/2010/09/kaiser-permanentes-innovation-on-the-front-lines/ar/1
- http://kpinnovation.org/projectmove.html
- http://kpinnovation.org/projects.html
- Exercise as Medicine Project: http://share.kaiserpermanente.org/tag/exercise-as-medicine/

Review the following:

- "Design Is in the Details"—Paul Bennett's TED Talk. Available online: https://www.ted.com/talks/paul_bennett_finds_design_in_the_details?language=en

- "How Great Leaders Inspire Action"—Simon Sinek's TED Talk on the Golden Circle principle of "Start with Why." Available online: http://www.ted.com/talks/simon_sinek_how_great_leaders_inspire_action?language=en

REFLECTIONS

- Download the dScout app (https://dscout.com/scouts) and try going on one of their missions for a service. What do you observe about this experience?
- View artists Halsey Burgund and Kelly Sherman's Patient Translations project at http://patient-translations.com. What are two other prototypes you might try to develop to capture the patient's perspective on his or her health care experience?

Case Story: Independence Blue Cross—Starting from Within

When a company gains the majority of market share in its sector, it can be very tempting for the company to rest on its laurels; it must define the new metrics of success and explore new benchmarks. Independence Blue Cross (Independence) is the largest health insurer in the Philadelphia region and when faced with this market leader positioning, it responded in two interesting ways. The first is that it launched an Innovation Center. The second is that it went to the members to prototype ways to best serve its members in light of the Affordable Care Act.

The broader mission of Independence is to enhance the health and wellness of the people and communities it serves while enhancing access to necessary health care. The Independence Blue Cross Center for Health Care Innovation (The Center) views itself as internal consultants, facilitating creative opportunities and problem solving, and is charged to focus on two areas: capability and culture. Capability refers to thinking differently and creatively around new ways to approach a job, a functional area, and to help Independence associates optimize their creative capacity at work. A culture of innovation is then built through teaching this capability. The goal is to create a culture where more managers and associates are interested in taking risks and trying new things. The ultimate goal is to provide practice for employees to become less risk averse and to develop new ways of implementing a process.

The Center's approach to designing services is to consult with business areas about their greatest needs and offer workshops, ideation sessions, and customer journey mapping. Sometimes they will identify unmet needs in random ways, for example, overhearing a conversation about an unmet need on the elevator. As they became more well-known in the organization, other Independence associates have approached them for help on projects. They apply the appropriate tools according to the challenge at hand. One example of a project is with the LGBT group of associates, where they will map three life events for LGBT people: (1) coming out to one's family; (2) being diagnosed with HIV/AIDS; and (3) making a decision to undergo a gender change. The Center is recommending how

to improve service delivery at those junctures in concert with the LGBT employee group and then will decide on how best to advertise it to users.

With a "learn and do" approach in workshop sessions, Michelle Histand, director of The Center, recalls that the real challenge was "How do we get our associates to think of applying these tools in their daily work? How do we continuously engage them? They forget. It is easier to apply when it is guided. We are really trying to create new habits, and create a process that will be sustainable" (Interview, Nixon & Histand 2014).

After only the first year of being open, Independence's engagement surveys indicated a story of incremental successes related to capability and culture. On a question about risk-taking in this engagement survey, there was a 14 percent increase when compared to responses on risk-taking from the year prior. This sent a message to Michelle and her team that they were making progress. Anecdotally, Independence associates report that they enjoy becoming engaged through The Center with comments such as "This is the best experience of my career" (Interview, Nixon & Histand 2014).

One of the challenges that came to The Center was about the pending deadline for citizens to register for the Affordable Care Act. Independence wanted to ensure that a large portion of people who had no health insurance understood their options. As Paula Sunshine, vice president of sales and marketing for consumer business, explained, "Intuitively we have embraced a lot of design thinking principles such as lateral thinking, prototyping, story and empathy. Without the involvement of the Independence Blue Cross Center for Health Care Innovation we would not have gotten there" (Interview, Nixon & Sunshine 2014).

When the Affordable Care Act (ACA) first launched, they were faced with a lot of consumers in Philadelphia who didn't realize they were potential customers of an emerging market. Thus, a design challenge was born: How might we build awareness of the options embedded in the ACA? There was essentially an education deficit. People did not understand the details of the ACA, and Independence was faced with the challenge of leading the charge in the region. But they did not want to solely rely on typical methods, such as buying advertisement space on radio or printing thousands of brochures.

Sessions in The Center helped them to develop the novel idea of how to utilize the "Independence Express" mobile truck in the community (see Figure 8.9). They decided to go to the user, instead of devising ways for the user to come to them.

The Independence Express truck can be found in strip malls and heritage festivals in the region. The biggest challenge was to convince people to give five minutes of their time (see Figure 8.10). When in prototype stage, they pondered "How do we want people to feel?" and "What is the give and take?" Lateral thinking took place by not thinking as a health care company or as an insurance

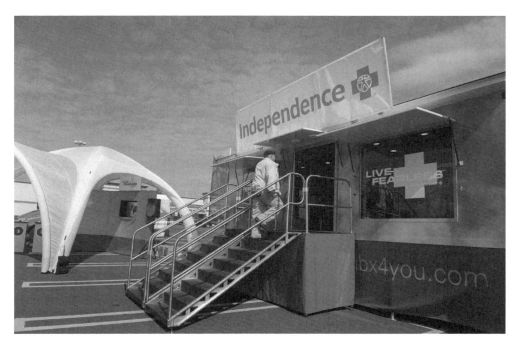

Figure 8.9 Independence Blue Cross Express Truck
Independence Blue Cross

Figure 8.10 Inside the Independence Blue Cross Express Truck
Independence Blue Cross

company, but instead as a participant in a festival. With that in mind they devised games, prizes, buzzers, and a carnival atmosphere. They learned very early to prototype and thus embrace the value of failing early and often. For example, once they settled on a game show idea, they took the truck out to a YMCA parking lot and played the game with whoever stopped by. They learned very quickly whether or not the lights were right, if the questions made sense, or if the sequencing was the best. "Once we got to open enrollment, we wanted to make sure that we were where our users were: so, for example, at church on Sunday, in Chinatown, and we had to bring enough utility to

help folks sign up for healthcare coverage" (Interview, Nixon & Sunshine 2014).

They also pivoted to using the same venues to help users understand what they bought and how to use the product because these were customers who may not have had health insurance in the past and needed help navigating this new system. The design-thinking principle of story played an important role because of the enrollment deadline for the ACA:

Part of our marketing strategy was to develop a 90 second video contest. We challenged young people to use storytelling to help explain to their friends the *importance of having health insurance. There was a $10,000 prize and the winner was based on the number of votes received.* (Interview, Nixon & Sunshine 2014)

Given how brands such as Dove and Chipotle have experienced great success by connecting to their users through meaningful stories, without ever mentioning the product, it was a smart and creative move for Independence to ask its users to create the video content. User-generated content is one of the most effective ways that brands demonstrate authenticity. Paula believes her team constantly returned to an empathetic stance because Independence's mission is to improve the health and wellness of the people they serve; they were driven to ensure that as many people as possible had access to know about ACA opportunities. They used journey mapping as a way to visually explore the very different path to care that individual insurers have versus those who receive insurance from/through their employer.

GO DEEPER

Read the following:
- "Platforming: Evolving the Paradigm of Branding" by V. Jacobs in *Design Management Review*. What are other good examples of brands that are excellent platforms for services?
- "Viewing Ascension Health from a Design Thinking Perspective" by N. W. Nixon in *Journal of Organization Design*.

REFLECTION
- View the IBX "90 Seconds Video Contest" entries on YouTube posted by Independence Blue Cross at https://www.youtube.com/user/ibxphilly. What ideas does this inspire in you about ways to crowdsource innovation for a service?

Case Story: The Vetri Family Foundation—Using Food to Delight and to Do Good

Philadelphia has become known as a favorite destination for foodies. If you spend any time in Philly, you are bound to experience a Vetri restaurant. Marc Vetri and partner Jeff Benjamin launched their first restaurant in the late 1990s. Marc Vetri is primarily responsible for the culinary side of the business, while Jeff Benjamin is responsible for the operational side. Their approach to the delivery of innovative services is interesting, not only in how they design the food, but also in terms of how they have used food as a means for social change in the Philadelphia public school system.

Their value proposition is to make people happy through food. Creating the best experiences through food starts with the way staff is trained—in itself a design process. Here are three areas that the Vetri group specifically designs for the best food service delivery.

Kitchen Design

Kitchen design is ultimately about helping each cook to be as efficient as possible. The Vetri kitchen is designed in a hub and spoke fashion—versus in a brigade or assembly line fashion. "In the brigade system the cook is only responsible for 1/3 of the plate. This is a bit boring—they are only painting a portion of the picture" explains Jeff Benjamin (Interview, Nixon & Benjamin 2014). Instead, with the hub and spoke design, the cook responsible for making the chicken, for example, makes all of the components and then brings the dish to central space—a central hub with spokes.

Experience Design

Vetri employs experience design very early on in the training of employees, mainly by utilizing role-play. Jeff will pretend that he is a customer, forcing the wait staff to think through questions, such as why the guest is dining (An anniversary? A date? A professional afterwork meeting?), and they then codevelop a standard. They try not to have a robotic approach because each diner is unique.

> We go through different scenarios. The approach has to be customized to a business dinner versus a date. Each evening prior to opening we go through each reservation with staff and talk about what we know about the guests … Over the years, this training has become part of the system. We're designing your event as it is going on. Sometimes something changes midstream—you can't predetermine how to approach a table—it can't be a canned experience. (Interview, Nixon & Benjamin 2014)

Thus, the ability to anticipate the diner's needs is essential in how the staff are trained to design each experience.

Menu Design

In selecting menu features, physical attributes (for example, the weight of the paper, or the choice whether or not to use an iPad) is important because these are strong visual cues. The style of font and placement of words are considered in relation to factoring in where the eye travels.

> Lots of thought goes into that because we are thinking about which items we want to sell in higher volume. We also consider the season—what is appropriate and what is available? Now that we've produced this dish, what are other items we can offer our guests? (Interview, Nixon & Benjamin 2014)

The design of the plate is also considered—whether it is too monochrome, or which colors are dominant is significant.

Ultimately, dining is a sensorial experience:

> At Vetri the music is hinting at you in the background. The soloist is the food. We have kind of created the orchestra. The ballet is our service—you see that visually. You smell the food. Should make you feel like you are in your mom's home. All of those things are background music to the soloist, which is the food on the plate. (Interview, Nixon & Benjamin 2014)

Their Vetri restaurant is a small room, warm colors are used, the tablecloths are cream not white "so that it does not feel antiseptic. You almost feel an embrace." Their Osteria restaurant, by contrast, is a casual environment: "We are trying to create a jovial, fun atmosphere, so there are higher ceilings to create louder volume by design; there's exposed duct work on purpose for a more industrial, relaxed, feeling" (Interview, Nixon & Benjamin 2014). Floral arrangements are also key—the restaurant must be mindful that the floral scent does not clash with the food and be compatible to wine and food parings.

Service design at Vetri is the means to truly innovate. They are not the first or last Italian themed restaurant—but the details in the design of their service delivery will help them to stand out.

Vetri also started a foundation in order to use the design of food service for social impact. The Vetri Foundation for Children was originally started to get involved with Alex's Lemonade Stand. It then grew to partner with area Philadelphia public schools and develop the Eatiquette program. Eatiquette, "a Vetri method for school lunch," has the lofty goal to transform children's eating experience to one where social interaction, communication, and learning about different cultures takes place (see Figure 8.11).

An interview with Vetri chef Tia McDonald revealed the genius behind this deceptively simple concept. There are several key factors that go into the Eatiquette experience. First, children eat at round tables (not rectangular ones), with real plates and flatware, and with pitchers and large salad bowls at the center of each table. "The indirect message is that they themselves are not disposable, and that we value sustainability," Tia explained. Additionally in this democratic structure, everyone can

Figure 8.11 Vetri Eatiquette program at Community Partnership School
The Vetri Foundation for Children

be a participant, children can more easily communicate and share. Long rectangular tables give the message of isolation and children-as-chattel model.

Teachers and staff have reflected on interesting unintended consequences in the children's behavior: noise levels have reduced dramatically; there are fewer fights because lines have been eliminated, and the children sit down immediately, served by their peer table captain; because the food is wholesome, teachers report back that the kids are more eager to re-engage with learning after lunch (see Figure 8.12). On the day I visited, lunch consisted of a broccoli salad, marinated barley, grilled cod and cherry compote for dessert. The kids' peer table captain dons a chef coat, arrives fifteen minutes early, sets the table, and sets out the entrees; *everyone* participates in the cleanup.

When I asked Tia to reflect on the role of design thinking in this innovative school lunch delivery program, she highlighted empathy and prototyping. The empathy she had to exhibit by being extremely focused on the user, the school children, was to realize that the problem she was trying to solve was to "teach them survival skills; and help them realize that things outside their immediate vision could be available to them." She was referencing the relatively exotic sounding foods that the children serve each other, such as a gazpacho soup. Children in the United States have become somewhat

Figure 8.12 Lunchtime via the Vetri Family Foundation Eatiquette program
The Vetri Foundation for Children

disconnected from the source of their food. By bringing them into the prep and service process, the students themselves develop more empathy and curiosity about the food system. The Vetri Eatiquette program uses their work in the summer Dream Camp as a way to prototype new recipes and service delivery systems.

Dream Camp is an extension of the ESF summer camp program, which provides five weeks of free camp to Philadelphia students between the ages of six and sixteen within a select income range. As Tia explained, "During the school year, we have mandates with the school district about what to serve. But at Dream Camp, we make the food, prepare the budget, and consult with the counselors and the students—they are integrated into our program." Tia's biggest aha moment was when she realized that the redesign of food service to children was having a huge impact—as in this story from a parent. A father shared that when going grocery shopping with his son, the boy selected cucumbers, cilantro, and tomatoes, which surprised the dad because his son never liked vegetables. The boy announced that he wanted to make gazpacho soup! Tia reflected, "I am doing the right thing. We are making a difference that is affecting the rest of their lives … We are affecting change. And I like being a change agent" (Interview, Nixon & McDonald 2014).

REFLECTIONS

- Explore the business model of Real Food Works (http://www.realfoodworks.com), which taps into the capacity of under-utilized upscale restaurant kitchens at off-peak hours to deliver healthy lunches to premium paying customers.
- Research Indian Dabbawalla lunch food delivery system by watching this video: http://vimeo.com/60748502. What does this decades old system teach you about food as a system? What about this designed food system could be incorporated into the ways we prepare food in Western societies?
- How have large and small restaurants, such as Chipotle (see the Cannes award-winning film *Back to The Start*: https://www.youtube.com/watch?v=aMfSGt6rHos) and Honeygrow (http://www.honeygrow.com), redesigned the ways we experience fast food?
- Do a scan of sensorial cues of fast-food restaurants. What colors are used for signage? How is the furniture designed? What about lighting, noise volume, ceiling height, and line cues? Catalog as many sensorial design cues as possible and write an explanation for why the fast-food restaurant might be purposefully designed in that way.

Case Story: Highlands Dinner Club—Where Open-sourced Culinary Laboratories Promote Social Innovation

Ben Walmer is a meal curator and has become a social architect of sorts. A licensed architect with a formal education in engineering, art, and psychology, he brings a very interdisciplinary approach to a phenomena that is spreading throughout major cities in

America—alternative dining groups. His gatherings around meals are not quite restaurants, and not exactly caterers, but are means to social innovations. Ben's company is the Highlands Dinner Club (HDC), and it was birthed out of a desire to celebrate an apartment renovation in Harlem, New York. He credits his appreciation of intelligent systems as well as his fascination with "food and shelter as fundamental points of innovation" as the source for HDC. Started in 2009 as an eight-course dinner party, it has since become more experimental. It is perceived as an ongoing culinary laboratory and a way to bring narrative and social networks to the process of executing projects.

How does Highlands Dinner Club work? Ben explains:

The purest way an event happens: someone asks "Hey, can we have an event? This looks interesting and fun!", and there is an open invitation for convivial interaction ... We are not caterers; we are not restaurants. We remain a performance and an experiment, and therefore, we can look past those constraints. For example, we have sent people a map, they've hiked two miles into the woods and then had a 12 course meal around a fire. (Interview, Nixon & Walmer 2014)

One of their first experimental events was in collaboration with a neighbor in Harlem who regularly fished and sold his caught fish out of a cooler on the sidewalk. They decided to drive to Hyannis Port together early one morning, catch 125 pounds of porgies, drive back to Harlem, and hold a gigantic fish fry the next day, which evolved into an outdoor party of 100 neighbors and invited guests from HDC's mailing list. The guests paid for their meal on a donations basis. That experiment led to Ben connecting to other similar foodies and in 2011 he was invited to the New York dinner club Whisk and Ladle in Brooklyn, New York, to cook for the *Michelin Guide* release party and for professional chefs.

Such events are an integration of design, systems thinking, and materials. As in architecture, procurement of materials is a significant part of the operations. Ben sees other connections between architecture and food:

They both take time. With food I get that quick gratification to carte blanche find the best materials ... and I get to see the end-user experience this product of the design teams happening in the same space, on the same day—it is a great thing to experience. (Interview, Nixon & Walmer 2014)

Their current business model is to be funded by a network of sponsors, underwriters, and donations from the final customer. Highlands Dinner Club utilizes an ensemble model and taps into seasonal retail. Ben sees clear connections between complex systems and food production—either through his HDC project, or those of an international scope such as Aggreco, which aims to build out agricultural projects around the world as a platform for socially sustainable businesses and agriculture. He was inspired by his farming relatives where he saw firsthand the role of improvisation, creativity, and tinkering in thinking through solutions when cultivating food directly off of the land. He sees it being fundamentally related to design thinking:

> *The process of integrating with your natural surroundings in order to produce food—building complexity to produce food on a market basis—each of those levels creates complexity. The food system is the most potentially data rich thing out there. This is the long view of our international work.* (Interview, Nixon & Walmer 2014)

Ben has two other projects: Roselle, a restaurant farmers' market, and METAble, a project he has prototyped in Kenya and Armenia to bring public policy and business stakeholders focused on sustainable development together around food. All of these projects embrace prototyping, experimentation, and story in order to develop innovative networks.

GO DEEPER
Review the following:
- Runaround Sous: http://chowhound .chow.com/topics/972140
- Food Thinking—"Where design thinking meets food": http://food-thinking.com
- The Whisk and Ladle in Brooklyn, NY: http://www.thewhiskandladle.com

REFLECTIONS
- Research aquaponics and hydroponics food projects, such as The Agrarian Group and METAble. In what ways are they designing a system of food delivery? How is what they propose different from larger-scale food production systems?
- What are other "pop-up" experiential eating services that you can observe, emerging in your part of the world? Why do you think this is occurring? Check out, for example, Cook, in Philadelphia, "a collaborative kitchen classroom": http://audreyclairecook .com

---

Conclusion

In this chapter we have looked at the full range of definitions of services and service design, and we have contextualized service as an improvisational structure and as a vehicle to deliver experiences. You have learned through the various case stories that people (i.e., customers) exist within a *system* of experiences. There can be fluid structures set up to best design service delivery. When we begin to view service design as a means of curation, we see even greater value and relevance in our current "experience economy," where service design has become increasingly important.

Acknowledgments

Thank you to all of the thought leaders and design professionals who took the time to be interviewed by me for this chapter: Jeff Benjamin, Kirtley Fisher, Kelly Herrenkohl,

Michelle Histand, Amy Kates, Tia McDonald, Paula Sunshine, and Christi Zuber. Service design is one of the most exciting extensions of strategic design thinking because of its social and fiscal impact on a business and in society. I acknowledge Alison Rieple, my principal advisor during my doctoral studies at the University of Westminster, who launched me on this path of exploring the design of services. Thank you as well to my students in the Strategic Design MBA program at Philadelphia University who keep my mind stretched; and to my husband, John, for his awesome support.

References

Alakoski, L., K. Ojasolo, and K. Pätilä, eds. (2007), *Service Innovation and Design*, Finland: Laurea Communications.

Barrett, F. (2012), *Yes to the Mess: Surprising Leadership Lessons from Jazz*, Boston: Harvard Business Press.

Barrett, F. J. and K. Peplowski (1998), "Minimal Structures within a Song: An Analysis of 'All of Me,'" *Organization Science*, 9 (5): 558–60.

Bedford, C. and A. Lee (2008), "Would You Like Service with That?" *Design Management Review*, 19 (1): 38–43.

Berry, L., V. Zeithaml, and A. Parasuraman (1990), "Five Imperatives for Improving Service Quality," *Sloan Management Review*, 31 (4): 29–38.

Bitran, G., J-C. Ferrer, and P. R. Oliveira (2008), "Managing Customer Experiences: Perspectives on the Temporal Aspects of Service Encounters," *Manufacturing Service Operations Management*, 10 (1): 61–83.

Brown, J. and P. Duguid (1991) "Organizational Learning and Communities of Practice: Toward a Unified View of Working, Learning, and Innovation," *Organization Science*, 2 (1): 40–57.

Chase, R. B. (1981), "The Customer Contact Approach to Services: Theoretical Basis and Practical Extensions," *Operations Research*, 29 (4): 698–706.

CIA World Factbook (2014), "Country Comparison GDP (Purchasing Power Parity)," Available online: https://www.cia.gov/library/publications/the-world-factbook/rankorder/2001rank.html

Clatworthy, S. (2011), "Service Innovation through Touch-Points: Development of an Innovation Toolkit for the First Stages of New Service Development," *International Journal of Design*, 5(2), 15–28.

Crossan, M. M. (1998), "Improvisation in Action," *Organization Science*, 9 (5): 593–99.

Csikszentmihalyi, M. (1990), *Flow: The Psychology of Optimal Experience*, New York: Harper.

Diller, S., N. Shedroff, and D. Rhea (2006), *Making Meaning—How Successful Businesses Deliver Meaningful Customer Experiences*, Berkeley, CA: New Riders.

Eckersley, M. D. (2008), "Designing Human-Centered Services," *Design Management Review*, 19 (1): 59–65.

Erlhoff, M., B. Mager, and E. Manzini (1997), *Dienstleistung braucht Design*, Cologne: Luchterhand.

Geertz, C. (1973), *The Interpretation of Cultures*, London: Hutchinson.

Gillespie, B. (2008), "Service Design via the Global Web: Global Companies Serving Local Markets," *Design Management Review*, 19 (1): 44–52.

Gronroos, C. (1984), "A Service Quality Model and Its Marketing Implications," *European Journal of Marketing*, 18 (4): 36–44.

Grove, S., R. Fisk, and M. Bitner (1992), "Dramatizing the Service Experience: A Managerial Approach," *Advances in Services Marketing and Management*, 1: 91–121.

Gupta, S., and M. Vajic (2000), "The Contextual and Dialectical Nature of Experiences," in J. Fitzsimmons and M. Fitzsimmons (eds.), *New Service Development—Creating Memorable Experiences*, 33–51, Thousand Oaks, CA: Sage.

Heskett, J. L., W. E. Sasser, and C. W. L. Hart (1990), *Service Breakthroughs: Changing the Rules of the Game*, New York: Free Press.

Heskett, J. L., W. E. Sasser, and L. A. Schlessinger (1997), *The Service Profit Chain*, New York: Free Press.

Hock, D. (2005), *One from Many—VISA and the Rise of Chaordic Organization*, San Francisco, CA: Berrett-Koehler Publishers, Inc.

Hollins, W. (1993), "Design in the Service Sector," *Managing Service Quality*, 3 (3): 33–37.

Hollins, W. (2006), "About: Service Design," *Design Council*, 24 (November): 1–33.

Jacobs, V. (2009), "Platforming: Evolving the Paradigm of Branding," *Design Management Review*, 20 (4): 16–21.

Koskinen, J. (2009), "Service Design: Perspectives on Turning-Points in Design," *Servicedesign.tv*, downloaded January 18, 2009.

Langeard, E., J. Bateson, C. Lovelock, and P. Eigler (1981), *Services Marketing: New Insights from Consumers and Managers*, Report no. 81–104, Cambridge, MA: Marketing Science Institute.

Lévi-Strauss, C. (1962), *The Savage Mind*, Chicago: University of Chicago Press.

Lovlie, L., C. Downs, and B. Reason (2008), "Bottom-line Experiences: Measuring the Value of Design in Service," *Design Management Review*, 19 (1): 73–79.

Maffei, S., B. Mager, and D. Sangiorgi (2005), "Innovation through Service Design—From Research and Theory to a Network of Practice, a Users' Driven Perspective," *Joining Forces Conference*, University of Art and Design Helsinki, September 21–23, 2005.

Mager, B. (2008), "Service Design," in M. Erlhoff and T. Marshall (eds.), *The Design Dictionary—Perspectives on Design Terminology*, 354–57, Basel: Birkhäuser.

Mager, B. and S. Evenson (2008), "Art of Service: Drawing the Arts to Inform Service Design and Specification," in Bill Hefley and Wendy Murphy (eds.), *Service Science,*

Management and Engineering—Education for the 21st Century, 75–76, New York: Springer.

Mangold, W. and E. Babakus (1991), "Service Quality—The Front-Stage vs. the Back-Stage Perspective," *Journal of Services Marketing*, 5 (4): 59–70.

Manzini, E. (1993), "Il Design dei Servizi—La progettazione del produtto-servizio," *Design Management*, 4, 7–12.

Meroni, A. and D. Sangiorgi (2011), *Design for Services*, Aldershot, UK: Gower Publishing.

Nixon, N. W. (2012), "Designing Experiential Services with an Improvisational Stance: Lessons from The Ritz-Carlton," *Touchpoint: The Journal of Service Design*, 4 (1): 32–35.

Nixon, N. W. (2013) "Viewing Ascension Health from a Design Thinking Perspective," *Journal of Organization Design*, 2 (3): 23–28.

Nixon, N. and A. Rieple, (2010), "Luxury Redesigned: How the Ritz-Carlton Uses Experiential Service Design to Position Abundance in Times of Scarcity," *Design Management Journal*, 5 (1): 40–49.

Nixon, N. (2014), "7 Rules for Improvising at Work," TEDx Philadelphia Talk, March. Available online: https://www.youtube.com/watch?v=UTS95OchFOE

Norman, D. (2004), *Emotional Design—Why We Love (Or Hate) Everyday Things*, New York: Basic Books.

Parasuraman, A., V. A. Zeithaml, and L. Berry (1988), "SERVQUAL: A Multiple-Item Scale for Measuring Consumer Perceptions of Service Quality," *Journal of Retailing*, 64 (1): 12–40.

Pine, J. (2004), "What Consumers Want," TED Talk. Available online: http://www.ted.com/talks/lang/eng/joseph_pine_on_what_consumers_want.html (accessed April 30, 2010).

Pine, J. B. and J. H. Gilmore (1999), *The Experience Economy—Work Is Theatre and Every Business a Stage*, Boston: Harvard Business School Press.

Pullman, M. and M. Gross (2004), "The Ability of Experience Design Elements to Elicit Emotions and Loyalty Behaviors," *Decision Sciences*, 35 (3): 551–78.

Roberts, K. (2004), *Lovemarks: The Future Beyond Brands*, New York: PowerHouse Books.

Roth, A. V., R. Chase, and C. Voss (1997), *Service in the U.S.: Progress towards Global Service Leadership*, Birmingham, UK: Severn Trent Plc.

Roth, A. V. and L. J. Menor (2003), "Insights into Service Operations Management: A Research Agenda," *Production Operations Management*, 12 (2): 145–64.

Saco, R. M. and A. Goncalves (2008), "Service Design: An Appraisal," *Design Management Review*, 19 (1): 10–19.

Shedroff, N. (1999), "Information Interaction Design: A Unified Field Theory of Design," in Robert Jacobson (ed.), *Information Design*, Boston: First MIT Press, 267–92.

Shedroff, N. (2001), *Experience Design*, Indianapolis: New Riders.

Stacey, R. (1991), *The Chaos Frontier: Creative Strategic Control for Business*, Oxford: Butterworth-Heinemann.

Stacey, R. (1992), *Managing the Unknowable—Strategic Boundaries between Order and Chaos in Organizations*, San Francisco: Jossey-Bass Inc. Publishers.

Taatila, V. P., J. Suomala, R. Siltala, and S. Keskinen (2006), "Framework to study the Social the Docial Innovation Networks," *European Journal of Innovation Management*, 9 (3): 312–26.

Zeithaml, V., A. Parasuranam, and L. Berry (1985), "Problems and Strategies in Services Marketing," *Journal of Marketing*, 49 (Spring): 33–46.

Manoj Fenelon (director of Foresight & Innovation at PepsiCo) helps imagine and design desirable futures for PepsiCo's beverage brands and businesses. He also sees himself as a go-between, exploring opportunities to create new value where business and societal interests intersect. Manoj is Indian by birth, a New Yorker by residence, and a frequent speaker at foresight and trends gatherings.

Manoj Fenelon

Focusing Question: How can design help business adapt to key shifts in the macro-environment that are changing the ground rules for value-creation and innovation?

This chapter explores the key questions:

- In what larger historical context should we locate the emergence of disciplines like design and foresight within business?

- Why is design uniquely positioned to help twenty-first-century businesses create value?

- How is design helping reshape branding, innovation, and business models across industries and economic sectors?

- What are the significant issues on the horizon that design (and design thinkers) should consider?

Foreword

The story of the absorption of design thinking into business is playing out in three acts. The first is already an accounting fact. Consider the case of PepsiCo—in its first full year of operation, PepsiCo's Design Group generated enough savings by *in*-sourcing creative services and better managing agency partnerships to more than pay for itself and its new SoHo digs. With its insistence on a holistic view that cuts across channels and points of interaction, design departments within CPG (consumer packaged goods) companies are poised to reverse a several-decades-long trend of the assembly-lining and outsourcing of creativity.

What now? Only the little task of changing corporate culture! The second act has design radiating outward from the function (group) to become a way of thinking and problem solving that is widely used across a range of business issues and settings. Students of design today can expect to be its ambassadors and catalysts within business organizations tomorrow. The handful of examples presented in this chapter for dissection and reflection demonstrate how far companies that *get* design can go with rethinking their products and brands. Hopefully they also show how design thinking can help businesses engage with complex, and otherwise befuddling, issues like sustainability and transparency.

Which brings us to "what's next?" This may sound audacious, but in short order, design may be called upon by business to redesign business itself. From radically different business models and corporate structures to fundamental rewiring of the motives and principles underlying business activity, capitalism will need alternatives because it is in crisis, falling far short in practice on its two major ideological claims: it has neither produced prosperity for all, nor does it go hand-in-hand with democracy. Design, if it so desires, can play a pivotal role in reimagining business, building strategies for growth and innovation on entirely different assumptions about how people want to live, and what they therefore need.

The reader should take away three things from this chapter. First, a sense that design thinking in today's business settings comes in different flavors and varieties, and it helps with a wide range of problems. The second and third takeaways function like a prologue and epilogue to the set of examples that make design's value to business concrete: The prologue offers the backstory of why design is emergent in business at this historical juncture, and the epilogue serves up topics that could help chart design's evolution within business.

The chapter starts with a reminder that design thinking can't be divorced from the concerns about quality of life and the social utility of business (and other large institutions) that animated its earliest proponents. It then reviews a collection of cases drawn from all corners of the business world (as well as a few from the nonprofit and public sectors), synthesizing the main ways in which design thinking is helping businesses create new value, connections, and even meaning.

Design in a Time of Ambiguity and Uncertainty

The Institute for the Future (IFTF), a forty-five-year-old, independent, nonprofit research organization, has a succinct way of describing the times we're living through: "a century of transformation, a decade of turbulence" (2012 Map of the Decade, 2012). Why transformation? Why now? The reason, according to Ian Morrison, a president emeritus with the institute, starts with understanding the future as a problem of two curves. The rocky transition as civilization attempts to shift from one curve to the other is what is causing terms like volatility, uncertainty, complexity, ambiguity (mnemonically VUCA), and resilience to fly around in important places, from the US Army War College to the halls of "Big Business."

The first curve (also established or incumbent) is loosely generalizable as the industrial paradigm through which a vast majority of the global economy's profits and revenues now flow. Signs of the decline of this paradigm are all around us, from business failures and capitalist crises to environmental disasters and massively iniquitous social outcomes. The second curve is the emergent wave of new businesses and new ways of doing business that are radically different from the first curve. The decline of the first curve entities and the emergence of those on the second curve are both fueled by three macro forces of change, in the areas of demography, technology, and political economy (see Figure 9.1).

The demographics of the world are shifting in ways that will have profound ramifications—most of Europe and North America is aging just as the balance of economic power shifts to the East and South, and as established economic and political orders enter crisis mode. Social safety nets premised on younger workers paying into a system that pays out to retirees are threatened by lower birth rates, persistent

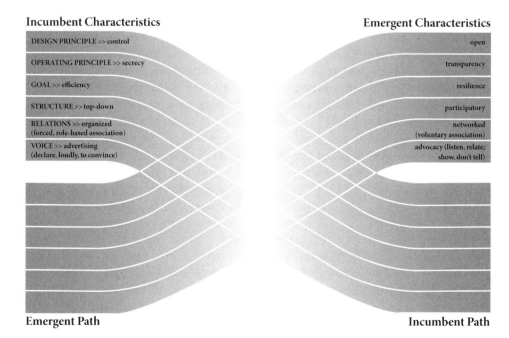

Incumbent Characteristics

DESIGN PRINCIPLE >> control

OPERATING PRINCIPLE >> secrecy

GOAL >> efficiency

STRUCTURE >> top-down

RELATIONS >> organized
(forced, role-based association)

VOICE >> advertising
(declare, loudly, to convince)

Emergent Characteristics

open

transparency

resilience

participatory

networked
(voluntary association)

advocacy (listen, relate;
show, don't tell)

Emergent Path

Incumbent Path

Figure 9.1 Curve view of the future
Source: Adapted from author's notes from the IFTF's ten-year Forecast Retreat, 2012)

and rising unemployment among youth, and the destruction of pension-plan value by investments gone wrong.

In technology, Moore's Law (Gordon Moore, a founder of Intel, predicted in the 1980s that semiconductor chip capacity would double approximately every eighteen months) is still going strong, helping to make everything faster, smaller, and better. Smartphones have put more computing power in our pockets than Ronald Reagan had at his command when he was president, more than spaceships had in the 1980s. Technology is also connecting us in ways previously unimaginable and at unprecedented scales. It is projected that 50 billion devices will be connected to the cloud by 2020 (Green 2013), more than five times the number of people on the planet then.

The triumphant narrative of capitalism as the engine of democracy and social progress has been fatally disrupted by the global financial crises of 2008 and the ensuing political fallout, as well as by the economic rise of China. Capitalism finds itself at a crossroads, as its pursuit of infinite growth runs up against the realities of a planet with finite resources.

The arc of progress (survival?) in the twenty-first century will be one of great transition from the first to the second curve, even as the radically different principles underlying the two set up all manner of disruptions and turbulence in the teen years of the century. It is in this volatile stew of forces for change that we must locate the emergence of disciplines, such as design and foresight, in society at large, but especially in business and particularly with innovation.

Design: The Soul of Business?

Design is an inherently integrative discipline that draws on the best of our analytical and intuitive abilities to create an entirely new way of thinking. Design dissolves polarities (e.g., passion vs. reason, thinking vs. doing, and art vs. science) that have anchored collective consciousness for the last 200-plus years.

Technically, design thinking represents a form of logic called abductive thinking that differs markedly from the other two forms that inform most business thinking and argumentation: deductive and inductive. In **deductive** (rule-applying) logic, one reasons from a general rule to specific instances (to borrow from Calvin & Hobbes: if heaven is a happy place, and tigers scare people, then tigers are likely not allowed in heaven). In inductive (rule-forming) logic, one reasons from specific instances to form a general rule (if tigers make some people happy, and heaven is where people are happy, it makes sense to allow tigers in heaven). **Abductive** logic is called upon in contexts where the rules are unknown or unknowable, to help make sense of the chaos. It often unearths new insights from the creative juxtaposition of known and unknown elements (perhaps tigers don't scare people in heaven, or maybe heaven doesn't exist).

By allowing for a multiplicity of perspectives and by fusing concerns of the mind with those of the heart, design also provides a platform for those in business to acknowledge and integrate an explicitly moral outlook on the issues and challenges of our times. And this moral compass will be necessary, even crucial, if design is to make a difference. With technology driving exponential growth in our capability to manipulate the environment around us, human progress/survival itself depends on how this technology is thought of and deployed.

Ronald Wright, in his book *A Short History of Progress* (and the documentary of the same name), talks about a recurring pattern in human history where past civilizations—each with their own technological achievements to rival ours—followed their respective ideas of "progress" to their graves. He calls this pattern a ***progress trap***. Just because something is technologically possible and feasible does not necessarily make it desirable and/or useful. Cue Evgeny Morozov's argument, in *The Net Delusion* (2011), that the same social media technologies that the net-erati tirelessly promote as emancipatory are just as (if not more) likely to become instruments of fraud, surveillance, and state repression.

If design is to shape the potential of technology to decidedly human and humane ends, it has to draw inspiration from the ethos that animated some of its earliest proponents. Two exhortations, decades apart, stand out as bookends of sorts for the humanizing influence of design thinking on business— Stefano Marzano's (1992) (ex-CEO of Philips Design) seminal call for designers to orient themselves toward improving people's quality of life and Wolff Olins's (2012) distillation of the five characteristics of future-facing brands and businesses. If the industrial order,

by and large, was one of increasing complication, the postindustrial order presents problems that are not just complicated but complex. Business strategy has to account for unknown unknowns, and come to terms with the fact that cause-and-effect relationships can be discerned only in retrospect. This environment puts a premium on action as the first step in sensemaking and problem solving, and explains why design-thinking principles, like rapid prototyping and iterative experiment-and-learn loops, are the talk of the business world.

GO DEEPER

Read and watch the following:

- *Flying over Las Vegas* by S. Marzano. Available online: http://www.usa. philips.com/philips5/shared/assets/ Downloadablefile/Flying-over-Las- Vegas-14327.pdf
- "Game Changers: Five Behaviors That Are Shaping the Future of Business" by Wolff Olins. Available online: http:// gamechangers2012.wolffolins.com/static/ report/files/WO_GameChangesReport .pdf
- Watch the documentary *Surviving Progress* by M. Roy and H. Crooks.

REFLECTIONS

- How does your business or what you do in business improve the lives of your customers? Can you articulate this clearly and simply, in terms that a child (or grandparents) can grasp?
- Try to make a list of the macro-socioeconomic, technological, and

political forces that are affecting your business. It may be interesting to compare notes on this topic with acquaintances and friends in other industries.

- Use the characteristics listed in Figure 9.1 to identify a few tensions that are behind the turbulence in your workplace. Engage a few of your trusted colleagues to expand the discussion.

Design in Action

This section introduces select examples that paint a picture of how design thinking is helping businesses large and small. It is not only helping them to improve products and services, but also to ask better questions, raise deep-seated assumptions, and reappraise their relationship with people and society. A way to frame this breadth and diversity of influence is to show design and designers active in all three dimensions of business value creation—the What (products, services, brands), the How (people, processes, structure), and the Why (values, purpose, strategy). The examples below are organized by this crude (but simple) scheme to afford the reader a richer understanding of design's impact on business.

The What—Helping Rethink Products and Brands

The Dockers Wellthread Collection: Reimagining How Clothes Are Made, Seed to Stitch

Paul Dillinger, vice president of global design at Levi Strauss & Co, is a walking, talking embodiment of what most people associate with design—style. Thankfully, for our purposes, Paul is also a living, breathing, case study of how design can help sustainability invigorate an apparel brand and company instead of being a drag on its fortunes.

The Dockers® Wellthread Collection grew out of Paul's First Movers Fellowship with The Aspen Institute. The institute's Business and Society Program has as its mission: "'to equip business leaders for the twenty-first century with a new management paradigm—the vision and knowledge to integrate corporate profitability and social value" (Aspen Institute 2015). The First Movers Fellowship brings together socially conscious *intra*preneurs within companies large and small; gently facilitated experiences function as a kind of innovation lab for fellows to develop projects for their respective companies that integrate business value (profitability) with social and environmental values. [Note: the author is a First Movers Fellow of the class of 2013.]

Paul used the experience to develop (to paraphrase him) a fully integrated design methodology for a sustainable, values-based approach to growing and making cotton T-shirts and pants—a way to not only make meaningful improvements in the lives of cotton growers and systemic sustainability improvements up and down the supply and manufacturing chain, but also to make simple, elegant apparel designed to last long and never go out of style. Levi's, in their wisdom, asked that he try out his toolkit on the Dockers brand, and Wellthread was spun from there.

Paul started, as good designers often do, with good questions:

- Why is there a "race to the bottom" in the fashion industry, where calculations of profit seem to run counter to notions of ethics, responsibility, and sustainability?
- Why are so many of us, as consumers, so comfortable with outsourcing our waste (literally) and even our guilt over the waste (the secondhand market)?
- Will people pay good money for clothes that are verifiably made in ways that mirror their values?

What Paul did with these questions stands as an inspiring example of how design can be a catalyst for organizational change, and help resolve corporate tensions between doing well financially and doing good in society.

Paul starts the story of his fellowship with a startling admission: "As a designer, I didn't know how I was going to fix an industry-wide problem (with sustainability and poor social practices), but I was sure that it was my problem (i.e., a problem of design)" (Dillinger 2014). But the genius of this admission is that it simultaneously opens up the possibility that another, more sustainable and humane way to make apparel that we all wear can be designed. This may sound like a trivial insight, but it is not. Legions of well-intentioned corporate personnel have fretted over the same apparel (and other) industry problems and run up against the limitations of their respective functional silos in trying to solve them.

As Paul points out, not recognizing the systemic nature of the "race to the bottom" dynamic leads to solutions, however well-meaning, that are far from equal to the scale and complexity of the issue. For instance, marketing has barely scratched the surface before it decides to run with the "made with organically grown …" campaign, but does organically grown mean it wasn't picked using child labor? Or how about when those trying to reduce water-use find themselves in a zero-sum game with those trying to reduce energy-use? And what about accidents such as the 2014 Rana Plaza collapse in Bangladesh? These are terrible tragedies occurring way beyond the company's control in their outsourcing chain.

Levi's are reinventing the way the world thinks about socially and environmentally sustainable apparel, holistically. Design interventions span sustainable farming practices (including specially written songs that serve as mnemonic aids for farmers to remember the right times to water and add fertilizers); more efficient; less harmful dyeing processes; and judicious touches, like loops and reinforced shoulders, that make it easier for pants and T-shirts to be drip-dried (instead of dried in the dryer).

The changes to the dyeing process are a case in point of the thoroughness that a design lens can bring: The Dockers Wellthread collection uses specialized garment-dyeing processes that reduce both water and energy use (vs. conventional processes). Using cold-water pigment dyes for tops saves energy on heating, and salt-free reactive dyes for pants eliminate the need for energy-intensive desalination in wastewater treatment. Design also brings creativity, which allows for solutions to emerge that were not part of the problem space to start with—Wellthread apparel is dyed in the factory, not in the mill—allowing not only more direct control on the part of Levi's over the implementation of the new processes, but also new supply-chain efficiencies because fabric can now be dyed to order.

Lastly, but perhaps most tellingly, at a time when conventional crisis-response stratagems would dictate staying far away from anything Bangladesh, Dockers Wellthread Khakis are made exclusively at a Bangladeshi plant, one of five factories where Levi's are piloting a new approach to improving the lives of apparel workers: surveys of locals about what they think would be meaningful and relevant improvements in their lot, leading to tailored local assistance programs that are transformative for the participants and cycle back to positive business results for the company.

Before we leave this example, it is worth pointing to the relative ease with which programs like Wellthread can take root in the friendly soil of a corporate culture that's already thinking about sustainability as a core business issue, not just as a CSR (corporate social responsibility) or PR (public relations) sidebar. Paul has an apt term for this state of affairs; he calls it "innovating downhill" (Dillinger 2015). For those not as fortunate in their institutional settings, Figure 9.2 offers a simple and elegant framework to take stock of the challenges a design project may face.

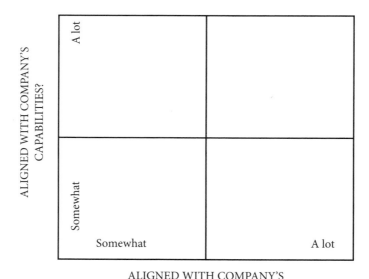

Figure 9.2 A simple tool to assess the cultural fit of your project
Source: Adapted from Aspen Institute's First Mover Fellowship seminar material)

We have seen how design can turn what were once crippling business tensions (e.g., profit vs. social/environmental well-being) into new opportunities. Although it's too early for sales figures to tell us much in this first example, the Levi Strauss Co. remains convinced that most people are with them on the need to reimagine how clothes are made, seed to stitch, and is committed to supporting its Dockers Wellthread Collection.

Chipotle: Empowering People to Positively Affect Food Culture

The next example highlights a company that has bet the farm, quite literally, on people caring about where their food comes from and how it is made—caring enough to pay a bit more and to prefer the brand over other brands that don't seem to care. A catalyst for the mainstreaming of conscientious eating in the United States: what a long, strange trip it has been for the United States, from Chez Panisse to Chipotle!

When the history of branding is soon revised, September 12, 2013, will mark some kind of a turning point. That day, the Mexican-kitchen chain that has captured the American fast-food imagination to the tune of 1,230 outlets and $2.3 billion USD released two very strange pieces of advertising: (1) *The Scarecrow*, a three-and-a-half minute animated video, posted online, featuring Big Food as the villain, and (2) a free, downloadable, interactive game that riffed on the same factory farms versus small-scale/family farms topic. They were strange because both had virtually no branding in any accepted sense of the term—the brand name appeared once, in small print, in the introduction to the game, and the logo once, after the video ended.

More strangeness was on its way; *USA Today* reported that *The Scarecrow* was mere prequel to "a series of four, TV show-length Big-Food-busting dark comedies, 'Farmed and Dangerous,' which the company planned to post online sometime in 2014" (Horovitz 2013). As other outlets reported on the making of the videos, news dribbled out about ultra-high-end production values and the participation of top animation and musical talents. What was going on here? Why was a fast-food chain spending good money on videos that fused the sensibilities of a Wes Anderson and a Michael Moore? And if it thought the results were cool and had viral-potential, why wasn't it slapping its brand and logo all over them?

As you may have guessed, there is more method than madness to Chipotle's approach to marketing and branding. In February 2012, the *New York Times* reported on the first shot across the bow for this restaurant industry upstart—another short animated film, *Back to the Start*, featuring puppets and an upbeat plot about a family farmer first switching to factory farming before realizing the error of his ways and switching back to more sustainable ways of raising animals. The video, originally released online and then in movie theaters, was scheduled for its latest reincarnation as the company's first national ad, two-minutes long, during the Grammy Awards telecast, and paired with an invitation to download, via iTunes, the accompanying song, a Willie Nelson cover of Coldplay's "The Scientist." Sixty cents out of every ninety-nine cents for the download went to fund the Chipotle Cultivate Foundation, started by the company's founder, Steve Ells, to promote sustainable farming practices and more family farms. It is somewhere between *Back to the Start* and the Cultivate Foundation that we start to see what Chipotle is up to:

1. It is clearly being driven by a larger purpose than profit. The company is quite profitable precisely because of not chasing profitability as a goal! Don't worry, there's a good explanation for this seeming paradox.
2. It senses that people are hungry for a conversation about food that's based on values, and has turned over its media time, paid and earned, to enabling and amplifying exactly that. This is not a work of altruistic entrepreneurship; it is savvy twenty-first-century marketing.
3. It is a brand that has very little to say about itself. Which, in a paradigm increasingly shaped by the people formerly known as consumers, is exactly what gets you talked about (and your content zipping around the inter-tubes). Branding for Chipotle is not about tightly defined positions and controlling the message, it is about letting go of the brand ego and becoming the scaffolding upon which people can build their own experiences, relationships, and meaning.

A bit more on each of these radical acts of design: Design is an intrinsically purposeful endeavor. The act of creating anything or solving a problem presupposes an overall sense of mission. And good brand designers everywhere are introducing (reintroducing?) conversations about purpose into boardrooms. Sound research and the imprimatur of a successful ex-CMO of Procter & Gamble are certainly helping their cause. In the "Go Deeper" section following this example, you will be prompted to read *Grow* by Jim Stengel (the ex-P&G-CMO). The book grew out of a remarkable study of long-term growth, synthesizing ten years' worth of financial data, Millward Brown Optimor's global database of brand-equity scores (> 50,000 brands), and additional research by the Anderson School of Management at UCLA.

The researchers' key finding: brands that focused their business priorities on the ideal of improving people's lives consistently outperformed brands that didn't, in delivering long-term value. As measured by stock value, profits, and customer ratings of brand strength, the fifty best performing (over a decade) brands were distinguished by their having an ideal. Chipotle is one of the Stengel 50, as the list has come to be called.

Here's how Jim Stengel (2011: 16) defines a brand ideal: "It is a shared intent by everyone in a business to improve people's lives. [It] is a business's essential reason for being, the higher-order benefit it brings to the world." Figure 9.3 summarizes Stengel's research, showing how being oriented toward an ideal drives preferential consideration for a brand.

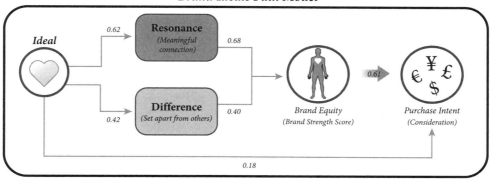

Figure 9.3 A path model for the influence of brand ideals driving purchasing intent. (The higher the number, the stronger the relationship between the two variables.)
Source: Stengel, 2011

Chipotle's purpose is not to grow profits. It is to encourage sustainable farming and family farms. Increasing profits happen to be one of the outcomes of doing that. Chipotle's brand ideal, per Stengel, is to empower people to positively affect food culture. But how does one do that in a thirty-second commercial? Well, one starts by ditching the thirty-second commercial (in fact, the entire idea of advertising itself) and starting a conversation. And it is in this light that *Back to the Start* and *The Scarecrow* show their true colors. The former is the brand being transparent and telling its own story of moving away from factory farming toward sustainable, small-scale farming. The latter is a pointed drawing of the battle lines between Big Food and sustainable farming. And if you're the only fast-food brand conscious enough to start this sort of a discussion, who needs the logos and font-fetishes of conventional branding! Chipotle's act of provoking discussion on this issue and removing itself

from the stage, simultaneously, is more powerful and resonant than any statement advertising can hope to make today.

It is not just the videos and short films; brand marketing at Chipotle is about inviting people into conversations, facilitating relationships, and orchestrating—with a light touch—shared intent and activism around where and how we grow food. Cultivate festivals are sprouting all over the country courtesy of the company and allied foundation—providing an open platform for likeminded people to gather in celebration of independent music and independent farms, the virtues of locality, rootedness, authenticity, and collaboration. This is the brand as platform or scaffolding (see Valerie Jacobs and Michael Wintrob in chapter 3), defining itself by higher-order values and principles and ceding control over the experience and meaning to people who see heart-to-heart with it. As Valerie puts it, channeling Liz Sanders—a design lecturer at Ohio State—brands cannot design experiences (or meaning), experience is inside people; brand design can only hope to furnish the opportunities, contexts, stimuli, and tools for people to create their own experiences and meaning. Time to throw away the rusty brand management tools of the last century; no more pyramids, wheels, positioning statements, and guardrails. Time to humanize branding: say hello, a bit about where you're coming from, and what you're about, then shut up and let your actions do the rest of the talking.

GO DEEPER

Read or watch the following:

- *Grow: How Ideals Power Growth and Profit at the World's Greatest Companies* by J. Stengel.
- "Beyond Corporate Social Responsibility: Integrated External Engagement" by J. Browne and R. Nuttall. Available online: http://www.mckinsey.com/insights/strategy/beyond_corporate_social_responsibility_integrated_external_engagement
- Paul Dillinger shares the story of his First Movers project at the 2014 Aspen First Movers Summit on YouTube. Available online: http://www.youtube.com/watch?v=WsXyIAACxmM&hd=1
- Dockers WellThread video on YouTube. *Available online: https://www.youtube.com/watch?v=3xGR_psgU0k&hd=1*

REFLECTIONS

- Use Figure 9.2 to assess the cultural fit of a project you are doing, or looking to do, in your organization. Where are

the gaps? What broad strategies can you think of to close them?
- Think of some examples of "false opposites" (e.g., it is hard to be sustainable and profitable in fashion) you have experienced or read about. Practice writing "How might we …" statements (e.g., How might we make apparel that is sustainable and sells well?) that reframe the problem as opportunity. This is good training to spot design problems masquerading as other sorts of problems.
- What values or ideals does your brand represent? Draft a statement of your best guess, and do some quick research by asking for reactions from a wide variety of people that interact with the brand.

The How—Looking at People & Process Differently

Let us shift to the How dimension of value creation in business and take up a topic that perplexes a lot of corporate leaders: innovation. Top questions on their minds include: What kinds of people, processes, and organizational contexts promote innovation? Can we train people who are not naturally innovative (whatever that means) to be innovative? How? And what about this *creativity* thing?

The IBM Global CEO study is published every two years. As its name indicates, it surveys and reports on the opinions of over 1,500 CEOs from around the world and across a range of industries. The key takeaway from the 2010 edition of the report: Chief executives believe that successfully navigating an increasingly complex and uncertain world will require *creativity* (in 2012, it was "leading through connections and collaboration"). These leaders felt the need to attract, develop, and promote creative leaders who could be comfortable with strategic ambiguity, question assumptions, consider previously unheard-of ways to transform the enterprise, and make drastic business model changes to realize their strategies.

All fine and dandy, but how does an organization cultivate such radicalism within the course of its normal functioning?

Before we attempt to answer that question, let's learn a little more about creativity—a quality that is both in high demand and hard to pinpoint (spec out in a job description, for example). The research of Charles Limb (2010), a neuroscientist at Johns Hopkins University, offers some interesting clues about how creativity works. Experimenting in his free time, our curious brain researcher puts jazz musicians and rappers, among others, through fMRI (functional magnetic resonance imaging) scanners, while having them perform both composed music/raps and improvisations. He hypothesizes that the differences in patterns of brain function between the two musical tasks will help us map the neural contours of creativity. His initial findings, while not conclusive, point in an interesting direction: Rather than correlating to raised activity in specific areas of the brain, creativity appears to be associated with the shutting down of regions in the forebrain that are responsible for analytic logic and top-down control of decision making.

Could creativity be something that does not have to be acquired because it is already there, except usually under a choke-hold from analysis? What does this imply for the development and training of creative leaders? What sorts of organizational settings and modes have to be "shut down" (metaphorically speaking) to enable creativity to flourish within?

The answers to these questions involve values that design holds dear—empathy, flexibility, freedom, and participation. The next two examples of design thinking in action are not about individual companies as much as they are about the paths less traveled that many companies are taking, in order to become innovative, adaptive, and resilient.

International Corporate Volunteering: Adventures in Empathy

The term "global-minded" is often bandied about in discussions of leadership, but what does it really mean? Is it just a fancy way of saying leaders who keep up with world news? Does it connote life/work experience in foreign cultures? If we use North/South here as a crude proxy for the economic blocs represented by the so-called advanced industrial countries and the rest of the world, respectively, then is it largely polite-speak for businesspersons from the global North getting acquainted with the realities of the South? Or a confession that social privilege has so distanced businessfolk from the realities of the global majority as to trigger remedial lessons in empathizing? Whatever your take, it is worth looking into one route companies are taking to develop more global-minded leaders—international corporate volunteering.

While it encompasses a broad range of programs with diverse ambitions, international corporate volunteering provides unusual contexts for associates to share experiences with, and develop empathy for, people from different geographies, histories, and social classes. Let's delve into the nuts and bolts of one such program, at PepsiCo, to better understand the phenomenon and the design-thinking principles embedded in it.

PepsiCorps is a month-long international-business experience that aims to deepen employees' commitment to the company's guiding philosophy: performance with purpose (see Figure 9.4). Associates worldwide (across functions) who are in the leadership-development window apply to participate in the program, and carefully selected teams of seven to eight are sent abroad to work on projects that leverage their business acumen to address challenges relating to clean water, sustainable agriculture, affordable nutrition, and women's development (focus areas for the company). The teams live and work with the communities they're helping, eschewing the typical perks of executive business travel in favor of immersion in the local culture and environment.

For instance, the very first team of PepsiCorps participants spent a month in Denu, Ghana, working with the local government and tribal councils of South Ketu District to improve villagers' access to clean and safe water and promote

Figure 9.4 Members of a PepsiCorps team with local officials in South Ketu District, Ghana
Manoj Fenelon

sustainable eco-tourism. One half of the team researched and recommended process improvements to the district's Water & Sanitation Board, and they held "train-the-trainer" sessions with local government officials to help with implementation. The other half brought together local government, tribal leaders, and other community stakeholders to develop a proposal and concepts for attracting eco-tourism investment from the central government and private parties. On Fridays the whole team volunteered at local schools, teaching personal-hygiene habits to over 1,000 elementary and primary schoolchildren. In linking the provision of basic utilities to economic development (eco-tourism revenues to ensure sustainable funding for water-access improvements), education and health, the team was exemplifying a systems-approach to community development. It was also, effectively, prototyping a new way for the company to be present in a world beset by troubling inequalities, while enabling its members to leverage their business skills and expertise to contribute tangible and enduring solutions to complex problems.

This leadership development program is remarkable for being conceived, created, and implemented from below, in this case by an unofficial group of eight junior associates working outside of their regular roles and responsibilities. In each of its first few years, the program has grown in size and scope, reflecting a healthy demand among PepsiCo's over 325,000 employees for training that happens outside of (as the stereotype goes) windowless conference rooms.

The program is now managed by the company's office of Global Citizenship and Sustainable Development, and it is hailed throughout the company as a pioneering alternative to more conventional corporate volunteering and leadership development programs. It has also been featured in the *Wall Street Journal* and earned the group that created it a seat at a White House roundtable on skills-based volunteering.

By emphasizing on-the-ground learning and creative problem solving in the face of extreme constraints, PepsiCorps and programs like it are seeding the sensibility and tools of design in ever-widening circles within the company. It is also interesting to note the diversity of ends that international corporate volunteering programs serve within various companies, each program uniquely designed to reflect the company's culture and strategic priorities. Some (e.g., IBM) seek to inculcate a general sense of service and citizenship among corporate employees; others (e.g., PepsiCo) seek to develop a new generation of leaders who are global-minded, purposeful, adaptable, and cross-disciplinary in their orientation to addressing complex problems; and still others (e.g., Dow-Corning) are framed as experiences to generate empathy and contextual learning for innovation to positively affect the lives of those at the bottom of the socioeconomic pyramid.

As PepsiCorps excites and inspires the PepsiCo community, the people involved with the program are already focusing on the next stage of the journey—what do you (or could you) do with a growing cadre of employees tuned into purposeful action in business? How do you connect them with roles and assignments that further a shared mission of doing well financially by doing good socially? That's a problem the company is happy to have.

The next example proves that corporations do not have to send employees thousands of miles away to make them more innovative and design oriented. They could do just as well by freeing them up to hang around basements and garages, or at the DIY maker-space nearest them.

Jugaad Innovation—The Art of Corporate Tinkering

India's Mars orbiter, Mangalyaan, sent into space in November 2013 and more than halfway to its destination (at the time of writing), is poised to give India a distinction that twenty-one other Asian countries have tried and failed to earn—the continent's first successful Mars mission. But there is much more to the story of Mangalyaan; it is perhaps the most compelling example, on the world stage, of *jugaad*—an Indian attitude and approach to innovation (and life) whose principles are being studied and applied by top multinational corporations and governments all around the world.

Jugaad, in Hindi, means being resourceful and thrifty in one's approach to solving problems. Coverage in the *New York Times* (Rai 2014) and *The Guardian* (Anand 2014) underlined the frugality behind India's Mars mission: Mangalyaan cost the Indian Space Research Organization (ISRO) about $75 million USD. By contrast, NASA's MAVEN Mars explorer (launched around the same time, ironically) cost $671 million USD. The former took fifteen months to build, the latter five years. Astonishingly, Mangalyaan was built and launched for 25 percent less than it took Warner Bros. and director Alfonso Cuaron to make the 2013 sci-fi thriller, *Gravity*. While the research capabilities of the Indian probe were considerably less than its NASA cousin's, the intense practicality of the jugaad approach to innovation is capturing headlines and attention inside the space industry and beyond.

To be clear, the spirit of jugaad is both deeply Indian—ingenuity as adaptive response to incredible constraints in a nation of over a billion people—and palpably universal, as similar odds are faced and beaten daily by billions, from Belgrade to Cairo to Detroit, Durban, Lagos, Manila, Mexico City, and São Paulo. It is also entwined with the spirit of design thinking—in its focus on contextual elements, modularity, and reuse—and the adoption of a learn-as-you-go testing approach.

In the case of Mangalyaan, jugaad manifested itself in the repurposing of launch capabilities and design elements already developed during other missions, rapid and more efficient testing, and some ingenious piggy-backing on favorable conditions. Take the launch plan, for example. *The Guardian*'s coverage quoted Bruce Jakosky, principal scientist on NASA's MAVEN mission: "They sent [the Mangalyaan probe] into orbit around Earth and used a series of small rocket motor burns to get into higher altitude. They used the last burn to break free of Earth's gravity to slingshot to Mars.

I thought it was a very clever way to do it" (Anand 2014). This is a specific application of a more general design philosophy: wringing the most out of what is already available (as opposed to building to a set of idealized specifications). As ISRO's chairman, K. Radhakrishnan, explained to *The Guardian*, "We used the launch vehicle that was available to us to the best of its capability, tailoring the launch time and angle to achieve the correct trajectory" (Anand 2014).

One window into the ethos behind Jugaad is in a campaign of the World Wildlife Fund (WWF). Thanks to the WWF and its partner, the Global Footprint Network, August 20 is now Earth Overshoot Day, a day that marks how quickly humans go through the amount of natural resources that the earth can sustainably regenerate in a year (World Wildlife Fund 2014). Add this looming scarcity to rising inequality, political instability, and declining trust in institutions, and we have the turbulent background against which jugaad can be seen almost as an expression of a collective survival instinct.

Another practitioner of Jugaad innovation is GE Healthcare. The *New York Times* quoted Terri Bresenham, the chief executive of GE Healthcare, South Asia, who is based in Bangalore, India, and oversees the country's largest R&D setup: "If necessity is the mother of invention, constraint is the mother of frugal innovation" (Rai 2014). GE Healthcare has come up with innovations that promote affordable access to infant health, cancer detection and heart disease treatment. It is also at the vanguard of a paradigm shift that is scrambling accepted notions of center and periphery

in world affairs, and rewriting the rules for innovation. Globalization as the spread of Western ideas, behaviors, and products is a spent force; the new globalization is multipolar in its flows of influence.

While this realignment in the global soft-power balance has been addressed before, notably in *Reverse Innovation: Create Far from Home, Win Everywhere* (2012) (by Vijay Govindarajan and Chris Trimble of the Tuck School of Business at Dartmouth, with a foreword by Indra K. Nooyi, CEO and chairwoman of PepsiCo), perhaps the most comprehensive telling of this phenomenon, to date, is in *Jugaad Innovation* (2012), a book by Navi Radjou, Jaideep Prabhu, and Simone Ahuja, based on research undertaken under the aegis of the Centre for India & Global Business at Cambridge University's Judge Business School. The research covers inspirations for jugaad, spanning entrepreneurial activity from Asia to Africa to South America, and its application in business and government settings to spur creativity and innovation. We will consider, briefly, the three pivotal conclusions the authors draw from their rich and varied observations, because they offer us a wire framework for the new innovation paradigm; in the "Go Deeper" section following this example, you will have a chance to dive into the myriad case studies chronicled in the book—from Ford Motor Co. to SNCF, the state-owned French national railway company.

1. Increased freedom, not increased budgets, is a key driver of innovation. This finding explodes the prevailing

myth that innovation is an expensive affair, driven by huge R&D investments and high technology. This is not to say that R&D and technology don't help with innovation; the unlock, it seems, is in how creative companies are with R&D and technology, not in how much they spend on them. A key corporate innovation imperative going forward, accordingly, will be to offer appropriate contexts and tools that promote employees taking innovation into their own hands.

2. Flexible methods trump stage-gated process-control when it comes to innovation success. At their most provocative, Navi, Jaideep, and Simone take an empirical axe to the very root of conventional business thinking on innovation—the notion that it is another corporate activity that can be managed and optimized via Six Sigma–like techniques. What if the very idea of innovation management is oxymoronic, they ask. Organizations will have to shift from "funneling" innovation efforts to creating an ecosystem of them, with symbiotic parts that are each adapted to specific needs like speed, disruption, scale, and so on. The relative comfort with ambiguity that is common to creative disciplines like design and foresight makes them well-suited to the task of helping business adapt to the new innovation paradigm. Using frameworks and processes for orientation and navigation without becoming trapped in them is an aspect of design thinking that business could use more of.

3. Participatory networks, not secretive silos, drive innovation. True to its historical roots in the most marginalized sectors of society, jugaad is inherently democratizing and abhors hierarchy and elitism. Transparency and collaboration (not secrecy and competition) are the organizing principles for a new wave of twenty-first-century innovation. From public prize competitions to various forms of open innovation (including incubation and acceleration services), companies large and small are experimenting with harnessing the power of informal networks and employees energized by the opportunity to participate.

Taken together, the principles of jugaad delineate some of the contours of the emerging paradigm of value-creation in business. It will be an upside-down world, vis-à-vis the industrial paradigm of the last two centuries. Consider something Navi often brings up in his talks: There are over 50 million people in the United States who are "un-banked" (with no link to a formal banking institution or service). It would seriously challenge the current definition of emerging markets to suggest that this slice of the US population is precisely that—an emerging market for a Kenyan-born concern like m-Pesa, an e-banking platform that allows people to do almost all their banking via text messaging. And yet, here we are. As William Gibson, the science fiction writer, put it so aptly, "The future is already here—it's just not very evenly distributed."

Jugaad Innovation also furthers our understanding of the How dimension by validating the popular suspicion that the most underutilized resource in most big companies may be the human kind. William McKnight, an early leader of 3M, warned us long ago: "If you put fences around people, you get sheep." Organizations that cultivate a sense of shared purpose among employees, and empower them to collaborate and create outside of narrow roles and responsibilities, will define the new frontier for growth and innovation. And design, a discipline that is fundamentally about people, is well situated to be a guide as business explores the question of how to get the most out of the people formerly considered cogs in the machine.

GO DEEPER

Read the following:
- *Jugaad Innovation* by N. Radjou, J. Prabhu, and S. Ahuja.
- "Capitalizing on Complexity: Insights from the Global Chief Executive Officer Study," IBM CEO Study Report 2010. Available online: http://www-01. ibm.com/common/ssi/cgi-bin/ssialias? subtype=XB&infotype=PM&appname =GBSE_GB_TI_USEN&htmlfid=GBE 03297USEN&attachment=GBE03297 USEN.PDF
- "Corporate Volunteerism Emerges from Infancy and Identifies Key Challenges" by A. Useem. Available online: https://www.devex.com/ news/corporate-volunteerism- emerges-from-infancy-identifies-key- challenges-80835

Watch the following:
- Charles Limb's TED Talk, "Your Brain on Improv." Available online: http://www.ted.com/talks/ charles_limb_your_brain_on_improv.
- The Pepsicorps Experience. Available online: https://www.youtube.com/ watch?v=yyZdc2CuVt8

REFLECTIONS
- Think of areas or topics on which your organization is disconnected from real life: These are typically topics on which there is much research (facts and figures) but little direct experience. Try to come up with easy ways for yourself, colleagues, and executives to stay connected to the real-life experiences of customers, consumers, and other stakeholders.
- Think of ideas for new products/ services/ways of working that you (or someone you know) abandoned because you (they) lacked the resources to pursue it. Would you be able to make a better case for more resources if you had a working prototype? Think of ways to apply jugaad thinking (make the most of what you have) to construct a minimum viable prototype of your idea.

The Why—Raising Questions on Purpose

So, design can help with making better things and making work itself better for the ones doing it. But the best that design can offer business may be yet to come. As capitalism strives to develop a conscience, it needs a discipline with deep humanist convictions to prod it to be more introspective and (re-?) ask the questions of Why. Why does business exist? Toward what purposes should its prodigious resources and capabilities be directed? And who is to decide that? Since capitalist propaganda unfailingly cites the system's relationship with democracy, it's only fair to ask why so little of the latter exists within the former's institutions.

None of the above is to suggest that design itself is above the need to evolve toward questions of Why. To borrow an analogy from Jerry Michalski (founder of REX, the Relationship Economy eXpedition), designers who think they're improving schooling by making the bell's sound more pleasing must graduate to asking about the meaning of school itself, and if a bell is even needed! The insistence on an empathetic worldview is a great start, but design can, and must, embrace a deeper moral dimension if it is to gain broader relevance during a decade of turbulence. This imperative frames the last two examples in this chapter—seeds of a newly conscious capitalism, and vectors along which design could extend itself to make companies more human.

B-Corporations—Beyond Shareholders to Stakeholders

The story of the B (for-benefit)-Corporation is about a group of successful entrepreneurs rallying around shared convictions regarding the purpose of business, and applying design thinking (consciously or not) to the questions of structure and governance necessary to guard and champion those convictions.

The story starts with small acts of courageous, principled resistance at the fringes of the dominant paradigm. While the broader economy was busy generating the outcomes leading to the 1 percent versus 99 percent meme, a handful of US companies were following an entirely different script—one that said profits did not matter above all else and needed to be balanced against obligations to be socially and environmentally responsible. Guided by ideals nobler than maximizing profits and shareholder returns, these companies were betting on a values- and mission-driven connection with their customers to achieve business success. They included Ben & Jerry's, The Body Shop, Izze, Patagonia, Seventh Generation, and Toms of Maine among others.

The success of these companies gradually attracted attention from larger conglomerates unable to muster, in practice, even a semblance of the authenticity endlessly discussed in their PowerPoint presentations. It was "if you can't beat them, join them" as corporate strategy, except the joining was seldom mutually desirable. In many instances, the small companies (and their founders) were vocal and open about their resistance to Big Business's advances, citing irreconcilable differences in values and concerns about the dilution of their broader social mission. Their protestations, they soon found, were no match for legal arguments. The prospective buyers simply upped their offers till enough of the small company shareholders were bought off. Directors of the small companies who resisted merging with Big Business could be sued by shareholders unhappy that their best interests were not being served, and were. Enough of these skirmishes ended with the forced sale of the small companies (and the selling-out of their missions) that the entrepreneurs were faced with this critical question: How do you protect the long-term interests of the company, along with those of the ecosystem and communities that sustain it, against the legally enforceable short-termism of some of the shareholders?

Their answer was an elegant one: rewrite the rules of the game itself, by codifying their tripartite balancing of profits, people, and planet in law. The result was a new class of explicitly for-benefit corporate entities, legally beholden to what have come to be known as "triple bottom-lines." (Companies do not have to be certified B-Corporations to be considered socially responsible or "good" [certainly not in any legal sense]). The B-Corp is legal scaffolding for an alternate vision of what business ought to be about— socially useful in purpose and delivering balanced returns to shareholders, as well as other stakeholders (employees, communities, the commons) in practice. It also marks the institutionalization of a profound shift in worldview within the dominant social institution of our times. The new worldview (re-) contextualizes business activity within the larger sphere of human aims and ambitions, and it is summarized in Figure 9.5.

B-Corporations are certified by the 501(c)3 nonprofit B Lab to meet rigorous standards of social and environmental performance, accountability, and transparency. B Lab imagines itself a movement-hub, providing legal and impact-research services besides the certifications. Thanks to its efforts, laws have been passed in twenty-two states and Washington, DC, establishing B-Corporations as a class of companies devoted to (and assessed on) using the power of business to increase social good. It also compiles and maintains the world's largest database of verified social and environmental impact data for private companies (1,100+ companies), the backbone of its B Analytics service, which serves companies, impact investors, and fund managers.

According to the B Corp website, there are over 1,035 Certified B-Corporations spread across sixty-plus industries and more than thirty-four countries,

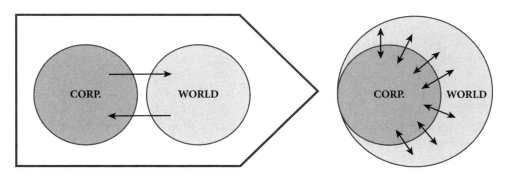

Figure 9.5 The corporation in relation to the world—a paradigm shift
Manoj Fenelon

collectively redefining what business success means, and how (and for whom) the economy works. While currently dwarfed by the scale and size of business-as-usual companies, this second-curve phenomenon will only grow because it is well adapted to what society is demanding of business—more transparency, and urgency in tackling the world's pressing problems.

If B-Corporations are an example of rewriting the rules of the game to account for purpose, then the next example is one of throwing away the rulebook altogether, when it comes to how to run a company.

Semco—The Key to Management Is to Get Rid of the Managers

Semco is a successful company, at least in its two modern incarnations. Starting as a centrifuge-maker in the 1950s, the company shifted heavily toward the service sector when Ricardo Semler took over from his father, Antonio Curt Semler, in the 1980s. The Semco Group came to have businesses in environmental consultancy, facilities management, inventory support, and real estate brokerage, while growing revenues from $4 million in 1983 to over $214 million in 2003. Semco Partners now manages a portfolio composed of fifty-fifty joint ventures with multinational companies doing business in Brazil. For all this, success is probably the least interesting part of the Semco story.

Ricardo Semler has been voted Brazil's Businessman-of-the-Year twice and named a Global Leader of Tomorrow by the World Economic Forum. He has taught at Harvard's and MIT's business schools and has been profiled by the BBC's *Re-Engineering the Business* series. Designing by subtraction, Ricardo has created one of the most intriguing management structures of our times by starting with assumptions about human beings and work that are starkly opposed to those that ground conventional thinking. Instead of a hangover from the industrial management era, which saw labor as a resource to be optimized efficiently, he takes a new approach that sees workers as human beings, and smart adults, who, when freed from top-down control, will naturally do what is in the best interests of the company, and do it exceptionally well.

The creativity behind how Semco is managed is crystallized in this insight: Why would you take people, who are functioning adults in the outside world, and treat them like children who cannot figure out much for themselves, when they come to work. Semco is what happens when you design environments around principles like fairness, openness, reciprocity, and trust; when you redefine work itself as the expression of our better natures. Here are some of the tenets of management, Semco style (Semler 1995):

- Everyone sets their own salaries and working hours (which are posted for all to see).
- There is no Human Resources group, all hiring and firing is done by consensus.
- There is no Information Technology group, everyone takes responsibility for their computers and other shared IT resources.
- All meetings are voluntary.

- The company's balance sheet and other vital records are open books for all employees.

Picture 3,000-plus people working like this and it gets a little easier to imagine better possibilities for the future for work. In the "Go Deeper" and "Reflections" sections at the end of this chapter, you will find avenues for exploring some of these possibilities. Semco is not just a more humane workplace but also a vastly more efficient one, and it is in this twinning that we find the seeds of a larger revolution and a North Star for the future role of design in business.

Afterword

We are at a pivotal moment in human history, with transformative (for better or worse) technologies within our grasp. If we think of business itself as a technology, the systematic application of the art, knowledge, and techniques available to humans, then the truest expression of design thinking within business may well be the redesign of business.

We surely know this about human nature—it is malleable and adapts to the environment. If people-potential is *the* most underleveraged resource in most businesses, what kinds of environments should we design to get the most out of people?

What role will morals and ethics play in the design discussions of the future? Are designers up to the challenge of helping companies be more introspective and reflective? Will design look into the corporate soul and find higher meaning and purpose than extraction and accumulation? Will Human Resources departments everywhere become the new hotbed of design activity? Will design drive new forms of collaboration guided by shared purpose—among corporations, governments, and other civil society actors?

Whatever else design has to teach the world of business, the biggest lesson may be this: Start with good questions.

GO DEEPER
Read the following:
- *Maverick* by R. Semler.
- "Ricardo Semler Won't Take Control" by L. Fisher. Available online: http://www.strategy-business.com/article/05408?gko=3291c
- "Creating Shared Value" by M. Porter and M. Kramer. Available online: https://hbr.org/2011/01/the-big-idea-creating-shared-value

REFLECTIONS
- Think about the rules and regulations that surround your work. What are the assumptions about human behavior that are built into them? How do these assumptions make you feel?
- How would you define your personal purpose? What have you come into the world to do? And how does that mesh with the purpose of your organization? How can you strengthen areas of congruence and address areas of conflict?
- One reason why the pro-social impact of business is not discussed often enough is because it is not measured in the first place. Think of opportunities to measure the social-good impact of what you're doing, and incorporate it into the ways your work is evaluated.

Acknowledgments

With much gratitude to Mauro Porcini, for adopting me into the world of design at PepsiCo; Paul Dillinger, for sharing your story and inspiring many others; the Institute for the Future, for research and guidance; and the founders of PepsiCorps, for being the little team that could.

References

2012 Map of the Decade (2012). Retrieved from http://www.iftf.org/fileadmin/ user_upload/downloads/IFTF_SR-1472_TYF_2012MOTD_reader_sm.pdf

Anand, A. (2014), "Shoestring Theory: India's Pioneering Budget Space Probe Is Halfway to Mars," *The Guardian*, May 1. Available online: http://www.theguardian.com/ world/2014/may/02/india-mars-probe-mangalyaan.

Aspen Institute (2015), "First Movers Fellowship Overview." Available online: http:// www.aspeninstitute.org/policy-work/business-society/corporate-programs/ first-movers-fellowship-program/overview

Browne, J. and R. Nuttall (2013), "Beyond Corporate Social Responsibility: Integrated External Engagement," McKinsey & Co. Available online: http://www.mckinsey.com/insights/ strategy/beyond_corporate_social_responsibility_integrated_external_engagement

Dillinger, P. (2014), "Aspen First Movers Summit." Available online: http://www.youtube.com/watch?v=WsXyIAACxmM&hd=1

Fisher, L. (2005), "Ricardo Semler Won't Take Control," www.strategy-business.com. Available online: http://www.strategy-business.com/article/05408?gko=3291c

Govindarajan, V. and C. Trimble (2012), *Reverse Innovation: Create Far from Home, Win Everywhere*, Cambridge, MA: Harvard Business Review Press.

Green, E. (2013), "Will the 'Internet of Things' Actually Be a Thing in 2014?" *The Atlantic*, December 18. Available online: http://www.theatlantic.com/technology/ archive/2013/12/will-the-internet-of-things-actually-be-a-thing-in-2014/282458/

Horovitz, B. (2013), "Chipotle targets Big Food, skips branding," *USA Today*. Retrieved from http://www.usatoday.com/story/money/business/2013/09/12/ chipotle-big-food-millennial-marketing/2798023/

IBM CEO Study Report (2010), "Capitalizing on Complexity: Insights from the Global Chief Executive Officer Study." Available online: http://www-01.ibm.com/common/ ssi/cgi-bin/ssialias?subtype=XB&infotype=PM&appname=GBSE_GB_TI_USEN&h tmlfid=GBE03297USEN&attachment=GBE03297USEN.PDF

Limb, C. (2010), "Your Brain on Improv," TED Talk. Available online: http://www.ted. com/talks/charles_limb_your_brain_on_improv

Marzano, S. (1992), "Flying over Las Vegas," Keynote speech at the Seventeenth World Design Conference of the International Council of Societies (ICSID) in

Ljubljana. Available online: http://www.usa.philips.com/philips5/shared/assets/Downloadablefile/Flying-over-Las-Vegas-14327.pdf

Morozov, E. (2012), *The Net Delusion: The Dark Side of Internet Freedom*, NY: Public Affairs.

Olins, W. (2012), "Game Changers: Five Behaviors That Are Shaping the Future of Business," www.WolfOlins.com. Available online: http://gamechangers2012.wolffolins.com/static/report/files/WO_GameChangesReport.pdf

Olson, E. (2012). "An Animated Ad with a Plot Line and a Moral," *New York Times*. Available online: http://www.nytimes.com/2012/02/10/business/media/chipotle-ad-promotes-sustainable-farming.html?_r=0

Porter, M. and M. Kramer (2011), "Creating Shared Value," *Harvard Business Review*, Boston: Harvard Business Publishing. Available online: https://hbr.org/2011/01/the-big-idea-creating-shared-value

Radjou, N, J. Prabhu, and S. Ahuja (2012), *Jugaad Innovation: Think Frugal, Be Flexible, Generate Breakthrough Growth*, San Francisco: Jossey-Bass.

Rai, S. (2014), "From India, Proof That a Trip to Mars Doesn't Have to Break the Bank," *New York Times*, February 17. Available online: http://www.nytimes.com/2014/02/18/business/international/from-india-proof-that-a-trip-to-mars-doesnt-have-to-break-the-bank.html

Roy, M. and H. Crooks (2011), *Surviving Progress*, documentary, Canada: Big Picture Media Corporation.

Semler, R. (1995), *Maverick: The Success Story Behind the World's Most Unusual Workplace*, New York: Grand Central Publishing.

Stengel, J. (2011), *Grow: How Ideals Power Growth and Profit at the World's Greatest Companies*, New York: Crown Business.

Useem, A. (2013), "Corporate Volunteerism Emerges from Infancy, Identifies Key Challenges," DevEx Impact. Available online: https://www.devex.com/news/corporate-volunteerism-emerges-from-infancy-identifies-key-challenges-80835

World Wildlife Fund (2014), "Living Planet Report 2014," *World Wildlife Fund*. Available online: http://wwf.panda.org/about_our_earth/all_publications/living_planet_report/

Wright, R. (2005), *A Short History of Progress*, NY: Carroll & Graf.

CONCLUSION
The Future of Work

In 2013 graduate students in Philadelphia University's Strategic Design MBA program collaborated with peers in the International Design Business Management program at Aalto University in Finland on a design research project. Its topic: The Future of Work. This project later looped back to a series of charrettes with thought leaders and practitioners in Philadelphia to collect more ideas on determinants the students had identified. The ways, means, and spaces in which we currently work have been transformed by a series of technical and economic drivers, such as digitalization, connectivity, and hyper-competition. This is compounded by constraints, such as global economic recessions, increasing disparities between the haves and have-nots, energy challenges, and access to health care and education. At the same time, human factors and customer involvement (from conceptual design to in-store retailing of products) are increasingly playing a major role as determinants in the sustainability and success of organizations, ecosystems, and entire societies. The value of this book is that each chapter grants a new way of thinking through meaningful engagement in the future of work, using strategic design principles: human-centered, collaborative, creative, systems-based innovation.

Increasingly, the value of work is created through collaboration and in environments that enable transformative practices. The realization that the best talent is not always (some say never) within your organization, drives collaboration and co-location of the established with the emerging. This is a trend that is fast gaining momentum. In this new world, the young and the old, the students and the established businesspersons, the top-down and the bottom-up coexist and co-create ideally to produce extraordinary value for the ecosystem of employees, firms, and society as a whole.

While these trends are clear, what is still shrouded in haze is the future of work. What are the best practices in collaborative work, and where is that work done? We need the strategic design-thinking frameworks to explore the future of work in various industries, to identify relevant skills, and to propose that leaders should think creatively about who they involve in this challenge. When assessing the future of work, determinants such as physical space, interpersonal interactions, organizational culture, creativity, and external touchpoints affecting workplace experience matter.

In the extended project, the Strategic Design MBA students thought through determinants, such as technology, energy, education, and health care, and explored the following ideas.

Transportation and Energy

- What if there was an app that could chart energy savings and thus incentivize more sustainable forms of transportation?
- What if commuters who took the train, bus, or biked to and from work could talk with one another and create a feedback loop?
- What if there were incentives that could convert car commuters into users of public transportation?
- How might commuters use connectivity platforms to stay connected to each other? For example, could a "Mentoring Train" allow passengers to know with whom they are traveling and to develop mentor/mentee relationships?
- What if commuter trains used real-time information sharing and served as lecture platforms, blurring the boundaries of formal education? The idea that you could learn while traveling to and from work and be inspired or stay connected to others was a consistent theme.

Education

- How might we make education lean and reduce the clutter that currently exists in the form of testing and other variables that exist outside of the classroom?
- Might there be the return of the apprenticeship model and more blurred lines between companies and institutions of higher education?
- Could meta-skills such as professional interaction, teaming, and interviewing come to the foreground?

Health Care

There will be a paradigm shift and wellness will be the focus instead of targeting disease. The following questions will matter:

- What role does stress play on your mental, physical, and overall lifestyle?
- Does traffic and a long commute contribute to that stress? What if there was a program that rewarded biking to work?
- What if you could track your bike commute through an app on a watch/bracelet? Can making a game out of a commute incentivize people to lose weight and get in better physical and mental shape?

All of these ideas and questions really build on the major focus of this book's introduction, that of *shared platforms*. Thus, there are three major lessons from this book. The first lesson is that an integrative approach, such as strategic design thinking, yields more innovative outcomes for a range of businesses and practitioners–in design, health care, government, finance, education, and so on. Theory and practice *can* intermingle and make sense in the aggregate.

The second lesson from this book is the value of focusing on the *process* and not just the final insight or outcome. The ways in which strategic design point us to the design of the intangible—that is, services in addition to tangible objects—certainly emphasize this point. And the third lesson is that this book embraces new opportunities for educators and for practitioners to converge. Hopefully, whether you are a student or a practitioner reading this book, you have gleaned that silos within academia and within your particular practice area are no longer efficient. By extension an integrative approach between academia and industry will yield much more exciting and interesting learning for all parties involved.

This book has taken you through the *Why*, *How*, and *What* of strategic design thinking. You now have an array of theories, frameworks, and practical tools to apply to your work in multiple sectors. The value proposition of strategic design thinking is that problem solving is an integrative process that embraces complexity and leads to innovative outcomes. In a world where boundaries are increasingly blurred, it is essential to have the lens of strategic design to embark on creative problem solving.

Onward, and enjoy your journey!

Reference

McGowan, H. (2015), "Redesigning Work, Employment and the Social Contract" (talk at Amplify Festival, June 2015). Available online: https://www.youtube.com/watch?v=G67RfVvOmvY

Index